Traditional Ecological Knowledge

This book examines the importance of Traditional Ecological Knowledge (TEK) and how it can provide models for a time-tested form of sustainability needed in the world today. The essays, written by a team of scholars from diverse disciplinary backgrounds, explore TEK through compelling cases of environmental sustainability from multiple tribal and geographic locations in North America and beyond. Addressing the philosophical issues concerning Indigenous and ecological knowledge production and maintenance, the authors focus on how environmental values and ethics are applied to the uses of land. Grounded in an understanding of the profound relationship between biological and cultural diversity, this book defines, interrogates, and problematizes the many definitions of Traditional Ecological Knowledge and sustainability. It includes a holistic and broad disciplinary approach to sustainability, including language, art, and ceremony, as critical ways to maintain healthy human–environment relations.

Melissa K. Nelson is an ecologist and indigenous scholar-activist. She is a professor of American Indian Studies at San Francisco State University. Since 1993, she has also served as the president of the Cultural Conservancy. She is the editor of *Original Instructions: Indigenous Teachings for a Sustainable Future* (2008) and is an active media maker, having produced several documentary short films and audio recordings.

Dan Shilling worked at the Arizona Humanities Council from 1984 until 2003, the last fourteen years as executive director, during which he developed award-winning environmental history/ethics projects. He is the author of *Civic Tourism: The Poetry and Politics of Place* (2007) and earned the prestigious Distinguished Alumnus Award from Arizona State University.

NEW DIRECTIONS IN SUSTAINABILITY AND SOCIETY

Series Editors

CHRISTOPHER BOONE
Arizona State University
NORMAN YOFFEE
University of Michigan

Editorial Board

Published in conjunction with the School of Sustainability at Arizona State University and The Amerind Museum and Research Center in Dragoon, Arizona, New Directions in Sustainability and Society features a program of books that focus on designing a resilient and sustainable future through a rich understanding of past and present social and ecological dynamics. Collectively, they demonstrate that sustainability research requires engagement with a range of fields spanning the social and natural sciences, humanities, and applied sciences. Books in the series show that a successful transition to a sustainable future will depend on the ability to apply lessons from past societies and link local action to global processes.

For more information about the series, please visit http://newdirections.asu.edu/.

Titles in the Series

Sustainability in the Global City edited by Cindy Isenhour, Gary McDonogh, Melissa Checker.
The Give and Take of Sustainability edited by Michelle Hegmon.

Traditional Ecological Knowledge

Learning from Indigenous Practices for Environmental Sustainability

Edited by

MELISSA K. NELSON
San Francisco State University

DAN SHILLING
Arizona State University

CAMBRIDGE
UNIVERSITY PRESS

CAMBRIDGE
UNIVERSITY PRESS

University Printing House, Cambridge CB2 8BS, United Kingdom

One Liberty Plaza, 20th Floor, New York, NY 10006, USA

477 Williamstown Road, Port Melbourne, VIC 3207, Australia

314-321, 3rd Floor, Plot 3, Splendor Forum, Jasola District Centre, New Delhi - 110025, India

79 Anson Road, #06-04/06, Singapore 079906

Cambridge University Press is part of the University of Cambridge.

It furthers the University's mission by disseminating knowledge in the pursuit of education, learning and research at the highest international levels of excellence.

www.cambridge.org
Information on this title: www.cambridge.org/9781108428569
DOI: 10.1017/9781108552998

First published 2018

A catalogue record for this publication is available from the British Library

ISBN 978-1-108-42856-9 Hardback
ISBN 978-1-108-45044-7 Paperback

Contents

Editors and Contributors

Editors: Melissa K. Nelson and Dan Shilling

Melissa K. Nelson, PhD, is a professor of American Indian Studies at San Francisco State University and president of the Cultural Conservancy, an Indigenous rights organization, which she has directed since 1993. She is Anishinaabe/Métis/Norwegian, an enrolled member of the Turtle Mountain Band of Chippewa Indians.

Dan Shilling, PhD, is a former project director with Arizona State University's Institute for Humanities Research. He joined the Arizona Humanities Council in 1984 and was named executive director in 1989 and served in that position for fourteen years.

Contributors

Jeannette Armstrong, PhD, is Syilx Okanagan. She currently holds the Canada Research Chair in Okanagan Indigenous Knowledge and Philosophy at University of British Columbia Okanagan and directs research at the En'owkin Centre. She is a literary author with a wide variety of published academic articles.

Gregory Cajete, PhD, is a Tewa Indian from Santa Clara Pueblo, New Mexico. He is Director of Native American Studies and a professor in the Division of Language, Literacy and Sociocultural Studies in the College of Education at the University of New Mexico. He has authored seven books.

Manuka Henare (Te Aupouri, Te Rarawa) is an associate professor in Māori Business Development in the Department of Management and International Business and Associate Dean. He is the foundation director of the Mira Szászy Research Centre for Māori and Pacific Economic Development and leads a number of multidisciplinary research project teams.

Carla Houkamau (Ngati Porou) is a senior lecturer in the Department of Management and International Business at the University of Auckland, Auckland, New Zealand.

Linda Hogan (Chickasaw) is former Writer-in-Residence of the Chickasaw Nation and Professor Emerita from the University of Colorado and is an internationally recognized public speaker and writer of poetry, fiction, and essays.

Robin Wall Kimmerer, PhD, is a mother, scientist, writer, and Distinguished Teaching Professor of Environmental Biology at the State University of New York College of Environmental Science and Forestry. She is founding director of the Center for Native Peoples and the Environment and is the author of the award-winning books, *Gathering Moss: A Natural and Cultural History of Mosses* (2003) and *Braiding Sweetgrass: Indigenous Wisdom, Scientific Knowledge, and the Teachings of Plants* (2013).

Dennis Martinez is an internationally renowned restoration ecologist and Indigenous rights leader of O'odham/Chicano/Anglo heritage. He is the founder and chair of the Indigenous Peoples' Restoration Network (IPRN), a working group of the Society for Ecological Restoration International (SER-I), and is codirector (with Agnes pilgrim of Siletz Confederated Tribes) of the Takelma Intertribal Project.

Joan McGregor has a PhD in philosophy and is Professor of Philosophy in the School of Historical, Philosophical, and Religious Studies at Arizona State University; she is also a senior scholar with the School of Sustainability.

Michael Paul Nelson, PhD, is the Ruth H. Spaniol Chair of Renewable Resources, Professor of Environmental Ethics and Philosophy, and the lead principle investigator for the HJ Andrews Experimental Forest Long-Term Ecological Research Program at Oregon State University.

Simon Ortiz, Dr. of Ltrs, is an Acoma Pueblo writer, poet, scholar, creative nonfiction writer, essayist, author, college professor, advocate, and supporter of Indigenous liberation and decolonization. Presently, he is a regents professor of English and American Indian Studies at Arizona State University.

Chellie Spiller (Māori and Pākehā) is an associate professor and associate dean (Māori and Pacific) at the University of Auckland Business School. She is coauthor of *Indigenous Spirituality at Work* (2015) and *Wayfinding Leadership* (2015).

Priscilla Settee, PhD, is an award-winning professor in the Department of Native Studies at the University of Saskatchewan and a member of Cumberland House Cree First Nations from northern Saskatchewan, Canada. She is the author of two books: *Pimatisiwin: The Good Life, Global Indigenous Knowledge Systems* (2013) and *The Strength of Women, Ahkameyimowak* (2011).

Rebecca Tsosie, JD is a regents professor at the James E. Rogers College of Law at the University of Arizona and also serves as Special Advisor to the Provost for Diversity and Inclusion. Professor Tsosie, who is of Yaqui descent, is a faculty member for the Indigenous Peoples' Law and Policy Program at the University of Arizona.

John A. Vucetich, PhD, is a professor of animal ecology at Michigan Technological University, where he teaches courses in Population Ecology and Environmental Ethics. He is codirector of the Isle Royale Wolf-Moose Project, the longest continuous study of any predator–prey system in the world.

Kyle Whyte, PhD, holds the Timnick Chair in the Humanities at Michigan State University. He is Associate Professor of Philosophy and Community Sustainability, a faculty member of the Environmental Philosophy & Ethics graduate concentration, and a faculty affiliate of the American Indian Studies Program and Environmental Science and Policy Program.

Rachel Wolfgramm (Ngai Takoto, Te Aupouri, Whakatohea, Tonga) is an interdisciplinary scholar and researcher and serves as a senior lecturer at the University of Auckland Business School in New Zealand. She is coauthor of *Indigenous Spirituality at Work* (2015).

Preface

In our own ways, we have both been studying, teaching, and working to foster an appreciation of the cultural dimensions of humankind's relationship to the natural world. Melissa teaches American Indian Studies at San Francisco State University, has directed the Cultural Conservancy for more than two decades, and she has been a long-time contributor to Bioneers and the Indigenous food movement. All these roles offer opportunities to explore the human–nature accord through Indigenous points of view. As executive director of the Arizona Humanities Council, Dan developed noteworthy state and regional public projects that examined the historical, artistic, and ethical dimensions of the West's majestic landscapes, threatened waters, and land-based economies.

So when anthropologist Norman Yoffee suggested that we collaborate on a research and publication project on Traditional Ecological Knowledge (TEK), a topic that touches on most of our interests, we leapt at the chance to bring this volume to conclusion.

We thank Norm for starting the dialogue, and Christopher Boone at Arizona State University's Global Institute of Sustainability (GIOS) for underwriting and nurturing the research that led to this publication. The seeds were planted during a three-day seminar at the Amerind Museum in Dragoon, Arizona (Figure 1), where, thanks to GIOS's support and Amerind's generosity, we were able to bring together most of the authors presented here for deep, extended, and engaging conversations about Traditional Ecological Knowledge and its role today in education, land management, conservation programs, public policy, and sustainability studies.

FIGURE 1 Amerind Museum and Research Center, Dragoon, Arizona, where the authors met for a seminar in 2013. (Photo used with permission of Amerind Museum.)

Other books and monographs survey the terrain covered in *Traditional Ecological Knowledge: Learning from Indigenous Practices for Environmental Sustainability*, although this collection is significant in that it includes the voices of leading *Indigenous* scholars and activists, who discuss this mixture of Native knowledge and western science in the classroom and the field, and who also contribute to community programs that incorporate the principles outlined here. All are teachers in their own way, introducing life-affirming ways to an engaged generation of educators, land managers, park rangers, tribal officials, researchers, government employees, farmers, ranchers, tourism directors, and other culture- and nature-based economies.

Given the number of tribal nations in North America alone, not to mention the many bands and clans *within* tribal nations, we realize a full survey of Indigenous attitudes toward the land, even on this one continent, is not possible. A broad hemispheric study would be even more challenging at this point. So while this volume does touch on the Māori and other world cultures, North America is the focus. Admittedly, it is a regional approach, but the path these authors have started down will certainly widen, inviting more voices and more perspectives, as TEK's influence continues to grow.

PART I

INTRODUCTION TO KEY CONCEPTS AND QUESTIONS

Introduction: The Soul of Sustainability

Dan Shilling

For know, whatever was created, needs
To be sustaind and fed.

–John Milton, *Paradise Lost*

Few modern concepts are as talked about, debated, and misconstrued as sustainability – to the point that the word's trendy, buzzword status has earned it the label "sustainababble" from critics skeptical of the evangelistic aura that often surrounds it. That goofy made-up term is not entirely off beam. Review the literature, as well as the many programs and agencies that feature "sustainability" in their name or description – from the most uncompromising environmental group to the World Trade Organization – and you may find it hard to say what it is or isn't, who supports it and who doesn't (sometimes making for odd bedfellows), who benefits and who misses out, how or even *if* it can be realized, or why we're doing the sustainability thing in the first place.

Something should be sustained, but what? The planet's nonrenewable resources, South America's economy, or a privileged country's lifestyle? And for what purpose? To aid developing nations, grizzly bears in Montana, Indigenous peoples, or a Fortune 500 company? And underneath it all, who gets to answer those questions?

This volume looks back, historically, in order to approach these and other tough questions – back to the land practices of Indigenous cultures. Ironically, it has taken decades for many sustainability scholars to consider the spiritual and ecological underpinnings that helped define Native peoples' relationships to nature, even though these relationships "sustained" most tribal nations, and the land on which they lived, for

thousands of years. Perhaps sustainability advocates have been preoccu-
pied with new technologies – cars that get more miles per gallon, solar
cells that cost less and do more – and therefore Indigenous practices are
deemed irrelevant. Or perhaps scholars and practitioners don't believe
Native peoples are a good model, since they, too, the argument goes,
ruined landscapes and annihilated species. Others contend that because
Indigenous groups lacked modern machines, they couldn't possibly
destroy their habitat. All three excuses are misplaced. First, sustainability
is foremost a *moral*, not technological, undertaking, beginning with how
our species relates to its surroundings. Second, while Native Americans
did exploit and sometimes spoil parts of the land, they continued for
13,000 years or more in North America without damaging the place *too*
badly, compared to what westerners have done in one-hundredth of that
time. Third, Native peoples may have lacked earth movers but they *did*
build huge cities and manipulated their environment in colossal ways.
Also, considering their hunting skills, especially after they acquired the
horse and rifle, American Indians probably *could* have wiped out the
bison, but they didn't, an act of ecological restraint and spiritual reverence. Had they practiced farming or fishing more intensively on fragile
lands and rivers, they *could* have destroyed their world and its resources,
but most didn't. Historian Donald Hughes (1983: 98) observes: "Indian
technology was certainly capable of doing more damage to the environment than was actually done." It wasn't so much the tools that were or
were not available to Native peoples that determined ecological health; it
was, instead, the wisdom to know what to do with the tools, a theme for-
ester Aldo Leopold would later adopt: "We end, I think, at what might be
called the standard paradox of the twentieth century: our tools are better
than we are, and grow better faster than we do. They suffice to crack the
atom, to command the tides. But they do not suffice for the oldest task in
human history: to live on a piece of land without spoiling it" (Flader and
Callicott, 1991: 254).

This anthology, then, considers sustainability through historical and
ethical lenses, beginning, as best we can, at the beginning, with Indigenous
peoples' practices and knowledges, in order to trace the development and
contemporary application of an idea.

Sustainability Is Big Business

From the Latin *sustinere* ("to hold"), the word has been around in some
form since the seventeenth century, but its modern usage, primarily

having to do with steady-state environmental and social conditions, only surfaced in the 1970s. A definition of sorts was established in the United Nations' 1987 report, *Our Common Future*, published by the UN's World Commission on Environment and Development. Commonly known as the "Brundtland Commission" (chaired by Norwegian Prime Minister Gro Harlem Brundtland), the document offered a concise if uninspired definition that remains a moving target for research, application, and ideological quarrels: "Sustainable development is development that meets the needs of the present without compromising the ability of future generations to meet their own needs" (World Commission, 1987: 8). Naysayers pounced on "sustainable development" – calling it oxymoronic – arguing that, no matter how sensitive or well intentioned, development is, by nature, *un*sustainable. John Ehrenfeld, a critic of conventional proposals and methodologies, puts it bluntly: "Sustainable development is fundamentally a tool that suggests new means but still old ends – development remains at the core of this concept" (Ehrenfeld, 2008: 6). Further, who defines "the needs of the present" or those of "future generations"? Are these needs the same from place to place? From culture to culture? Will they change over time? As if those terms and concepts aren't vague enough, is there a bundle of words more definition-challenged than "without compromising the ability of"? To be sure, each piece of the UN's definition can be picked apart, turned inside out, and rendered contradictory or so toothless that it is meaningless, leaving practice open to abuse and exploitation.

In the wake of this bickering, scholars and practitioners have offered dozens of alternative definitions, to the point that some scholars list more than a hundred. A distressing irony – given that, in practice, sustainability is premised on social and ecological bonds – is that many of the suggestions remain stovepiped in single disciplines, lacking any hint of the connective tissue biologist E. O. Wilson (1998) calls "consilience." That is, ecology is *the* study that underpins sustainability, yet our discussions and practices often lack the integration ecology implies. The American monk Thomas Berry celebrated Wilson and other enlightened scientists for "providing some of our most powerful poetic references and metaphoric expressions," through their *integration* of cultural perspectives and scientific discoveries – a tool for addressing, let alone solving, the challenges that threaten a sustainable existence (Berry, 1988: 16).

Despite the disputes, imprecision, disconnections, and, at times, seemingly *un*sustainable temper of the dialog, sustainability today stretches across countless sectors, not only the predictable environmental landscape. The term's popularity alone, whether earned legitimately or not, is one reason to pay attention. It's here, get used to it.

Indeed, a quick online book search of "sustainability" reveals dozens of titles released within the last few years alone, covering business development, economic theory, urban planning, history, social justice, environmental ethics, biology, and other sciences. Step beyond the publishing world and broaden the search to include NGOs and other groups that operate in the sustainability arena, and literally thousands of hits appear: government programs, environmental agencies, think tanks, business councils, and a glut of consultants – from million-dollar firms with offices worldwide, to a guy in a bathrobe working out of his basement – all promising to make your town, company, procedure, or product sustainable. Even cities whose development history lies in the deepest circle of unsustainable hell – Phoenix and Las Vegas, for example – trumpet their commitment to the word through countless "green" programs. Large international organizations, among them Sustainable Cities, host conferences, publish journals, manage blogs, offer onsite workshops, and conduct research projects around the globe, all aimed at helping the public sector manage municipalities – from Chattanooga to Dakar, Bucharest to Curitiba – more sustainably.

Similarly, in higher education it's difficult to find an academic program that does not treat the topic in some form: law, literature, urban studies, geography, history, botany, ethics, political science, the arts, economics, ethnic studies, philosophy, and so on. Open almost any college guide, and you're apt to find "The Sustainability of" prefacing more than one course title, from undergraduate to doctoral level. Beyond individual classes, entire schools exist within colleges of liberal arts or departments of business, devoted to exploring their respective fields through the lens of sustainability. Across an ever-widening spectrum of disciplines, higher education is training future architects, economists, cultural leaders, educators, scientists, and corporate executives in the language of a term whose meaning and implications remain elusive. When these students graduate, chances grow more likely each year that their new employer, whether a business, nonprofit organization, or public agency, will eventually ask them to serve on a "green," "eco," "smart," or "sustainability" committee or initiative. Go to work for Xerox and you'll receive a "Sustainability Report" in the employee packet, along with the company's "Report on Global Citizenship" and a copy of "The Sustainability Handbook."

To cite one industry example, consider travel and tourism, a sector with an unusually heavy ecological footprint, dependent as it is on petroleum and other fossil fuels to move, feed, lodge, and entertain visitors. For decades critics have insisted that tourism can damage cultural and social networks, not only the natural environment. Today, many students majoring in hospitality are required to take a class in sustainable tourism, an industry niche traceable to the 1980s. Like organic food, sustainable tourism started modestly among environmental and antiglobalism activists; today it is a common, if not mainstream, topic among industry leaders who hope to rebrand tourism's commodified, wasteful, and even destructive image. When today's hospitality graduates enter the profession, they'll likely encounter an array of consultants, workshops, associations, websites, and publications promising to help them operate sustainably, whether they work for an airline, hotel, rental car agency, chamber of commerce, or tourism attraction. Think back to your last stay at a major motel chain: chances are a sprightly green and blue notice in the bathroom urged you to use towels more than one day: "Waste less water so Holiday Inn can help save the planet!" Motels and other industry players who meet environmental benchmarks established by international accreditation organizations such as Green Globe receive a certificate of sustainability, provided they are dues-paying members. The best among them are recognized at awards dinners and featured in the Sustainable Traveler Index website or the popular Lonely Planet guides. Given that socially conscious travelers are a growing consumer segment, and therefore a lucrative target market, green labeling and industry honors are now common throughout the hospitality sector, if for no other reason than they present another handy public-relations tool, which is what critics say their main purpose *is*.

A concept celebrating interrelatedness and ratcheted up by climate disturbances, resource depletion, and the public's realization that the ecosystem *does* matter, and that its parts are both finite and threatened, sustainability now touches nearly every academic discipline, social issue, political agenda, and professional sector. Even in economics, some of the field's neoclassic standard bearers, a surly bunch generally unfriendly to the notion of finite systems and to what they often deem anecdotal rather than hard evidence, have reluctantly yielded to natural capitalism, industrial ecology, creative economics, ecoefficiency, ecological economics, and the triple bottom line – popular theories that combine seemingly irreconcilable terms to suggest the profit motive is not incompatible with, and in fact may contribute to, healthy natural and social ecosystems.

Sustainability is big business, another apparent oxymoron. But do the people, organizations, governments, schools, and corporations that have adopted the term – skeptics might say hijacked the term – also embrace its core purpose and principles? Or have they written their mission language and strategic plans to serve a less demanding, self-serving agenda? Where does one even look for the term's "core purpose and principles," against which goals, methods, and outcomes might be measured? Where do we locate the soul of sustainability and, if it turns up, what do we do with it?

Not a New Idea

Previous to Brundtland, scientists, conservationists, philosophers, and planners, among others, likely referred to "stability," "balance," "harmony," "permanence," or "the economy of nature" to map out the conceptual terrain bordering on sustainability. Long before the word earned a semblance of popular recognition, however, the *idea* was in the air, if not fully fleshed out. Indeed, one might say people during the Pleistocene Era lived sustainably in that they sensed their existence was linked to the environment's well-being. Granted, their ecological wisdom may have been grounded as much in stories as in a scientific understanding of their dependence on trees and bees, but that does not obscure the fact that the earliest civilizations in the New World, to use one example, endured at least twenty times longer than the current occupants, who have inflicted far more ecological damage in a *much* shorter span. That period, beginning in the mid-eighteenth century with the Industrial Revolution, represents less than one percent of *Homo sapiens'* time on the planet, yet this blip of a moment has experienced more environmental degradation than the previous ninety-nine percent combined.

Staying with the so-called New World, because the collision of cultures is so apparent, among the reasons for their longevity, the first Americans' way of life, typically mobile, did less harm to the earth and kept populations in check. Pre- and nonagricultural societies rarely enclosed and plowed large swaths of land, which tends to undercut sustainability by exhausting nutrients and sabotaging biotic diversity. Seldom did they clear and destroy entire forests to build permanent settlements or graze livestock – the most ecologically damaging of which, cows, pigs, and sheep, hadn't yet set hoof on the continent. A limited number of possessions to store and carry was a prerequisite of a nomadic culture, meaning that large prey, for example, were usually only hunted when their meat, hides, claws, and bones could be used fairly soon.

Stories, mobility, and millennia's worth of wisdom served hundreds of generations of aboriginal peoples, and much of that wisdom carried over into the Agricultural Era, beginning about 10,000 years ago, when some Native Americans settled into communities; started harvesting corn, squash, and beans; built irrigation systems; established governments; developed trade with other villages; erected cities; and, like every other civilization, told themselves stories to explain their existence. Drawing on their pre-agricultural past, many of those narratives still honored nature's "sacred hoop," of which humans, so the creation stories told, were but one member. Tribal people "acknowledge the essential harmony of all things," writes Paula Gunn Allen in her elegant discussion of the sacred hoop, "and see all things as being of equal value in the scheme of things, denying the opposition, dualism, and isolation (separateness) that characterize non-Indian thought … Further, tribal people allow all animals, vegetables, and minerals (the entire biota, in short) the same or even greater privileges than humans" (Allen, 1996: 243).

The communal knowledge of, personal bond with, and spiritual relationship to the natural world represented by the sacred hoop is largely absent from today's inquiries about place and, by extension, from most discussions of sustainability, which more than a few observers across a broad swathe of disciplines regret. Biologist E. O. Wilson urges scientists to celebrate and engage the universe's essence, which he describes in terms that are as humanistic as they are technical. Poet Gary Snyder (1974) believes modern civilizations must rediscover and keep to Native pathways, a challenge he maps out in his verse and prose. Political scientist Murray Bookchin advises a return to a "vision of social and natural diversity" (Bookchin, 1995: 7). Social justice activist Vandana Shiva (1995) endorses a globalism that exports an Indigenous compassion for the planet's diversity, rather than a narrow industrial lust for its resources. Philosopher John Ehrenfeld (2008) warns that sustainability will remain elusive and largely unmet unless developed nations reorient their values. Scientist Janine Benyus (1998) counsels technicians to learn from Native insights, which often mimic nature's systems – in the same way architect Ian McHarg (1967) urges urban planners to "design with nature." Businessman Paul Hawken writes that economists must embrace a restorative approach where the market "creates, increases, nourishes and enhances" regional cultures (Hawken, 1993: 81). Farmer Wendell Berry asks us to remember that "the answers to the problems of economy are to be found in culture and in character" (Berry, 1990: 198).

Earlier western writers also sensed the need to rediscover our spiritual and cultural connections to nature, not only new technologies, if humans are to leave their environment unspoiled. Further, they believed

Indigenous people exhibited a proper alignment to model. Henry David Thoreau (1937) and Mary Austin (1903), for instance, celebrated "Indian wisdom"; Ralph Waldo Emerson found similar views in Eastern literature – an interrelatedness with nature that obliges humans to leave a livable world for civilizations to come (Buell, 2004: 172).

Many of these views are captured in a relatively new enterprise linking Western science with "Traditional Ecological Knowledge," or TEK. Santa Clara Pueblo scholar Gregory Cajete writes in *Native Science*, "Western society must once again become nature-centered, if it is to make the kind of life-serving, ecologically sustainable transformations required in the next decades" (Cajete, 1999: 266).

The Fierce Green Fire and Sustainability

Similar ethical and humanistic building blocks were championed by Aldo Leopold, who is sometimes considered an early modern voice for sustainability, even though he never uses the term. Leopold's "land ethic," however, is little more than a modern interpretation of traditional peoples' concept of nature as a community, of which humans are just one member: "In short, a land ethic changes the role of *Homo sapiens* from conqueror of the land-community to plain member and citizen of it" (Leopold, 1949: 204). This passage certainly breaks with what Descartes, Bacon, and other earlier philosophers believed about the human–nature relationship, what Manifest Destiny sanctioned, what Gifford Pinchot's utilitarianism endorsed, or what many of Leopold's contemporaries felt Genesis decreed. But *the core of Leopold's land ethic was not new*; he may have dressed it in twentieth-century ecological garb, and delightfully so, but the underlying moral obligation he revels in would have been familiar to earlier cultures of the Southwest, something Leopold realized later in life, when his words are tinged with regret for previously shutting down, rather than listening to, earlier cultures: "This same landscape was 'developed' once before, but with quite different results. The Pueblo Indians settled the Southwest in pre-Columbian times, but they happened *not* to be equipped with range livestock. Their civilization expired, but not because their land expired" (Leopold, 1990: 206–07). Rather than attempt to "fix" an impenetrable and unpredictable nature, Leopold senses he can and should learn *from* it, echoing Black Elk: "The buffalo is wise in many things, and thus, we should learn from him and always be a relative with him" (Brown, 1989: 72).

As a new ranger with the U.S. Forest Service in 1909, Leopold was transfixed by the ebbing embers of a "fierce green fire" in a dying wolf's eyes on an Arizona hillside (Leopold, 1949: 130). Over a forty-year career, he would build on that experience to disturb our certainty about the land community not a little – unearthing a deeper relationship with the natural world, metaphorically grounded in the green fire, where nature, culture, and science coalesce. Indeed, Leopold's long transition, from a haughty resource manager to a humbled lover of land, mirrors the conceptual transformation vital to sustainability today – from an unabashed and even violent utilitarianism to a personal, metaphysical, and, one might argue, *Indigenous* appreciation of place: "I doubt if there exists today a more complete regimentation of the human mind than that accomplished by our self-imposed doctrine of ruthless utilitarianism. The saving grace of democracy is that we fastened this yoke on our own necks, and we can cast if off when we want to, without severing the neck" (Flader and Callicott, 1991: 259).

Over time, the slow fusion within Leopold spawns a land ethic that is, in part, a western interpretation of Native ecology, made understandable and palatable to a dominant culture steeped in progress, boosterism, and scientific certainty. Given the political and social realities of his place and time (1887–1948), it is unlikely Leopold could stand before the Madison Chamber of Commerce, the Wisconsin governor, or the scientists he regularly addressed and declare, "We came from the earth … our mother," as did the Nez Perce prophet Toohoolhoolzote, let alone describe a conversation between a mountain and a dead wolf. But that is what his land ethic proposes – a "community" in the civilizing and mystical sense of the word, venerated by Indigenous cultures and framed by a new ecological understanding.

Leopold sought an "ethic" that was noticeably absent from Sinclair Lewis's Main Street, but whose roots he could trace to earlier cultures. While some may find his most enduring statement muddled, and critics point out that Leopold's science was sometimes wrong, those reproofs overlook the case advanced by philosopher J. Baird Callicott (1989) throughout *In Defense of the Land Ethic*, which is that the defining feature of the land ethic – that our relationship to nature must be based on something other than use – is not only valid but essential, perhaps even more so today. It is a quality that follows directly from Native American views, where land was seldom valued as a commodity to be surveyed, fenced, or purchased.

While it is impossible to identify *the* Native American philosophy
or attitude toward nature that helped to shape the views of Thoreau,
Leopold, or today's TEK advocates, just as there is no single Euro-
American view, we can point to a few common threads that weave their
way through the tapestry of many aboriginal beliefs about the natural
world, among them:

- Reciprocity and respect define the bond between all members of the
  land family.
- Reverence toward nature plays a critical role in religious ceremonies,
  hunting rituals, arts and crafts, agricultural techniques, and other day-
  to-day activities.
- One's relationship to the land is shaped by something other than economic profit.
- To speak of an individual owning land is anathema, not unlike owning
  another person, akin to slavery.
- Each generation has a responsibility to leave a healthy world to future
  generations.

These are not Romantic myths, New Age manifestos, or fables of a pre-
historic Noble Savage, as detractors claim; nor do they suggest an idyllic
fairytale where Indians and fellow creatures harmoniously cavorted in a
pristine garden before The Fall. The millions of people in the Americas
before European contact used natural resources, built cities, diverted
waterways, exploited animals, warred with one another, transformed
ecosystems with fire, and sometimes harmed the earth. Complicating
interpretation, the continent was home to hundreds of sovereign
nations, most with multiple clans and villages; so to say all Native/
Indigenous peoples in all places followed the same ecological blueprint
is a nonstarter.

Having said that, more than 10,000 years of history testifies that the
prevailing standards shaping most Indigenous relationships to the natural
world were *restraint* and *reverence* – restraint because, as people close
to the land, they understood and embraced their dependence on Earth's
resources; reverence because all was a gift from the Creator, whose animated universe meant animals, trees, and rocks were another "people."
The Walpi spoke of snake, lizard, and water people; Diné farmers called
maize "corn people," singing to each plant as they might nurture a child;
and Lakota hunters blessed and gave thanks to the "buffalo people," who
fulfilled their role in the chain of life by offering food, clothing, tools, and
ornaments.

Among Indigenous belief systems that reflect this conviction, the Iroquois Confederacy constitution, an oral account more than 500 years old first recorded in the nineteenth century, decrees that human actions should account for families seven generations beyond: "The thickness of your skin shall be seven spans ... Look and listen for the welfare of the whole people and have always in view not only the present but also the coming generations" (Gayanashagowa). In effect, the Iroquois outline a vision for a sustainable world, and while "sustainability" today has become a trendy and sometimes hollow buzzword, it became a genuine theme for Thoreau and other nature writers, even though the word never appears on their pages, and later philosophers of space, such as Aldo Leopold: "It thus becomes a matter of some importance ... that our dominion, once gained, be self-perpetuating, rather than self-destructive" (Flader and Callicott, 1991: 183).

That self-perpetuation, Leopold believed and earlier cultures practiced, is grounded in an *ethical* relationship to the land – the relationship that the essays in this book plumb.

WORKS CITED

Allen, Paula Gunn. "The Sacred Hoop." *The Ecocriticism Reader: Landmarks in Literary Ecology*, edited by Cheryll Glotfelty and Eric Fromm. Athens: University of Georgia Press, 1996, 241–63.

Austin, Mary. *The Land of Little Rain.* New York: Modern Library, 1903.

Benyus, Janine M. *Biomimicry: Innovation Inspired by Nature.* New York: Harper, 1998.

Berry, Thomas. *The Dream of the Earth.* San Francisco: Sierra Club Books, 1988.

Berry, Wendell. *What Are People For?* San Francisco: North Point Press, 1990.

Bookchin, Murray. *Toward an Ecological Society.* Montreal: Black Rose Books, 1995.

Brown, Joseph E. *The Sacred Pipe: Black Elk's Account of the Seven Rites of the Oglala Sioux.* Norman: University of Oklahoma Press, 1989.

Buell, Lawrence. *Emerson.* Cambridge: Harvard University Press, 2004.

Cajete, Gregory. *Native Science: Natural Laws and Interdependence.* Santa Fe: Clear Light, 1999.

Callicott, J. Baird. *In Defense of the Land Ethic: Essays in Environmental Philosophy.* Albany: State University of New York Press, 1989.

Ehrenfeld, John. *Sustainability by Design: A Subversive Strategy for Transforming Our Consumer Culture.* New Haven: Yale University Press, 2008.

Flader, Susan and J. Baird Callicott, Eds. *The River of the Mother of God and Other Essays by Aldo Leopold.* Madison: University of Wisconsin Press, 1991.

Gayanashagowa, the Great Binding Law: Constitution of the Iroquois Nations. [online] URL: Constitution.org.

Hawken, Paul. *The Ecology of Commerce: A Declaration of Sustainability.* New York: HarperCollins, 1993.

Hughes, Donald J. *North American Indian Ecology*, 2nd ed. El Paso: Texas Western Press, 1983.

Leopold, Aldo. *A Sand County Almanac and Sketches Here and There.* New York: Oxford University Press, 1949.

McHarg, Ian. *Design with Nature.* Hoboken: Wiley, 1967.

Shiva, Vandana. *Earth Democracy: Justice, Sustainability, Peace.* New York: South End Press, 2005.

Snyder, Gary. *Turtle Island.* New York: New Directions, 1974.

Thoreau, Henry David. *Walden and Other Writings of Henry David Thoreau,* edited by Brooks Atkinson. New York: Modern Library, 1937.

Wilson, Edward Osborne. *Consilience: The Unity of Knowledge.* New York: Alfred A. Knopf, 1998.

World Commission on Environment and Development [Brundtland Commission]. *Our Common Future.* Oxford: Oxford University Press, 1987.

2

Native Science and Sustaining Indigenous Communities

Gregory Cajete

This collection of essays presents an elegantly coherent synergy of voices and perspectives of some of the leading scholars of Traditional Ecological Knowledge (TEK). These voices, many of whom I am proud to call colleagues, have provided deep and invaluable insights into: the ways Indigenous stories provide "original instructions" for how to care for and relate to the land; the nature of reciprocity, exemplified by our relationship to plants, as an ethical foundation for "inhabiting a landscape of gifts"; the deep understandings of other than human consciousness we may learn from our relationship to animals as co-creators of the natural world; the role that "Indigenous knowledges" continue to play in sustaining Indigenous tribes today; the convergence of science and evolving recognition of TEK; the continuing need for ecological restoration guided by Indigenous thought; and the evolving role that Indigenous women are playing as contemporary "keepers of knowledge."

The work and insights of each of the contributors are priceless and come at a time when new perspectives for living more harmoniously with the natural world are so desperately needed. For we live at a time when dramatic climate change, environmental degradation, and social upheaval are beginning to manifest challenges of sustainability never before faced by humankind. I call this the time of the *"rise of the Indigenous mind."* It is a time when Indigenous people all over the world are voicing similar thoughts. In this context, TEK may be viewed as a part of a broader Indigenous paradigm that I call *Native Science,* which includes Indigenous relationship to land, plants, animals, community, self, cosmos, spirit, and the creative animating processes of life. It is the rise of the view of the "kincentric" multiverse that Dennis Martinez so practically reflects in his description of Indigenous relationships to their natural landscapes. In all this, Native Science reflects an ancient consciousness that is once again emerging as an expression of a deeper wisdom that still exists in the Indigenous world and which must be rediscovered and applied in a modern global context.

This rise of the Indigenous mind coincides with the rise of the importance of *sustainability* as a guiding theme through which TEK is steadily growing in prominence; it is particularly significant in the discourse on global climate change and the social and environmental crisis we face. Native Science is a foundational expression of the Indigenous mind, which is first and foremost a relational orientation, knowledge base, and process for sustaining people, community, culture, and place through time and generations.

What Is Native Science?

Native Science is a metaphor for a wide range of tribal processes of perceiving, thinking, acting, and "coming to know" that have evolved over millennia of human experience with the natural world. Native Science is born of a lived and storied participation with a natural landscape and reality. To gain a sense for the essence of Native Science one must also participate with the natural world; to understand the foundations of Native Science one must become open to the roles of sensation, perception, imagination, emotion, symbols, and spirit as well as concepts, logic, and rational empiricism.

Much of the essence of Native Science is beyond words and literal description. It is the authentic and holistic experience of nature as a direct participatory act around which Native Science has evolved. In terms of biology, Native Science may be seen as an exemplification of "biophilia" or the innate instinct that we and other living things have for affiliation with other life and with the animate world. There can be numerous other definitions, but in its core experience Native Science is based on the natural perceptive knowledge gained from using the whole body/mind of our senses in direct participation with the natural world.

In reality, Native Science is a broad and inclusive term that can include not only traditional ecological practices but also categories such as metaphysics and philosophy; art and architecture; practical sustainable technologies and agriculture; and ritual and ceremony practiced by Indigenous peoples both past and present. More specifically, Native Science encompasses such areas as astronomy, farming, plant domestication, plant medicine, animal husbandry, hunting, fishing, metallurgy, geology, and an array of other studies related to plants, animals, and natural phenomena. Yet, Native Science extends beyond even these areas to include spirituality, community, creativity, and appropriate technologies that sustain environments and support essential aspects of human life. In addition, Native Science may also include exploration of basic questions such as the nature of language, thought, and perception; the movement of time-space; the nature of human knowing and feeling; the nature of proper human relationship to the cosmos; and other such questions related to natural reality. Native Science is the collective heritage of human experience with the natural world and in its most essential form, a map of natural reality drawn from the experiences of thousands of human generations that have given rise to the diversity of human technologies and even to the advent of modern mechanistic science.

Why Is Native Science Important?

In today's world, the appreciation and understanding of the nature of Native Science is essential to the re-creation of a "participatory" science of life that is so desperately needed to balance the imbalance of science and technology and its continuing social and economic crisis consequences. For Native peoples themselves, the revitalization of Native Science is an essential component of cultural revitalization and preservation. It is the participation with the communal tribal landscape that evolved directly from relationship to a place or places in their historic past and in their present that defines them as a people.

The modern mind has lost its sensate bearings, its orientations to its roots, and to the natural world of process of which it is a part. It is the "ecological aware and participatory mind" that modern science must encompass, for it is that mind, that way of thinking, understanding, and participating with the natural world, that holds the best and most life-sustaining solutions to the current disconnection of science from the ground of its own being. The "new science" must be actively engaged in the reintroduction of the participatory mind. It must once again become a mind that authentically renews its orientation to the primal world of life and living process. It must be a mind that recalls and reestablishes the basis of human awareness in the larger ecology of the world.

Science must once again become the story of this awareness and relationship to the animate living world. Language must once again be understood as the body-based vehicle that refers to the animate landscape, which first gave rise to its expression. The thought that guides our actions and comprises our contemplation must be understood as a part of the dynamic expression of the physical as well as metaphorical air animating all nature. The intelligence that guides, focuses, and expresses our unique nature must be understood to be present in all things in nature. Therefore, a plant, an animal, a mountain, or a place may be said to have intelligence, its own mind and psyche, which is unique to it and with which our human intelligence continually interacts.

Native Science in its diverse forms of historic as well as contemporary expression presents templates for the kind of reconstruction and evolution of modern science required to address the issues and needs of a twenty-first-century world in the throes of ecological crisis and for which it shares responsibility for creating. Ecologically and socially responsible science must become the hallmark of twenty-first-century technology if we are to face the monumental environmental, social, and spiritual challenges of the next millennium. A new story of science must be created that once again assists us in:

> ... living in storied relation and reciprocity with the myriad things, the myriad beings, that perpetually surround us ... Only if we can renew that reciprocity – grounding our newfound capacity for literate abstraction in those older, oral forms of experience – only then will the abstract intellect find its real value. It is surely not a matter of "going back," but rather of coming full circle, uniting our capacity for cool reason [science] with the more sensorial and mimetic ways of knowing, letting the vision of the common world root itself in our direct, participatory engagement with the local and the particular. (Abram, 1996: 270)

The perspectives of Native Science that are being voiced by Indigenous peoples have great potential for developing insight and guidance for the creation of the kind of environmental ethics and deep understanding that must be gained in the critical times ahead. The serious study of Indigenous perspectives of environmental relationship to land, plants, animals, and natural resources provides much needed models for understanding environmental sustainability as a working process.

Native Science engenders in its very process and content the revitalization of our human "biophilic" sensibilities. It also provides a way to connect with the Indigenous soul deep within each of us. As a system of thought and process of application it can provide an expansive paradigm for applying scientific understanding. Indeed, the "perception" of science must expand to make it the whole and comprehensive form of human knowledge it needs to become.

For Indigenous people themselves, the revitalization of Indigenous knowledge through a truly self-determined education provides the most direct route for Native sovereignty. Nowhere is the path more direct than in the connection that Indigenous people feel for their communities and their homelands.

Community Is the Medium and the Message

"*Mitakuye oyasin*," as the Lakota say, "we are all related," a metaphor that personifies what Indigenous people perceive as community. Relationship is the cornerstone of tribal community and the nature and expression of community is the foundation of tribal identity. Through community Indigenous people come to understand their "personhood" and their connection to the "communal soul" of their people. The community is the place where the "forming of the heart and face" of the individual as one of the people is most fully expressed, the context in which the person comes to know relationship, responsibility, and participation in the life of one's people. *Community is the medium and the message!*

Community is also the context in which each community member assimilates culture and its underlying philosophy. In its most basic sense, culture is the way in which a group of people have come to relate to a place and its natural processes. While Native peoples all over the world are diverse in their expressions of culture, their fundamental way of relating to the natural world is remarkably similar, a commonality of ways that allows for generalizations to be made regarding Native Science.

Native community is the context in which the affective dimension of traditional education unfolds, the place where one comes to know what it is to be related. It is the place of sharing life through everyday acts, through song, dance, story, and celebration; of learning, making art, and a place of sharing thoughts and feelings where each person can, metaphorically speaking, become complete. Community is the place through which Indian people express their highest thought.

Native community is about living a so-called symbiotic life in the context of a symbolic culture, which includes the natural world as a vital participant and co-creator of community. That is to say, the life of the Indigenous community is interdependent with the living communities in the surrounding natural environment. Historically, Indigenous communities mirrored the stages of creative evolution and the characteristics of the animals, plants, natural phenomena, ecology, and geography found in their place through a rich oral tradition. Through the oral tradition, story becomes both a source of content, as well as methodology. Story enables individual and community life and the life and process of the natural world to become primary vehicles for the transmission of Native culture. The culture's vitality is literally dependent on individuals, in community with the natural world. Indigenous cultures are really extensions of the story of the natural community of a place and evolve according to ecological dynamics and natural relationships.

Traditional Indigenous people have always expressed their symbolic culture through the continuous retelling of the myth-dreams that concern their deepest connections within nature. The Native community conveys a message about a human society interacting with nonhuman life in a neighborly world. In this sense, community itself becomes a story, a collection of individual stories that unfold through the lives of the people of that community. This large community of story becomes an animate entity vitalized through the special attention given it by its tellers and those who listen. And when a story's message is fully received, it induces a powerful understanding that becomes a real teaching. Cosmology, the lived story of place, kinship, and environmental knowledge, forms the foundation for the expression of Native Science in Native communities.

People realized themselves by being of service to their community and by caring for their place. They sought the completion of themselves as tribal men and women, the communal and spiritual ideal, an ideal whose depth of expression is almost never achieved in contemporary communities. "Tribal man is hardly a personal 'self' in our modern sense of the word. He does not so much live in a tribe; the tribe lives in him. He is the tribe's subjective expression" (Deloria, 1973: 201).

Native Science Evolves from Native Community

Native Science builds on our innate sense of awe of nature's majesty, the core experience of spirituality. From this sense of awe flow the stories of creation, the philosophy of living, the foundation of community and the "right" relationship with all aspects of nature. Native cosmology and philosophy, the truest reflections of Native Science as a way of life, were the lived experience and practice within a community. Native Science, both in its contemporary and historic sense, is contextual and relational knowledge; it attempts to model traditional ways of teaching, knowing, and understanding relationships that are based on the existing makeup of the natural world.

Ecological communities revolved around practiced relationships at multiple levels of personal, family, and community life. The child born into this web of relationship first experienced the ecology of tribal community with the mother, father, and extended family; later, this learning extended to include clan and tribe. In the natural environment that formed the backdrop for all relational possibilities, the child learned the multiple roles of family, clan, plants and animals, and the special place in which he or she lived. These were not haphazard; they mattered to the survival of the community and to the continuation of the special relationships the community had established with its particular part of the natural world. The community was the common focus of intention and attention in the social psychology of every Native person, young and old.

The natural principles observed in the working of relationships with the natural world were incorporated into the physical and social structure of a village. This might be metaphorically pictured as people huddled around something with rapt attention, or as people holding hands in a circle. Native Science was an attempt to create closer and closer resonance with those aspects of the natural world that individuals and tribes felt to be important. This "resonance" is *relationship*, originally grounded on and inspired by people's feelings for the night sky and the cosmos. Everything has its source in the natural world; therefore, learning about and preserving natural resources, the sources of one's life in all senses of the term, are important parts of Indigenous science as well as of the arts.

Through participation in the tribal community as well as in the greater community of nature, Native people experienced being at home with and in nature. Being in a community in natural places that brought forward this sensibility further engendered this connectedness. The concept of biophilia – the idea that human beings have an instinctual understanding and need for affiliation with other living things –, reflects what Native people have always known: affiliation is a part of being human, as well as that which underlies the transfer of knowledge from one generation to the next. Native life in community is a primal pathway to knowledge of relationships with the natural world. People establish and reestablish contacts with entities within nature, such as plants, animals, and natural forces.

Finding and growing food presented ecological principles that had to be reinforced. Native peoples constantly reminded themselves where their food came from. Every member of the community was responsible for gathering, hunting, or fishing, so each person came to know the intimate relationships humans had to maintain with the sources of their food. By following their traditional ways of food gathering, young and old came to understand that foods are prepared and must be respected in certain ways. The entire realm of Native foods provides a context in which all dimensions of Native Science are expressed. The preparation of food is itself an art in which all members of the community and family participated. Feasting and celebration formed the backdrop for telling stories, for friendly interaction, trade, family and community bonding, learning, and giving thanks for the life.

Native hunting and gathering at both the levels of process and experience placed Native people in constant participation with their sources of food. There are few other experiences that can develop empathy for the natural world in this way. Native hunting and gathering became both art and applied science and reinforced the sacred covenant that Native communities had long established with the places in which they lived.

Gardening provided another context for applied science through which people established and worked their special relationship with plants. Coming to know land entails coming to know, in very intimate ways, its plants. Similar to human communities in their diversity, plants prefer places based on their needs for certain soils, sunlight, water, and space. Reliance on readily available food sources forms the foundation for Native ethnobotany and the deep understanding that has evolved among Native people with regard to plants and their ecologies.

Native Science is a people's science, a people's ecology. People come to know and understand their relationships to the physical environment in which they work by what they do to live in that environment. Native technologies are often elaborate and ingenious. These technologies were ways of dealing with issues that come up in the process of living in a particular place – the desert, ocean, forest, mountaintop, wherever the place may be.

Traditional Native architecture presents yet another example of applied science. Each traditional structure evolved from the special relationship people had developed with their environments. Native structures were themselves reflections of the special features and available resources of the landscape of which they were a part. The stories, artistic forms, and the technologies involved with the construction of these structures were a testament to the long negotiated relationship with their land and resources. As people built, they learned stories behind the structures, materials used, and construction techniques. Appropriate symbols and uses of various structures all reflect Native Science, not to mention the lessons of cooperation, responsibility, and the role that each member of the community played in the construction of traditional shelters.

Mimicking the processes observed in nature, the community learned how to be reciprocal and responsible in relationships. Everyone had their work, a place, and a purpose in the community. Everyone had something to share as well as something to learn, so young and old came to understand this mutual, reciprocal principle of Native Science. Close observation of plants, animals, landscape sights and sounds, changes in wind and humidity – everything surrounding people is part of Native Science, as it is in the Western scientific tradition. It is the Native emphasis on participation and experience that embeds the sense of kinship with all nature in the minds, hearts, and souls of all members of the community. Learning to be confident in one's ability to live within nature is a key motivation and feature of maturity.

Beginning with the most basic skills, children learned to live respectfully in their environment, in ways that will guarantee its sustainability. By first watching and then doing, Native children learned the nature of the sources of their food, their community, and their life relationship. They learned that everything in life was a matter of kinship with all of nature. Education involves a constant flow of information; it is multigenerational and cross-generational: young teach old; old teach young; sister teaches younger sister; brother teaches younger brother; aunts, grandmas, and grandpas teach children. Mentoring relationships between the young and old are essential. Moreover, mentoring relationships do not have to be between people alone; they can also be between humans and plants and natural forces and spirits and all manner of things not usually recognized in Western science. Sometimes knowledge of self and new knowledge useful to the people as a whole occurs in the form of dreams.

Practical understanding develops in many ways. The key to learning was continual experience of the natural world through work, play, ritual, food gathering, hunting, and fishing. In some tribes, young people had to plan long journeys, and so apply their knowledge. Skills of observation, seeing, smelling, listening, tasting, healing, and intuition may someday be used for disciplines such as those of the herbalist, masseuse, hunter, maker of art, and animal tracker. These understandings were often based on practicing in a game, like that of learning how to walk without the use of eyesight by depending on another. The latter, sometimes called "night walking," requires that the person set out in the dark and depend exclusively on balance, listening, and touch to move about.

Being provided the opportunity and time to reflect has always been an important aspect of Native education. It was understood that knowledge and creativity have their source in every person's inner being and in their personal journeying and thinking. Self-reliance, even in young children, is based on the belief that all persons have the ability to know and to share, to bring forward great strides in understanding and knowledge. Consequently, there are many myths revolving around the learning experiences of young people, as well as their roles in bringing new knowledge to the people.

Indigenous science and knowledge encourage and direct curiosity, or the human instinct of learning. Children learn by doing and experiencing, such as in planting, hunting, preparing food, and helping to put up a traditional shelter. Indigenous education methodologies, then, include role-playing, or learning relationships or roles that humans play, as well as the ways of animals. As children mature, they take on the ways of animals and remember to remember human roles in traditional dances that are artistic representations of relationships with all the things that matter affecting Native people's lives and traditions. Even traditional costumes reflect symbolic representations of their relationship to these entities, and the people dance and sing their relationships, to revitalize their understanding.

Participating with nature through play, work, hunting, gathering, fishing, gardening, and traveling reinforces the innate "biophilia" or sense for affiliation with the natural that is essential to the development of the mind, body, and spirit of children. After all, these relationships are the ultimate source of continuity for any culture.

Native Science has a mythic tradition and connection. Myths express relationships involved in building compacts with animals and natural forces in a particular place. Each traditional art form embodies the cosmology, philosophy, and mythic themes of a tribe. For example, in the Haida tradition of the American Northwest, dance and totemic art reenacts the formation of clans and the relationships of those clans to bear, eagle, raven, and whale. Traditional art forms provided a context for remembering the important lesson of wise use of materials, the sources of those materials, their appropriate use within the tribe, and developing the skills of listening, close observation, patience, and memory.

Even gambling games were a part of the learning process because of their grounding in myth, but also because of the skills of mathematical reasoning and strategy that they develop. Now, in Western science, evolving chaos theories reflect conceptual orientations related to gambling that Native people understand.

Personal relationships with plants, animals, and natural forces constitute a Native Science orientation. Talking to trees, for instance, is an introspective exercise rooted in Native traditions. Scientists develop relationships or a feeling for the phenomena they study. Barbara McClintock, a Western scientist famous for studying corn reproduction, is unusual in the sense that she wrote about her relationship with corn. In their dances and related traditions Indigenous people celebrate relationships to the plant and animal world by effectively becoming one with their spirits or their world. Humans are not separated from their environments or from the other creatures inhabiting those environments as they are in Western science. Knowledge must be both a source of joy as well as one of gravity or respect, because responsibility to the surrounding life is ignored only at great peril.

The research on Native Science is only in its initial stages as an area of serious study. Nevertheless, preliminary exploration has already revealed tremendous data in such areas as plant medicines, archeo-astronomy, and philosophical areas related to quantum theory. This is only the beginning of a new and creative evolution of science. Yet it must be a *dialogue* and not the replay of the past in which Native peoples have been exploited for their resources and ideas but receive little in return. The issues of intellectual and cultural property rights as they relate to plant medicines provides one case in point. There are many others. The ideas and processes of Native Science are equally important as conceptual well-springs for helping to bring about the integration of science and spirit that is essential to the marriage of "truth" – the ideal goal of science – with "meaning" – the ideal goal of spiritual practice. Native peoples must be given credit for their intellectual achievements and benefit from the encouraging research that has been accumulated with regard to Native Science.

Native community mirrors the natural order of nature through its forms of organization and in its focus on knowing and cultivating key social and ecological relationships. Native communities evolved in response to the requirements of surviving in particular environments and maintaining sustainable relationships therein. While many Native communities were forced to adopt Western forms of community after being displaced from their ancestral lands, the spirit of Native community continues to be expressed in many ways among Native people. The few Native communities that have not been displaced continue traditions of participation with their landscape, and serve as examples of the meaning and possibilities of the conscious integration of human community with natural community. As we proceed through the twenty-first century, Native cultures are attempting to reestablish their ancestral focus on one's relation with a homeland.

Likewise, environmentalists advocate relationship with natural places through the concept of bioregionalism. Still, this concept does not go as deep as the Native expression of natural community. What traditional Native models have to offer is a perspective of community that goes beyond the social "isms" and theories of community. Traditional Native models of community get to the heart of social and natural relationships as an expression of human biophilia and the reality of human society as a part of, rather than separate from, nature. These are ancient ideas, but they are also timeless ideas. Native Science, Indigenous community, and the kincentric universe must be allowed to rise in our collective consciousness once again. In the perilous world of the twenty-first century, it may well be a matter of our collective survival. Indeed, *The "Indigenous Mind" Is Rising!*

WORKS CITED

Abram, David. *The Spell of the Sensuous: Perception and Language in a More-Than-Human World.* New York: Vintage Books, 1996.

Armstrong, Jeannette. *Constructing Indigeneity: Syilx Okanagan Oraliture and Tmixwcentrism.* Electronic Publication. Greifswald: University of Greifswald, 2010.

Barnhardt, Ray and Angayuqaq Oscar Kawagley. "Indigenous Knowledge Systems and Alaska Native Ways of Knowing." *Anthropology and Education Quarterly*, 36 (1), 2005, 8–23.

Bartlett, Cheryl M., Albert Marshall, and Murdena Marshall. "Two-eyed Seeing and Other Lessons Learned within a Co-learning Journey of Bringing Together Indigenous and Mainstream Knowledges and Ways of Knowing." *Journal of Environmental Studies and Sciences*, 2 (4), 2012, 331–40.

Cajete, Gregory. *Native Science: Natural Laws of Interdependence.* Santa Fe: Clear Light, 2000.

   Look to the Mountain: An Ecology of Indigenous Education. Skyland, NC: Kivaki Press, 1994.

Deloria, Vine, Jr. *God Is Red.* New York: Dell Publishing, 1973.

Hayward, Jeremy W. *Letters to Vanessa: On Love, Science, and Awareness in an Enchanted World.* Boston: Shambhala Publications, 1997.

Kimmerer, Robin W. "Weaving Traditional Ecological Knowledge into Biological Education: A Call to Action." *Bioscience*, 52 (5), 2002, 432–38.

Martinez, Dennis. "Protected Areas, Indigenous Peoples, and the Western Idea of Nature." *Ecological Restoration*, 21 (4), 2003, 247–50.

Nelson, Melissa K., Ed. *Original Instructions: Indigenous Teachings for a Sustainable Future.* Rochester, VT: Bear & Company, 2008.

Peat, F. David. *Lighting the Seventh Fire: The Spiritual Ways, Healing and Science of the Native American.* Secaucus, NJ: Carol Publishing Group, 1994.

Settee, Priscilla. "Honoring Indigenous Science Knowledge as a Means of Ensuring Scientific Responsibility." Master's thesis. Winnepeg: University of Manitoba, 1998.

Skolimowski, Henryk. *Eco-philosophy: Designing New Tactics for Living.* Boston: M. Boyars, 1981.

Wildcat, Daniel R. *Red Alert! Saving the Planet with Indigenous Knowledge.* Boulder, CO: Fulcrum, 2009.

Wilson, Edward Osborne. *Biophilia.* Cambridge, MA: Harvard University Press, 1984.

3

Mishkos Kenomagwen, the Lessons of Grass: Restoring Reciprocity with the Good Green Earth

Robin Wall Kimmerer

Introduction

When we look about us on the earth, what we see is colored by our worldview and the languages that we use to describe our observations. A landscape of streams and lakes, mountains and rich valleys, shared by thousands of species of plants and animals, is understood through the lens of the western materialist worldview as a wealth of ecosystem services or natural resources. In contrast, through the lens of traditional Indigenous philosophy the living world is understood, not as a collection of exploitable resources, but as a set of relationships and responsibilities. We inhabit a landscape of gifts peopled by nonhuman relatives, the sovereign beings who sustain us, including the plants.

In the ancient teachings of the Anishinaabek, it is said that when Nanabozho, the original man was placed upon the earth, he was filled with wonder at the strangeness and the beauty of the world, which was at that time, unknown to him. The Creator had instructed him to wander to the Four Directions, as a humble student, learning all that he could from the others who were already living there in harmony with one another. He was given the responsibility of speaking with every kind of being and learning from them what gifts they had to share with the people who would be coming. Every plant he encountered taught him of its worth, the way its roots could be eaten, the medicines it made, how its bark was ready to become lodges, its branches baskets, its berries to sweeten life. From these teachings, he followed the Creator's instructions and bestowed a name on every species. As he traveled the earth, the plants took care of him, providing him with the materials for his canoe, the cordage for his fish net, food for his belly and medicines to protect him. In each of the sacred directions, he encountered a powerful plant that would be his teacher. (Benton-Banai, 2010)

The Nanabozho stories from the beginning of the world reflect the understanding of humans, not as dominators, but as humble students of the earth's other beings. Nanabozho was instructed to respect all the beings of the earth, and in ways both comical and profound he learned many lessons of what that meant. A fundamental tenet of traditional plant knowledge is that the plants are understood, not as mere objects or lower life forms as the western "pyramid of being" might suggest, but as nonhuman persons, with their own knowledges, intentions, and spirit. Not only are the plants acknowledged as persons, but they are also recognized as our oldest teachers. It is said that the plants have been here far longer than we have; they know how to make food and medicine out of light and air and then they give it away. They unite the earth and the sky and exemplify the virtues of generosity, providing us with all that we need to live. They heal the land and feed all the others in creation, i.e., the ecosystem. No wonder they are revered as teachers by we humans who are just learning how to live on the earth. In fact, humans, who lack the generous gifts of plants and animals, are often referred in Indigenous cultures as "the younger brothers of creation." If plants are our teachers, what are they teaching us and how can we be better students? These are among the responsibilities of humans. Traditional plant knowledge is the product of this orientation to humility, to careful attention to being a student of plants. This essay explores, in a small way, some lessons learned in that ongoing process, through listening to teachers, both human and plant.

Plants clearly embody the flow of gifts that sustain the animal world, including humans. In some Anishinaabek teachings plants are recognized as the second level of creation, on whom all other life forms rely. Rocks, soil, and water, upon whom the plants depend, comprise the first level, animals the third, creating a chain of being that reflects contemporary scientific principles of trophic pyramids of energy flow. In my culture, it is said that every being has its own gifts and the Creator instructed the plant people to use their gifts to help the humans who were coming. As Nanabozho, the culture hero, trickster, and great teacher of the Anishinaabe learned, plants have continued to fulfill that responsibility. In fact, in our language, *min,* the word for "berry" and the word for "gift," are closely related.

Acknowledgment of human reliance on the gifts of plants is inescapable in a subsistence economy, where daily needs of food, medicine, tools, clothing, containers, shelter, and more, are met by the plants. The calendar months in the growing season are often named for what the plants are providing at that time – for example, the strawberry moon, the maple sugar moon, the blueberry moon, wild rice moon, blackberry moon. Seasonal cycles of ceremony honor those life-sustaining gifts. The people were guided by the powers of the sacred herbs and healed by the medicines. From the willows of the cradleboard to the cedar of the grave, plants offer their gifts to people. In other ways, simultaneously material and spiritual, people understand their debt to the plants. So close is the reliance that plants are honored in many creation stories, as the origin of the people, like the Wabanaki who emerged from the ash tree, or Mayan peoples made of corn meal. In these cultures plant–human relationships had a central place in the life of an individual, the family, the community, and the nation – a profound connection that is difficult to visualize in an industrial society in which plants, if acknowledged at all, are often viewed only as commodities or adornments to the built landscape.

This orientation to the world as an ongoing gift exchange between the human and the more-than-human world is foundational in Indigenous environmental philosophy. It raises the question, "How does one respond to a world made of gifts?" The answer is likely very different from the response engendered by the notion of a world of commodities or property. Gift economies generate cultures of reciprocity in which humans have a moral, spiritual, and material responsibility to reciprocate the gifts received. Native peoples of the eastern deciduous forest share elements of a creation story that is emblematic of the question, "What is our responsibility in return for the gifts of the earth?"

In the beginning, there was the Skyworld, where people lived much as they do on earth today. There grew the great Tree whose branches bore all the seeds, fruits, medicines, grasses, every kind of plant. One day, a great wind came and toppled the tree, opening a hole in the Skyworld where its roots had been. In curiosity, a beautiful young woman, called Gizhgokwe in our language, the Skywoman went to the edge of the hole to look down. She lost her footing and began to slip, grabbing on to the Tree branch to stop herself.

She fell like a maple seed pirouetting on an autumn breeze. A column of light streamed from a hole in the Skyworld, marking her path where only darkness had been before. But in that emptiness there were many, gazing up at the sudden shaft of light. They saw there a small object, a mere dust mote in the beam. As it grew closer, they could see that it was a woman, arms outstretched, long black hair billowing behind as she spiraled toward them.

The geese nodded at one another and rose as one from the water, in a wave of goose music. She felt the beat of their wings as they flew beneath and broke her fall. Far from the only home she'd ever known, she caught her breath at the warm embrace of soft feathers. And so it began. From the beginning of time, we are told that the very first encounter between humans and other beings of the earth was marked by care and responsibility, borne on the strong wings of geese.

The world at that time was covered entirely by water. The geese could not hold Skywoman much longer, so they called a council of all beings to decide what to do, loons, otters, swans, beavers, fish of all kinds. A great turtle floated in the watery gathering, and he offered to let her rest upon his back and so, gratefully she stepped from the goose wings onto the dome of the Turtle. The others understood that she needed land for her home. The deep divers among them had heard of mud at the bottom of the water and agreed to retrieve some. The loon dove to get a beakful, but the distance was too far and after a long while he surfaced with nothing to show for his efforts. One by one, the other animals offered to help, the otter, the beaver, the sturgeon. But the depth, the darkness and the pressures were too great for even these strongest of swimmers who came up gasping for air and their heads ringing. Soon, only the muskrat was left, the weakest diver of all. He volunteered to go while the others looked on doubtfully. His little legs flailed as he worked his way downward. He was gone a very long time. They waited and waited for him to return, fearing the worst for their relative. Before long, a stream of bubbles rose from the water and the small limp body of muskrat floated upward. He had given his life to aid this helpless human. But, the others noticed that his paw was tightly clenched and when they opened it, there was a small handful of mud. Turtle said "Here, put it on my back and I will hold it."

Skywoman bent and spread the mud across the shell of the turtle. Moved by gratitude by the gifts of the animals, she sang in thanksgiving and then began to dance, her feet caressing the earth with love. As she danced her thanks, the land grew and grew from the dab of mud on Turtle's back. Like a good guest, she had not come empty-handed. She had in her hand, the broken branch from the Tree of Life and so over the new land, she spread the seeds from the Tree in the Skyworld, sowing the land with the gift of the plants. And so, the earth was made. Not by one alone, but from the alchemy of the plant and animal gifts, and human gratitude and reciprocity. Together they created what we know today as Turtle Island. The following is a rephrasing of a story from Kimmerer:

Our oldest teachings remind us that gratitude is the thread that binds us together. They were her life raft at the beginning of the world, and now so much closer to the end, we must be theirs (Kimmerer, 2013a).

Creation stories offer us a metaphoric glimpse of the principles that guide interactions of traditional Indigenous peoples with the natural world. The goal of this chapter is to explore the ways in which the relationships of human reciprocity with the plant world are manifest. Consider how the thinking and practices developed by our ancestors can be a guide for our path forward. The approach must be both ancient and urgent in order to meet the challenges of human societies facing unprecedented levels of anthropogenic environmental change and uncertainty. By reflecting on ancient teachings, we aspire to find strategies that enable us to heal our damaged relationships with the more-than-human world, so that we might all continue.

Cultures of Gratitude Lead to Cultures of Reciprocity

Native environmental philosophy acknowledges that our human lives are utterly dependent on the lives of other beings and thus our first responsibility is for gratitude. As the Skywoman story suggests, recognition of the world as gift is an invitation to thanksgiving, and indeed many Indigenous cultures have been characterized as "cultures of gratitude."

The expression of gratitude may be emotional and spiritual but it also engenders very practical outcomes, with adaptive evolved survival values. The practice of gratitude can in a very real way lead to the practice of self-restraint, avoiding rampant exploitation. The evolutionary advantage of cultures of gratitude is clear. Indigenous story traditions are full of cautionary tales about the failure of gratitude. When people forget to honor the gift, the consequences are always both spiritual and material. In story, the spring dries up, the corn doesn't grow, the animals do not return, and the legions of offended plants and animals and rivers rise up against the ones who neglected gratitude. The western storytelling tradition is strangely silent on this matter. So we find ourselves in an era when centuries of overconsumption have depleted natural resources and left human societies materially and culturally impoverished by a deep disconnection from the living world.

Gratitude is most powerful as a response to the earth because it provides an opening to reciprocity, to the act of giving back. How do cultures engage in reciprocity with the more-than-human world? How do we give back in return for the gifts of the earth? As the Skywoman story and millennia of lived experience attest, this was a central question for our ancestors, as it is for us today. Traditional knowledge is rich with teachings about how to reciprocate. The imperative of reciprocity is explored in what Melissa Nelson refers to as our "Original Instructions," i.e., ethical systems that govern relations with the human and the more-than-human world. The exercise of reciprocity can take many different forms.

Ceremonies are a form of reciprocity that renews bonds between land and people and focuses intention, attention, and action on behalf of the natural world, which is inclusive of the spiritual world. From the First Salmon ceremonies of the Northwest to the great Thanksgiving Address of the Haudenosaunee, ceremony represents a ritual gift of spiritual energy, power, and beauty that is offered in reciprocity for the gifts, and contributes to a balance between humans and the more-than-human world. Plants, of course, often play vital roles in ceremony, as ritual foods and objects, and as vehicles for interface with the sacred. Consumption of plant foods in ceremony reinforces the appreciation of the ways that plants and animals give up their bodies to feed our own, in a sacred transaction of life for life.

It is important to remember that spiritual ceremonies, in addition to their power in unseen dimensions, may also have important immediate, direct effects on the physical world and thus constitute a form of "practical reverence." For example, the traditional four-day ceremony to honor the ripening of wild rice includes a prohibition on gathering during that ritual time. The abstention from harvest during ceremony yields pragmatic consequences for the flourishing of the rice, which benefits from four days of seed-drop to reseed the rice beds, before people come to gather. Likewise, salmon ceremonies that permit the salmon to run upriver without impediment, welcoming them back to their natal waters, ensure that an adequate number of fish return to the spawning grounds.

Prescriptions of Reciprocity: The Honorable Harvest

Of course, acknowledging the complete dependence of humans on other beings creates tension. It is understood that humans must take other lives in order to sustain our own, so the way in which plants and animals are harvested becomes very important, and they should be taken in such a way that that the life received is honored. This inherent contradiction, implicit in our heterotrophic biology, is resolved in Indigenous philosophy by practices of reciprocity, by giving back.

In the western worldview, plants are seen as either "wild" and therefore free for the taking, or they are owned as "property" that can be bought and sold. From this perspective of plants as "natural resources," whatever protocols exist to govern harvest are typically oriented toward maximizing efficiency. In the best management practices, harvesting is done in a way that does not damage the resource for future harvest, ensuring its sustainability. However, when plants are valued not as commodities but as sovereign persons who generously offer their gifts, additional protocols arise as part of traditional harvesting practices.

As clever consumers, we humans recognize our own tendency to take too much, to confuse our wants and our needs. Traditional Ecological Knowledge is rich with teaching stories explaining the consequences of taking too much. All too often Nanabozho ends up with an aching belly, but sometimes the negative result extends to others. When Heron taught Nanabozho a new fishing technique, he passed along a caution: "This way is so quick," Heron said, "it's easy to take too many, so catch only what you need for supper." But Nanabozho, so pleased with his new technology, filled his drying racks with more fish than he could ever eat. He went yet again to the lake to get even more, and while he was gone, Fox came and devoured every last bite of dried fish. It was a hungry winter for Nanabozho, and when he went to replenish his stocks the lake was now empty (see Johnston, 1995).

Such teaching stories are part of the Honorable Harvest, a set of unwritten guidelines, both ethical and practical, which govern human consumption. The canon of the Honorable Harvest guards against over-exploitation, protecting the future of the plant or animal, as well as the human future. These ancient practices resonate today, prescribing an alternative to the dominant consumptive materialist worldview in which humans are understood primarily as consumers and not as contributors to the well-being of other organisms.

Plant harvesting practices of the Honorable Harvest provide examples of reciprocity between culture and plant populations (Kimmerer, 2013a). Naturally, harvesting protocols differ among cultures, bioregions, and different kinds of plants. However, within this great, locally adapted diversity, traditional harvesters of wild plants often share similar teachings, passed down between generations, about the proper ways to gather so that the plant people and the human people will both continue to flourish.

I can share here some of what I have learned by listening to plant knowledge holders, paying attention to the teachings of the plants themselves, and through the actual practice of gathering. It represents my limited understanding of what I have gratefully learned, and it acknowledges that there are many different representations of these teachings.

I have been taught that when we go gathering, we don't just seek out a resource-rich patch and begin taking whatever we want. To gather properly, our hearts and minds must be clear of negative thoughts and we go only with good intentions. When we encounter the plant we are looking for, we introduce ourselves and explain our purpose. I was taught to greet the first one, but never to take it, for it might be the last. Instead, it is left alone to perpetuate its family and to carry the knowledge that a respectful person has come seeking. If one does find additional plants, then a traditional gatherer speaks to those plants, asking for permission to harvest, hoping to learn if the plants will share their gift with humans.

If one asks permission, then one must also listen for the answer. This kind of listening may involve many different kinds of perception. It might include the strictly empirical observation of whether the population is large and healthy enough to support harvest. It may be based on previous monitoring of the patch, its harvest history and population trajectory. The evaluation may also include detailed observations of other signs in the forest that are interpreted as positive or negative responses and often entail intuitive understanding about whether the plant is or is not willing to share itself. This subtle communication, which is readily interpreted by a practiced and attentive harvester, might include the apparency of the plant, the play of light, variations in resistance to harvest, and sensation of an emotional response between plant and harvester.

If the plant is selected for harvest, then the Honorable Harvest calls for a further set of respectful practices. I have been taught that one never takes more than she needs for the expressed purpose. Regardless of need, never take more than half of what is available. I'm told that in the old times, the harvester would somehow mark the patch to indicate to others that it has already been harvested and should now be left to rest. Often, certain patches were known to be the responsibility and gathering ground of a certain family and others would respect those boundaries. The harvesting method employed should be one that inflicts as little damage as possible to the surrounding vegetation, i.e., one doesn't use a shovel if a digging stick will do. If the ground is disturbed, the harvester repairs the damage.

Whatever plants are taken must be fully used and not wasted, so as to honor the gift. Used plant material is returned respectfully to the earth when its purpose has been met. Just as the plant shares with the people, we are instructed to share what we have harvested, for it does not belong to us, but to the plants themselves. The harvester is also obligated to express gratitude for the gift received and to reciprocate the gift. Traditional harvesters often leave a small gift such as tobacco or another valued item. Giving tobacco is the most common practice, which mirrors the giving of tobacco to human elders and teachers, in return for knowledge and as a sign of respect and a vehicle for unspoken communication. Taking without giving back is considered a breach of the Honorable Harvest.

Many plant gatherers also reciprocate the gift of the plant through specific postharvest practices. For example, a harvester who digs a rhizome may break the rhizome into pieces and replant them, or separate small bulbs from large ones and transplant them to new places nearby to spread the population. Often seeds are scattered, the plots are weeded to reduce density, and the soil is aerated by digging and replacing the disturbed soil. Shrubs may be pruned, small trees coppiced, sedge beds weeded and tilled by harvest. These practices exemplify "practical reverence," an action that has both spiritual and material dimensions which contribute to the well-being and longevity of the plant population.

The Honorable Harvest represents a prime example of the holistic, integrative nature of Traditional Ecological Knowledge (TEK), in which detailed empirical knowledge, material practices, ethical and spiritual responsibilities, and indigenous values of kinship and mutual responsibility are all engaged as a way of expressing a reciprocal relationship with the plant world. This cultural canon, devised by generations of knowledge holders, may seem simple on the surface but in fact represents a sophisticated symbiosis of philosophy and practice, which couples values and actions to yield a formula for mutual thriving, an integration not yet achieved by western models of sustainability. Coupling "taking" to the moral responsibility for "giving back in equal measure" is a missing link in western economic models, in which the good of the human person and the good of the land are seemingly philosophically independent, and the intrinsic good of nonhuman persons is absent from the economic equation.

Kyle Whyte, a Potawatomi professor of environmental philosophy, states, "The intent of indigenous governance is to make the values and relationships in our creation stories manifest" (Amerind seminar, April 2013). The Honorable Harvest serves as an example of "policies" in which the values expressed in the creation stories – of mutual responsibility, of reciprocity, of the coupling of human and nonhuman well-being, and of returning the gift – are actualized. They resonate with the teachings of a gift exchange between people and nature, which underlie the story of Skywoman. The practices are not legislated, but rather are reinforced by living with shared values, where ethical prescriptions are in harmony with biophysical necessity. Contemporary movements that support ecological economics (Costanza et al., 1996; Daly and Farley, 2011; Hawken, 1993) couple patterns of human consumption to ecological principles and ethics, reflecting the same necessities to which our Native ancestors adapted through the canon of the Honorable Harvest.

This exploration makes no claim that the canon of the Honorable Harvest is universally practiced in Indigenous communities. Indeed, there are far too many instances in which the erosion of TEK through the legacies of colonization and imposition of western economic forces have replaced traditional philosophies. Knowledge of these concepts and practices is at risk of disappearing, just when it is most needed. The landscape bears witness to the impact, not only in plant harvesting but also in resource extraction of all kinds. We face a tremendous challenge, and a tremendous need to reclaim the ethic of the Honorable Harvest, not only in practices of berry picking, but also as constraints and guides on humans' unrestrained consumption of the living world, be it water, fossil fuels, minerals, forests, soil, or plants.

Mishkos Kenomagwen: The Teachings of Grass

The teachings of the Honorable Harvest and concern over disappearing species brought my students and me under the tutelage of a great plant teacher, sweetgrass. Sweetgrass, or *wiingaashk* in the Potawatomi language, bears the scientific epithet of *Hierochloe odorata*, meaning the sacred, fragrant holy grass. Sweetgrass is known as one of the four sacred plants of the Anishinaabe and a plant deeply connected to our creation stories. Benton-Banai writes that when Nanabozho traveled to the North, he met *wiingaashk* and learned that this grass is of the "hair of Mother Earth." Its scent would protect and comfort him on his journeys and bring goodness to his path. Sweetgrass is said by many to be one of the first plants to appear on Turtle Island, perhaps arriving in the hand of Skywoman herself. Strands of sweetgrass are traditionally plaited into braids, just as one tenderly braids the hair of a loved one, as a tangible sign of loving care expressed for Mother Earth. In addition to its respected symbolic value, sweetgrass is used as a smudge, a ceremonial plant, a medicine, and as a component of traditional basketry, often as a decorative counterpart to baskets constructed of black ash splints. So important is this plant, it is a known to be a cultural keystone species, write Garibaldi and Turner (2004), for many Indigenous peoples throughout its range.

We were approached by Mohawk basketmakers who reported their observations that the plant seemed to be in decline. Its abundance within known harvesting locales was diminishing, and suitable gathering sites were becoming fewer every year. This case study is the result of research conducted by graduate students Daniela Shebitz and Laurel Reid, with support from our collaborator and traditional practitioner Theresa Burns, a Mohawk basketmaker.

Drawing on the traditional knowledge of sweetgrass distribution and what appeared to be its decline, we conducted an inventory of historically known sweetgrass occurrences, based upon herbarium records at universities throughout the northeast. These sites were revisited and the presence or absence of current sweetgrass populations was recorded, as well as changes in habitat. Shebitz and Kimmerer's (2004, 2005) recurrence data supported the basketmakers' hypothesis of population decline in previously known sites; many populations of sweetgrass known from historic records were gone. Shebitz and Kimmerer (2004) examined the trend and attributed the losses to habitat destruction, to successional replacement, and to habitat fragmentation. Sweetgrass is typical of open, early successional habitats and is outcompeted when shrubs and forest encroach. As a rhizomatous perennial, with poor seed viability, it extends its population by vegetative growth, making it highly susceptible to loss from barriers such as roads in a fragmented habitat. Interestingly, Shebitz documented that the pattern of sweetgrass loss among historically known sites was not geographically random. A significant concentration of historically known sites with persistent sweetgrass populations occurred surrounding the Mohawk reservation where numerous basketmakers continue traditional harvest. Her results were suggestive of the oral expression often heard among plant gatherers: "If we don't use it, it will go away. If we use it respectfully, it will stay with us and flourish."

Basketmakers were also interested in the impacts of harvesting on intact sweetgrass populations, expressing their concern that unsustainable harvest levels may contribute to decline and disappearance, and that violations of the Honorable Harvest might be responsible for the reduced populations. The basketmakers described two different and potentially competing harvest methods, referred to as "the traditional and proper method" by different sweetgrass pickers. Some gatherers harvest sweetgrass by pinching individual blades from the base of the plant. Others harvest a few stems at a time by a quick snap and pull at the plant base, which removes a cluster of shoots, often including small roots. These are known as the pinch and the pull methods, respectively.

Graduate student Laurel Reid created experiments to assess the potential outcomes of these two harvesting methods. Using a restored sweetgrass meadow as a research site, she set up a series of experimental harvest plots. Each plot was fully censused prior to harvest to determine stem density, height, and biomass. The plots were then randomly assigned to one of three harvest treatments, representing either pinch, pull, or the unharvested experimental control. In the harvested plots, 50 percent of the grass stems were removed by either pinching or pulling in an evenly distributed pattern throughout the plot, reflecting the basketmakers' dictate, "We never take more than half." After harvest, sweetgrass stems in all plots were individually tagged in order to monitor rates of growth, mortality, and new tiller production through the year. The experiment spanned two full cycles of summer harvest and postharvest monitoring.

The western science paradigm, which regards humans as primarily antagonistic to the success of other species, would suggest that the unharvested controls would have the greatest growth and reproduction, while mortality would rise with increasing intensity of harvest. However, that was not the case.

In the year following the first harvest, a notable response occurred in the harvested plots. Instead of the harvesting-induced decline anticipated by conservation biologists, an elevated rate of regrowth occurred, which not only replaced all the harvested shoots, but the density of new shoots was nearly 80 percent higher than the control. The plots harvested by both the pull and the pinch method yielded a strong increase in new shoots. The control plots, in contrast, experienced the lowest level of new tiller production and a significant increase in mortality. During the second year of the experiment, the difference in new shoots was even greater, more than doubling the rate of regrowth in the control in the plots where tufts of sweetgrass were pulled. In every case, the harvested plots fully regained the shoots that had been harvested, for a sustained yield over two years, despite harvesting 50 percent of the plants annually. The control plots continued to decline and experienced a higher rate of competition with colonizing forbs. Regardless of harvest type, the harvested plots were much more vigorous than the control. These experimental studies demonstrate that sweetgrass plants respond positively to traditional harvest, resulting in sustained or even stimulated regrowth rates. The only negative outcomes occurred when harvest was absent.

The results of the experiment can be expressed in two different idioms, each consistent with the cultural context of two different knowledge systems. While the results ran counter to conventional scientific wisdom, scientific approaches search for a mechanism to explain the unexpected outcome. The materialist, process-oriented interpretation explains that the stimulation observed in sweetgrass growth is due to a physiological shift known as "compensatory growth," in which the biomass lost to harvest is rapidly replaced by increased growth. This rapid regrowth has been observed in a number of grass species subject to herbivory, where the new shoots arise from subterranean apical meristems, or growing points. The greater stimulation observed after the "pull" harvest may be attributed to breakage of the rhizome, which stimulates tillering from buds located along this underground stem. The postharvest recovery is also associated with reduced resource competition, as light, water, and nutrients become more available when plant density is reduced. The decline in vigor of the control plots is likely to be associated with the accumulation of a mulch of dead, unharvested stems, which may accelerate nitrogen immobilization in the biomass and thus reduce nutrient availability. The mulch layer may also provide a microclimate favorable for competitors or pathogens. In sum, the mechanistic explanation for the findings can be stated: Harvest causes increased population growth as a result of reduced density, increased resource availability, and compensatory growth following biomass removal.

The relational explanation, grounded in Traditional Ecological Knowledge, recognizes agency of the plants in relation to human attitudes and practices. The experimental results are in full accord with the theories shared by traditional herbalists and gatherers (e.g., Ortiz, 1993), expressed in the oral tradition and repeated here: *If we respect a plant and use it well, it will stay with us and flourish. If we disrespect or ignore it, it will go away.* Not using a plant, failing to gather the gifts it offers, is understood as disrespectful in a worldview that recognizes plants as non-human persons, each with its own gifts and responsibilities. Indeed, the decline of the unharvested control and the stimulation of the harvested plants support this interpretation.

The response of the plants themselves, represented in the data, demonstrates that both cultural interpretations are valid in describing the phenomenon and represents mutually reinforcing explanations. The convergence in interpretation supports the Indigenous teaching that plants are the teachers. In this case, the sweetgrass was the teacher and the lesson could be expressed in two complementary frameworks, in the language of both TEK and Scientific Ecological Knowledge (SEK). The two explanations converge around the understanding that the human activity of harvesting is simultaneously beneficial to humans and plants. The study exemplifies the Indigenous notion of the role of humans as active participants in the well-being of the landscape. In this case, the removal of humans, as often dictated by modern conservation guidelines, would lead to the decline of sweetgrass, as human harvesting is vital to its success. This finding helps to explain the distribution of sweetgrass around Indigenous territories where basketmakers are active.

It is important to recognize that not all plants are capable of compensatory growth, and not all respond positively to harvest. Many slow-growing, long-lived plants of stable habitats have life-history characteristics that make them particularly vulnerable to harvest and overexploitation. Skilled Native harvesters do not uniformly apply the same techniques and harvest levels to all species, rather adjusting the specific protocols based on the Honorable Harvest to the nature of the plant, so that certain species are rarely harvested and when taken are tended in species-specific ways.

The case of sweetgrass is but one of a growing number of studies (e.g., Anderson and Rowney, 2002) in which academic ethnobotanists are finding that TEK is rich with examples where harvesting activities are linked to the well-being of the plant population, a phenomenon well known to the harvesters themselves. Among elder holders of traditional plant knowledge, one frequently hears expressions such as, "That plant has disappeared because no one picks it anymore," or, "That tree has gone away because people forgot how to use it," or the admonition, "We better go out digging or else there won't be any more for our grandchildren." In this sense, using a plant is a practice of respect, rooted in the notion of the plant as person. In order to maintain reciprocity and the integrity of the gift economy, there must be receivers of gifts, in order to honor the givers. Failure to accept the offered gift, i.e., not harvesting the fruits/roots/seeds that are offered, is viewed as disrespectful.

Ethnoecologists have documented a great many examples of sustainable harvesting practices in which human needs are met, while preserving and enhancing the regenerative capacity of the plant resource itself. Kat Anderson (2005), in her book *Tending the Wild*, and Deur and Turner (2015) in *Keeping It Living* contend that harvesting relationships between plants and people can maintain and even enhance the vitality of the plant population. The loss of tending relationships with certain plant species has been associated with decline of cultural keystone species.

The experiment clearly demonstrates that to restore sustainable sweetgrass populations, one must also restore the harvesting relationships that enable it to flourish. Restoring sweetgrass, without also restoring the disturbance regime provided by harvesters, would be an exercise in futility, because the well-being of the plants and the people are linked.

This mutualism between harvester and harvested presents an important counterpoint to the dominant paradigm of western conservation practice, which frequently recommends the elimination of harvest in order to protect vulnerable populations, rather than prescribing the restoration of harvesting relationships. Understanding the significance of mutualistic relationships between harvesters and plants of cultural significance can inform a new perspective on restoration in which human relationships, termed "cultural services," become a goal of restoration as well as restoration of ecosystem services.

Restoration: A Contemporary Practice of Reciprocity

Ecological restoration is a potent contemporary response to the question, "How do we enter into reciprocity with the living world?" We can use our considerable human gifts to heal the land, enacting the responsibilities of the Honorable Harvest in a landscape from which we have taken too much.

Through the relatively recent history of ecological restoration (Cairns and Heckman, 1996), the goals of this healing practice have developed and evolved (Higgs, 2003; Hobbs and Norton, 1996). The goal has greatly broadened from its beginnings as the direct revegetation of damaged land by installing artificial vegetation assemblages, heavily subsidized with inputs of water and nutrients, to emulating nature, with encouragement of self-sustaining communities with intact ecological structures and functions. But it would be a mistake if we confined our efforts to the realm of restoring ecosystem structure and function alone (Nabhan, 1991). Further advances have highlighted the incorporation of human values and biocultural restoration (Egan et al., 2011; Long et al., 2003). Expansion of restoration goals to include the mutualistic role of humans as active participants in land healing through cultural practices has been informed by Traditional Ecological Knowledge (Anderson and Barbour, 2003; Kimmerer, 2000; Long et al., 2003; Martinez, 2003) and is termed "reciprocal restoration" (Kimmerer, 2012).

Reciprocal restoration is the mutually reinforcing restoration of land and culture, such that the repair of ecosystem services contributes to cultural revitalization, and renewal of culture promotes restoration of ecological integrity. In Indigenous communities, these reciprocal relationships may include the return of subsistence activities, the practice of traditional resource management, the restoration of traditional diets, language revitalization, and the exercise of spiritual/ethical responsibility. Concepts of reciprocal restoration also apply to mainstream society by re-engaging people with land, renewing place-based connections, and supporting cultural practices that sustain the land. Integrating TEK can support this new direction in restoration ecology, as a model for restoration of reciprocal relationships.

Restoration of Knowledge: People of the Seventh Fire

After centuries of institutionalized attempts to suppress Indigenous ways of knowing, TEK is increasingly being embraced as a partner to scientific knowledge (Berkes, 2008; Berkes et al., 2000; Drew and Henny, 2006; Martin et al., 2010; Mauro and Hardison, 2000). TEK is also sought out by policy makers and scientists as a source of models for sustainability (Berkes, 2004; Berkes et al., 1995; Huntington, 2000), particularly as the limitations of western scientific approaches become apparent in an era of increasing uncertainty produced by anthropogenic climate change and resource depletion.

The call to bring traditional environmental philosophy to bear on contemporary social and environmental issues is widespread (Deloria, 1995; Kimmerer, 2013b; LaDuke, 2005; Nelson, 2008; Wildcat, 2009). Environmental leader and Onondaga Nation clan mother, the late Audrey Shenandoah, taught, "This is why we have been able to hold on to our traditional teachings, because there would come a time when all of the world's people will need to learn it for the earth to survive."

The history of knowledge loss and the contemporary responsibility to restore that knowledge is embedded in ancient teachings. Anishinaabe peoples speak of the Prophecies of the Seventh Fire (Benton-Benai, 2010), which describes the migration story of our people, from the time of the First Fire among our Wabanaki relatives at the mouth of the St. Lawrence River. They left in response to a sacred message that counseled the people to move west as a safeguard against the great changes that were to come to Turtle Island. Over many generations, the people followed the guidance to move until they came to "where the food grows on the water," the land of wild rice. The Seventh Fire teachings record the history both of the migration and the changes that befell the people upon the arrival of newcomers. It foretells the time when people will be separated from one another, from traditional lands, from spiritual ways, from language. Teachings speak of the great hardships and losses endured along the path, up to a time when the air is not fit to breathe and we can no longer lift a cup of clean water from streams, to a time when plants and animals turn away from us. All of this has come to pass.

We are told that all the world's peoples, Native and newcomers alike, will stand at a fork in the road and face a choice about the future. One path is the soft green path of life. The other is a burnt path, sharp and black. Elders say these two choices represent the spiritual path that honors life and compassion, and the materialist path of greed and selfishness – stark choices between the world understood as a sacred gift and the world in which Mother Earth is seen as a mere object to exploit. We stand at that crossroads. The prophecies are clear that in this time a new people will arise, the People of the Seventh Fire. These People will need great courage and understanding to lead the way. The teachings say that in order to walk forward on the path of life, we must first turn around and walk back along the trail that our ancestors followed and pick up what was left behind for us: fragments of land, remnants of stories, plant and animal relatives, and our languages and teachings, such as the Honorable

Harvest. With these treasures in our bundles we will be prepared to walk the green path and put the world back together. These teachings of loss and renewal, of gathering and traditional knowledge, speak directly to the covenant of reciprocity – of reciprocity between generations and of a renewed reciprocity between people and the land.

To my mind, the teachings of the Prophecies of the Seventh Fire speak of healing – healing the land and our relationships to land. This is the next step in answering the question, "How do we enter into reciprocity with the living Earth?" We do it by healing the damage we have done through unrestrained consumption, by violating the precepts of the Honorable Harvest. In the spirit of reciprocity and the Seventh Fire teachings we are called to restoration. A wealth of knowledge and practices related to the restoration of the structure and function of ecosystems can help revive the ecosystem services upon which all life relies. However, it is not only the land that is broken but our relationship to it. Our responsibility is not only to restore the land, but also to heal our relationship with land, restoring the covenant of respect, responsibility, and reciprocity.

On many damaged lands, the plants rush in to heal the broken ground. They carry the gifts for colonizing the open space, building soil, reestablishing the food chain and nutrient cycles, and restoring productivity. If we are open to a kind of intellectual biomimicry, the plants provide us with metaphors and models for the work of healing humankind's relationship to land. The plants can be teachers, but we must know how to be students.

Plant Knowledge Revitalization

At the same time that TEK is becoming accepted as a rich source of practices and philosophies for sustainability, the continuing erosion of knowledge in Indigenous communities, particularly plant knowledge, is of significant concern. Many grandparents could identify and use more than a 100 plants, but today it is estimated that the average American can identify fewer than 10 plants, let alone understand the ecological and cultural gifts that they hold. American youth, including Native students, can correctly identify as many as 100 corporate logos, but only a handful of plants (Nabhan, 2003). This is a dangerous form of intellectual colonization that efficiently converts living beings to inanimate products, while undermining knowledge of the life systems that support us.

Loss of plant knowledge erodes ecological and cultural resiliency, as communities without this knowledge can no longer reliably adapt to resource shortages or ecological and economic shifts through dependence on subsistence resources for food, medicine, and materials. Diminishing plant knowledge impedes a community's ability to observe and detect critical changes in vegetation and thus respond in a timely way to mitigate the impacts. Accelerating uncertainty and disruption induced by climate change compounds the risk.

Decline in plant knowledge is part of a generalized disconnection from the natural world in an industrialized society where the sources of our sustenance are hidden behind industrial processes, rather than visible in the living world. Increased reliance on market sources for foods, medicines, and materials also decreases reliance on the land and the knowledge of how to use it. Replacement of subsistence activities by a wage economy contributes significantly to knowledge loss, as do erosion of familial ties to land.

The societal ills associated with disconnection from nature have been well documented (e.g., Louv, 2008) and can have adverse consequences for physical, mental, and community health as well as ecosystem health. Louv and others have analyzed the widespread factors that undermine acquisition and transmission of land knowledge, primarily in the dominant society. However, Indigenous communities, while retaining cultural ties to the land, are also subject to these harmful influences, as well as the forces of cultural and knowledge erosion engendered by a history of forced assimilation, removal from traditional homelands, and urban relocation policies aimed at deculturation.

As material relationships with plants disappear, access to their lessons and the practices that contribute to knowledge generation also diminish. Plant gathering on the land provides a venue for cultural sharing of knowledge, songs, stories, and values such as those embodied in the teachings of the Honorable Harvest. If people don't harvest plants, the natural settings for sharing practices of mutual responsibility and reciprocity are lost, as are the teachings that contain resonance, meaning, and application far beyond the berry patch.

While our fluency with plant knowledge is diminishing, in both Native and non-Native communities, I have been taught that the knowledge itself is not lost. Humans may have forgotten, but the knowledge is resident in the land itself. Thus, knowledge revitalization depends as much on gaining the skills for learning from the land as it does on transmitting specific information. We need to ensure that we are educating people with the capacity to learn from the land again, to retrieve the knowledge that is held for us by the plants. Ideally, plant knowledge is conveyed by the plants themselves, through direct interaction. Learning from experienced community members is also a fundamental component of Indigenous pedagogy. Traditional protocols for knowledge seeking, which include careful observation, direct experience, fasting, and conversing with plants, are part of the skill set in knowledge revitalization. This means that language revitalization, restoration of ceremonies, and the protection of intact ecosystems must go forward so that people continue to have access to their teachers, the plants.

Plant knowledge revitalization must also incorporate responsibility for the knowledge. In western modes of scientific inquiry, generating knowledge for the sake of knowledge alone is an accepted, even celebrated, practice. However, in Indigenous pedagogy, knowledge is always coupled with responsibility. Knowledge might be withheld unless the recipient has demonstrated an understanding of the responsibilities attendant to that knowledge.

Much botanical knowledge is meant to be shared, modeling the generosity of the plants who offer their gifts widely, like the fast-growing plants that surround human settlements and thrive with human use. These common, easily regenerated species invite widespread use of their considerable gifts. These plants, like some kinds of plant knowledge, are resilient and less in need of strict protection. However, like rare, slow-growing plants of the deep forest, not all knowledge is to be freely disseminated, due to the risks of misinterpretation, inaccurate transmission, misuse of the knowledge, or because the knowledge is sacred and proprietary. To be properly used, these species, like species of knowledge, require particular protection and deep knowledge for proper use.

Knowledge of plant benefits must be coupled to a cultural context of respect, responsibility, and reciprocity. Without the agreed upon constraints of the Honorable Harvest, a harvest can lead to deleterious consequences for the plants and their users. The disappearance of many medicine plants at the hands of those who commodify them attests to this risk. These are frequently the slow-growing plants of specialized habitats whose homes have been threatened by uncontrolled development and must be harvested with great care. It is imperative that gatherers understand, as our ancestors did, that harvesting protocols differ with different plants. Not all species can regenerate easily after harvest, the way sweetgrass does. Thus, efforts in plant-knowledge revitalization should include careful consideration of the attendant responsibilities for ethical education to protect plants and community knowledge against biopiracy. The cultural exchange cannot be knowledge alone but the wisdom to use that knowledge responsibly.

Restoring plant knowledge and the worldview in which it is embedded is a key element of the practice of reciprocity. Knowledge revitalization is an exercise of intergenerational reciprocity, as well as reciprocity with the plants themselves. When plants are understood as teachers, it is an act of reciprocity to be an attentive student and to pass on the teachings of the plants.

One of the dominant factors that contributes to the erosion of traditional plant knowledge in Native communities is the replacement of knowledge transmission by direct interaction with plants and community knowledge holders with institutions of public education. In most educational settings, if plant knowledge is conveyed at all, it is exclusively through the objective, materialist lens of western science. Revitalization of plant knowledge is made more difficult by educational systems that privilege science as a way of knowing, while dismissing and often undermining Indigenous knowledge. Systematic exclusion of Indigenous knowledge and its integrative worldview from public education also truncates the experiences of every student, limiting the scope of exposure to alternatives to the dominant materialist worldview, producing an intellectual monoculture.

The teaching stories of Nanabozho are memorable because they vividly capture the struggles between spiritual and physical impulses, which all humans experience. Nanabozho often gets into trouble when his physical appetites overwhelm clear thinking, when arrogance and hubris lead him astray. Fortunately, other nonhuman beings step in to put him back on the balanced path. It is said that humans have at least four ways to understand the world – with mind, body, emotion, and spirit. We do not fully comprehend unless we are using all four (see Cajete, 1994). Skilled medicine people engage traditional plant knowledge using all these dimensions. However, scientific plant knowledge intentionally restricts itself to the intellect and tools of physical measurement.

Science itself, a process of systematic inquiry and knowledge generation about the natural world, is the intellectual gift of all people. As I have stated, TEK is "the intellectual twin to science" and indeed Native science was practiced long before the western scientific worldview arrived on Turtle Island (Kimmerer, 2002: 433). Native plant science contributed to generating the deep knowledge of plant medicines, agriculture, land management, and ecological processes that our people employed to survive and adapt.

Scientific approaches are extremely powerful in generating knowledge of mechanisms of action and detecting and measuring phenomena beyond the scope of human observation – a vital part of higher education. We can legitimately celebrate this way of knowing as a powerful tool for understanding and manipulating the world we inhabit. There are many questions for which science is the most appropriate and effective tool. But it is not the only tool, nor are all important questions amenable to scientific solutions. Science is a tool for knowledge, but not necessarily for wisdom.

Science can tell us how something works, but its strict objectivity is only one dimension in a decision-making framework that must also include values, ethics, and spiritual perspectives. Science is a superb tool for answering true/false questions, but it does not have the capacity to address questions of right/wrong. Indeed, many of the complex issues we face today lie at the intersection of nature and culture, and leaders and policy makers, as well as scientists, acknowledge that science alone is not sufficient to address them.

The protocols of the Honorable Harvest illustrate how traditional knowledge holistically integrates the very dimensions that science seeks to exclude. The harvesting practices are simultaneously based on a strong understanding of the biophysical factors that influence plant regeneration, as well as the ethics of respect, kinship, and reciprocity rooted in a spiritual understanding of the proper relationship between human and plant responsibilities. Incorporation of these values generates an understanding of human-plant interactions that can lead to behaviors and social norms that sustain both plants and people. The science behind plant harvesting can produce descriptive knowledge, while traditional knowledge also produces prescriptive wisdom.

Our cultural evolution toward sustainable societies cannot proceed without examining the limitations of the scientific worldview and its broader application, not just as an inquiry about the natural world, but as the foundation of social and economic institutions. Respectful exploration of the themes fundamental to the Indigenous worldview may enrich our moral imaginations, explaining how we might live in societies based on reciprocity, and modeled for us by plants. Cultivating the conditions for the coexistence of knowledge systems and the adaptive solutions that they may hold should be a priority as humans push against the limits of sustainability. What we need is not the intellectual monoculture of scientism, but an intellectual pluralism. A polyculture of ideas is especially important at this critical time as we search for strategies of resilience in the face of accelerating ecological and cultural shifts of unprecedented magnitude.

How then do we cultivate a knowledge polyculture that supports the revitalization of plant knowledge, the Indigenous worldview, and connections to the natural world that restore the covenant of reciprocity? How do we make the values inherent in creation stories manifest in our relationship with the living world? If we consider the Indigenous notion that plants are important teachers, we can look to them for guiding metaphors. Among the best teachers I know for guidance on pluralism and symbiosis are three wise and beautiful beings, known by many as the Three Sisters – corn, beans, and squash.

The Three Sisters garden is a manifestation of Native science, an innovation that embodies the Indigenous worldview of relationship, kinship, and reciprocity in a polyculture of three different species. Accustomed to straight rows of single species, early colonists who saw the mixed fields of Three Sisters concluded that Native peoples had no real agriculture as William Cronon noted in his classic 1983 environmental history, *Changes in the Land.* In a striking parallel to their disregard for alternative knowledge systems, they judged that the only legitimate agriculture was by definition their monoculture, failing to recognize the power of botanical pluralism in the sustainable Indigenous polyculture.

The genius of Indigenous agriculture was to harness the power of complementarity, by cultivating together three carefully selected species. The corn, essentially a giant grass, stands tall and strong, growing quickly in the summer heat using specialized C4 photosynthesis. The vertical spiral of leaves up the stem uses light efficiently, yielding easily harvested ears of corn. However, the high productivity of maize also requires a rich source of nutrients. Consequently, nitrogen-fixing beans were planted with corn, providing needed fertilizer by enriching the soil. In return, the corn stalk provides support for the twining bean that climbs the corn and positions its leaves, flowers, and fruit in the open spaces between the corn leaves, creating a tower of food from the reciprocity between beans and corn. The third sister, the squash, spreads large, prickly leaves over the ground at the base of the corn. The shade of the squash leaves suppresses weeds and keeps the soil moist, while the rough leaves discourage herbivores.

Indigenous farmer-scientists created a system in which the three species facilitate each other's growth through cooperation, rather than reducing each other's success in the intense competition found in monoculture systems. Complementarity is also found below ground, where the architecture of the three different root systems occupy different regions of the soil, again promoting efficiency of resource use by avoiding competition or interference with one another. As a result, the calories produced by this polyculture exceed the yield that would result from planting them alone. The nutrients in corn, beans, and squash are also complementary; eating all three species produces a nutritionally complete diet, while one alone is insufficient for human health. The polyculture forms an archetypal manifestation of the Indigenous worldview, revealed in the practice of sustainable agriculture that fed thriving Indigenous cultures.

Standing in a Three Sisters garden, we are surrounded by a powerful metaphor for a potentially productive relationship between TEK and western science. The principle of complementarity is an essential element of the garden model. The well-documented (Barnhardt and Kawagley, 2005; Berkes, 2008; Petch, 2000; Procter, 2000; Simpson, 2000) dichotomies that distinguish TEK and SEK have long been viewed as a source of conflict and indeed the cultural gulf is wide. But in a garden model, the goal is to use those disparities as complementary assets instead of liabilities, collaborators instead of commensals or competitors. The potential for complementarity between SEK and TEK has been widely recognized (Bartlett, 2005; Bartlett et al., 2007, 2012; Becker and Ghimire, 2003; Kimmerer, 2002, 2013b; Moller et al., 2004).

Corn is a cultural keystone species (see Garibaldi and Turner, 2004) for many Indigenous nations of the Americas, and it is the primary element of the Three Sisters garden. The garden model for a knowledge polyculture acknowledges and honors the historical and cultural precedence of TEK as the "elder" knowledge. Its broader scope, simultaneously encompassing both social and biological systems, material, and spiritual perspectives, enables it to serve as an intellectual scaffold, the primary organizing architecture for knowledge symbiosis. In the garden, corn is planted first, and only when the corn is six inches tall are the beans planted. The elder corn is well established so that its strength and direction can guide the growing bean. This practice can also extend to cultivation of a productive relationship between knowledge systems, by acknowledging the principles of traditional knowledge as foundational to the knowledge of mutualism, rather than relegating them to the status of cultural anecdotes.

Native farmers observed that corn alone is not as productive as when grown with other plants. A diet of only corn is not nutritionally complete, because a complementary amino acid is missing. Beans are members of the legume family, which complements the nutritional value of corn's particular gift: the ability to take nitrogen from the air and manufacture protein. This protein, which is packed into seeds, leaves, and roots, is also released into the soil, where it acts as fertilizer, promoting the growth of corn and squash. The bean nourishes both people and soil.

Scientific Ecological Knowledge (SEK) is the analog of the bean plant in the knowledge symbiosis. Driven by curiosity, powerful in its understanding and scope, science can deeply nourish our understanding of the physical mechanisms that underlie the patterns and processes of the natural world, for which TEK has reduced capacity. Science can be life-enhancing, engaging our human capacity for wonder, innovation, problem-solving, and meaning-making.

The holism and depth of TEK, embedded in culture and the specificities of place, entails certain trade-offs in focus and capacity. TEK as a body of knowledge and as a process, philosophy, and practice is inseparable from its cultural context. TEK is not designed to illuminate underlying physical mechanisms and extend those causal relationships beyond boundaries of space, time, and cultural context. SEK is designed for testing hypotheses in a controlled systematic manner, which yields a different set of insights, related to validating knowledge in the context of true or false. Its ability to bypass subjectivity and bias, to let us test assumptions and find them lacking, to discard the false in search of the true – all of these capacities are present and essential to expanding understanding of the strictly physical world. The scientific method is conducted with the intention of transcending cultural contexts. (However, the assumption that separation from a subjective, cultural context is possible is itself a cultural construct.)

By its very design, SEK helps us understand only those things for which it possesses measuring tools. The best scientists understand that there is much we do not know and cannot measure – yet. True science is based on humility – recognition of the limits of human observation. Technology becomes the tool of science in creating means by which human understanding is freed from the constraints of our own perceptions, enabling us to explore remote galaxies and the inner workings of a cell. However, if science abandons humility, by dismissing what it cannot comprehend, by replacing respect, responsibility, and wonder with arrogance and hubris, then like overgrown bean vines, its very productivity endangers life rather than sustaining it.

Can we imagine a new kind of knowledge generation modeled after the complementarity of a Three Sisters garden, in which the practice of scientific inquiry is embedded in the Indigenous worldview? What would knowledge generation look like, if we created a mutualism in which the climbing "beans" of scientific inquiry are guided by the "maize" of Indigenous principles?

Science Embedded in Indigenous Worldview: Beans Guided by Corn

What are the principles of Indigenous knowledge that have the potential to guide a mutualistic relationship with western science? I think of these principles as the widespread and sturdy leaves of the maize, evenly spaced in a natural, harmonic order that creates around the corn stem a spiral ladder to guide the wandering bean. These principles create a conceptual framework for conducting science from the perspective of the Indigenous worldview. Just as the corn leaves encourage the progress of the bean's exploration, those principles might influence the trajectory of SEK, toward the conduct of science that generates knowledge that promotes the well-being of peoples and the earth.

The corn and beans in a Three Sisters garden symbiotically support and strengthen each other, as TEK and SEK can do in a knowledge mutualism, generating understandings of different kinds, of different aspects of the human experience and relationship with the living world. In the garden model, the mutualism is balanced, which maintains the integrity of each species of knowledge. TEK remains a proudly subjective, qualitative, holistic, long-term, and relational knowledge that encompasses mind, body, emotion, and spirit. SEK adheres to its tradition of a proudly objective, quantitative, short-term, reductionist, and materialist knowledge that privileges its intellectual schema for strictly empirical knowledge. Together, they can create a new kind of knowledge that will lead us to true, embodied sustainability.

The growth and development of a knowledge mutualism, in which SEK and TEK are as balanced as beans and corn, is far from reality. The goal is to plant the seeds and tend them, with that vision as an aspiration. But they do not grow alone.

Squash: Creating the Climate for Wisdom to Grow

At the base of the intertwined corn and beans is a thick cover of squash leaves. Its presence regulates the climate for the symbiosis. The big broad leaves intercept the sunlight that falls among the pillars of corn, so that no energy is wasted. The leaves cast a deep shade that suppresses the growth of weeds and keeps the soil moist. Its fruits are few but large and complement the nutritional ecology through synthesis of vitamins that the others cannot provide. Fed by the bean's nitrogen, the squash canopy provides habitat for a diversity of tiny predators that keep damaging pests in check. The ecological role of the squash is to create the conditions under which the corn and beans can flourish. And yet, the squash is the slowest to germinate, and when young requires the greatest care. (Kimmerer, 2013a)

In the Three Sisters garden of knowledge mutualism, squash represents the educational climate of mutual respect, intellectual pluralism, and critical thinking in which both TEK and SEK can grow. The layer of squash plants metaphorically creates what Ermine (2000) and Ermine et al. (2004) refer to as the "ethical space of engagement," a place between worldviews that "opens up the possibility for configuring new models of research and knowledge production that are mutually developed through negotiation and respect for cross-cultural interaction." The ethical space ensures that "value systems do not operate in the shadows" (Bartlett et al., 2012). Like the squash, this space can take a long time to root and needs considerable attention in order to grow.

Spiritual understanding is a fundamental component of TEK and must be part of knowledge revitalization if this knowledge system is to maintain its integrity. The importance of creating a space to include and honor spiritual understanding has been identified as a key pedagogical element for integrating TEK and SEK in higher education.

There is another element to the metaphoric as well as pragmatic role of squash in this knowledge polyculture – as an exchange or translational layer between the knowledge generated by humans and the knowledge held by the more-than-human world. Of all three plants, squash lies closest to the earth, at the boundary between the seen and the unseen. Both SEK and TEK, to varying degrees and with different modes, recognize that human knowledge of the natural world is limited by the biases of human perception and experience, by inadequate tools for observation and analysis, by our restricted ability to translate from intelligences other than our own, and perhaps most importantly by the limitations of our imaginations. The shady, weed-free space created by squash can be an analog for an educational space purposefully created to encounter the knowledge of all our relations, seen and unseen. It is a space governed by ethical and moral responsibilities to the human and more-than-human communities. It can function as a boundary or a filter through which Earth knowledge becomes human knowledge – a filter of humility, compassion, respect, and responsibility. The squash layer represents the recognition that knowledge is not our own but is the collective wisdom of the living world to which we are accountable.

As teachers, students, scholars, and practitioners, we are responsible for being the gardeners, for tending to the needs of all the species of knowledge, and, most importantly, for cultivating an intellectual landscape so multiple species of knowledge can continue to flourish as robust, dynamic individuals.

Higher education should create the space for this garden to develop, and it should strive to train competent gardeners, i.e., students literate in all three species of knowledge, not just in harvesting the fruits of those knowledges but in protecting and regenerating each of them. Just as different species of plants need different kinds of care, fertilization, and protection from pests, each knowledge system needs a specific kind of care. Each needs special tending to enrich its adaptive capacity and regenerative potential in an always changing biocultural landscape. The role of educational communities should be to help provide an environment that strengthens both SEK and TEK, an environment that enables reciprocity and creative synergy between them.

We can say of knowledge, as well as of plants, "If we use it respectfully, it will stay with us and flourish; if we ignore it or disrespect it, it will go away." The plants have taught us this, and humans should humbly remember and return these considerable gifts to the plants and the knowledge they have shared with us, so that we all might continue on this good green Earth.

WORKS CITED

Anderson, M. Kat. *Tending the Wild: Native American Knowledge and the Management of California's Natural Resources.* Berkeley: University of California Press, 2005.

Anderson, M. Kat and Michael B. Barbour. "Simulated Indigenous Management: A New Model for Ecological Restoration in National Parks." *Ecological Restoration,* 21, Dec. 2003, 269–77.

Anderson, M. Kat and Davie Rowney. "The Edible Plant *Dichelostemma capitatum*: Its Vegetative Reproduction Response to Different Indigenous Harvesting Regimes in California." *Restoration Ecology,* 7, 2002, 231–40.

Barnhardt, Ray and Angayuqaq Oscar Kawagley. "Indigenous Knowledge Systems and Alaska Native Ways of Knowing." *Anthropology and Education Quarterly,* 36 (1), 2005, 8–23.

Bartlett, Cheryl M. "Knowledge Inclusivity: 'Two-eyed seeing' for Science for the 21st Century." Proceedings of the workshop on Learning Communities as a tool for resource management. November 4–5, 2005. Halifax.

Bartlett, Cheryl M., Albert Marshall, and Murdena Marshall. "Integrative Science: Enabling Concepts within a Journey Guided by 'Trees Holding Hands' and 'Two-eyed Seeing'." *Two-Eyed Seeing Knowledge Sharing Series,* Manuscript No. 1, 2007.

"Two-eyed Seeing and Other Lessons Learned within a Co-learning Journey of Bringing Together Indigenous and Mainstream Knowledges and Ways of Knowing." *Journal of Environmental Studies and Sciences*, 2 (4), 2012, 331–40.

Becker, C. Dustin and Kabita Ghimire. "Synergy Between Traditional Ecological Knowledge and Conservation Science Supports Forest Preservation in Ecuador." *Conservation Ecology*, 8 (1), 2003, [online] URL: www.consecol.org/vol8/iss1/art1/

Benton-Banai, Edward. *The Mishomis Book: The Voice of the Ojibway*. Minneapolis: University of Minnesota Press, 2010.

Berkes, Fikret. "Rethinking Community-based Conservation." *Conservation Biology*, 18 (3), 2004, 621–30.

Sacred Ecology, 2nd ed. New York: Routledge, 2008.

Berkes, Fikret, Johan Colding, and Carl Folke. "Rediscovery of Traditional Ecological Knowledge as Adaptive Management." *Ecological Applications*, 10 (5), 2000, 1251–62.

Berkes, Fikret, Carl Folke, and Madhav Gadgil. "Traditional Ecological Knowledge, Biodiversity, Resilience and Sustainability." *Biodiversity Conservation*, edited by C. A. Perrings, K. G. Mäler, C. Folke, B. O. Jansson, and C. S. Holling. Dordrecht, Netherlands: Kluwer Academic Publishers, 1995, 281–99.

Cairns, John and John R. Heckman. "Restoration Ecology: The State of an Emerging Field." *Annual Review of Energy and the Environment*, 21 (1), 1996, 167–89.

Cajete, Gregory. *Look to the Mountain: An Ecology of Indigenous Education*. Asheville, NC: Kivaki Press, 1994.

Costanza, Robert, Olman Segura Bonilla, and Juan Martinez Alier. *Getting Down to Earth: Practical Applications of Ecological Economics*. Washington, DC: Island Press, 1996.

Cronon, William. *Changes in the Land: Indians, Colonialists, and the Ecology of New England*. New York: Hill and Wang, 1983.

Daly, Herman E. and Joshua J. Farley. *Ecological Economics: Principles and Applications*. Washington, DC: Island Press, 2011.

Deloria, Vine, Jr. *Red Earth, White Lies: Native Americans and the Myth of Scientific Fact*. Golden, CO: Fulcrum, 1995.

Deur, Douglas E. and Nancy J. Turner, Eds. *Keeping it Living: Traditions of Plant Use and Cultivation on the Northwest Coast of North America*. Seattle: University of Washington Press, 2015.

Drew, Joshua A. and Adam P. Henne. "Conservation Biology and Traditional Ecological Knowledge: Integrating Academic Disciplines for Better Conservation Practice." *Ecology and Society*, 11 (2), 2006. [online] URL: www.ecologyandsociety.org/vol11/iss2/art34/

Egan, Dave, Evan E. Hjerpe, and Jesse Abrams, Eds. *Human Dimensions of Ecological Restoration: Integrating Science, Nature and Culture*. Washington, DC: Island Press, 2011.

Ermine Willie. *The Ethics of Research Involving Aboriginal Peoples*. Unpublished Masters thesis. Saskatoon: University of Saskatchewan, 2000.

Ermine Willie, Raven Sinclair, and Bonnie Jeffery. *The Ethics of Research Involving Indigenous Peoples*. Saskatoon: Indigenous Peoples' Health Research Centre, 2004.

Garibaldi, Ann and Nancy Turner. "Cultural Keystone Species: Implications for Ecological Conservation and Restoration." *Ecology and Society*, 9, 2004. [online] URL: www.ecologyandsociety.org/vol9/iss3/art1/

Hawken, Paul. *The Ecology of Commerce: A Declaration of Sustainability.* New York: Harper, 1993.

Higgs Eric. *Nature by Design: People, Natural Process, and Ecological Restoration.* Cambridge, MA: MIT Press, 2003.

Hobbs, Richard J. and David A. Norton. "Towards a Conceptual Framework for Restoration Ecology." *Restoration Ecology*, 4 (2), 1996, 93–110.

Huntington, Henry P. "Using Traditional Ecological Knowledge in Science: Methods and Applications." *Ecological Applications*, 10 (5), 2000, 1270–74.

Johnston, Basil. *The Manitous: The Spiritual World of the Ojibway.* New York: HarperCollins, 1995.

Kimmerer, Robin Wall. *Braiding Sweetgrass: Indigenous Wisdom, Scientific Knowledge and the Teachings of Plants.* Minneapolis: Milkweed Editions, 2013a.

"The Fortress, the River and the Garden." *Contemporary Studies in Environmental and Indigenous Pedagogies*, edited by Andrejs Kulnieks, Dan R. Longboat, and Kelly Young. Boston: Sense Publishers, 2013b, 49–76.

"Native Knowledge for Native Ecosystems." *Journal of Forestry*, 98 (8), 2000, 4–9.

"Searching for Synergy: Integrating Traditional and Scientific Ecological Knowledge in Environmental Science Education." *Journal of Environmental Studies and Sciences*, 2 (4), 2012, 317–23.

"Weaving Traditional Ecological Knowledge into Biological Education: A Call to Action." *Bioscience*, 52 (5), 2002, 432–38.

LaDuke Winona. *Recovering the Sacred: The Power of Naming and Claiming.* Cambridge, MA: South End Press, 2005.

Long, Jonathan, Aregai Tecle, and Benrita Burnette. "Cultural Foundations for Ecological Restoration on the White Mountain Apache Reservation." *Conservation Ecology*, 8 (1), 2003. [online] URL: www.consecol.org/vol8/iss1/art4

Louv, Richard. *Last Child in the Woods: Saving Our Children from Nature-deficit Disorder.* Chapel Hill, NC: Algonquin Books, 2008.

Martin, Jay F., Eric Roy, Stewart A. W. Diemont, and Bruce G. Ferguson. "Traditional Ecological Knowledge (TEK): Ideas, Inspiration, and Designs for Ecological Engineering." *Ecological Engineering*, 36 (7), 2010, 839–49.

"Protected Areas, Indigenous Peoples, and the Western Idea of Nature." *Ecological Restoration*, 21 (4), 2003, 247–50.

Mauro, Francesco and Preston D. Hardison. "Traditional Knowledge of Indigenous and Local Communities: International Debate and Policy Initiatives." *Ecological Applications*, 10 (5), 2000, 1263–69.

Moller, Henrik, Fikret Berkes, Philip O'Brian Lyver, and Mina Kislalioglu. "Combining Science and Traditional Ecological Knowledge: Monitoring Populations for Co-management." *Ecology and Society*, 9 (3), 2004. [online] URL: www.ecologyandsociety.org/vol9/iss3/art2/

Nabhan, Gary Paul. *Singing the Turtles to Sea.* Berkeley: University of California Press, 2003.
"Restoring and Re-storying the Landscape." *Ecological Restoration,* 9 (1), 1991, 3–4.
Nelson, Melissa K., Ed. *Original Instructions: Indigenous Teachings for a Sustainable Future.* Rochester, VT: Bear & Company, 2008.
Ortiz, Beverly R. "Contemporary California Indian Basketweavers and the Environment." *Before the Wilderness: Environmental Management by Native Californians,* edited by Kat Anderson and Thomas C. Blackburn. Menlo Park, CA: Ballena Press, 1993, 195–211.
Petch, V. "Traditional Ecological Knowledge: An Anthropological Perspective." *Aboriginal Health, Identity, and Resources,* edited by Jill Oakes, Rick Riewe, Skip Koolage, Leanne Simpson, and Nancy Schuster. Winnepeg: Native Studies Press, 2000, 137–49.
Procter, Andrea. "Traditional Environmental Knowledge: An Analysis of the Discourse." *Aboriginal Health, Identity, and Resources,* edited by Jill Oakes, Rick Riewe, Skip Koolage, Leanne Simpson, and Nancy Schuster. Winnepeg: Native Studies Press, 2000, 150–64.
Shebitz, Daniela J. and Robin Wall Kimmerer. "Reestablishing Roots of a Mohawk Community and a Culturally Significant Plant: Sweetgrass." *Restoration Ecology,* 13 (2), 2005, 257–64.
"Population Trends and Habitat Characteristics of Sweetgrass, *Anthoxanthum nitens*: Integration of Traditional and Scientific Ecological Knowledge." *Journal of Ethnobiology,* 24 (1), 2004, 93–112.
Simpson, Leanne. "Anishinaabe Ways of Knowing." *Aboriginal Health, Identity, and Resources,* edited by Jill Oakes, Rick Riewe, Skip Koolage, Leanne Simpson, and Nancy Schuster. Winnepeg: Native Studies Press, 2000, 165–85.
Whyte, Kyle. Paper presentation, TEK Seminar, Amerind Museum, Dragoon, Arizona, April 27, 2013.
Wildcat, Daniel R. *Red Alert! Saving the Planet with Indigenous Knowledge.* Golden, CO: Fulcrum, 2009.

4

What Do Indigenous Knowledges Do for Indigenous Peoples?

Kyle Whyte

Introduction: Indigenous Peoples, Planning, and Knowledges

In this chapter, I aim to engage with the broad community involved in conversations about the ways in which knowledge exchange can occur between Indigenous peoples' knowledge systems and the fields of climate, environmental and sustainability sciences. I will begin with an introduction that is longer than what I would normally write because I feel it is important that I lay out some of the context that matters to me. I will make some connections among concepts of self-determination, Indigenous planning, climate, environmental and sustainability sciences, and Indigenous knowledges before I preview what will come in the rest of this essay. In the end, my argument is that scientists who seek to exchange knowledge with Indigenous peoples should not only understand what Indigenous knowledge systems can do for them, but also have a sense of the significance of these knowledge systems for Indigenous governance today. Hence the question-based title of this essay: What do Indigenous knowledges do for Indigenous peoples?

The context I wish to share starts with the idea that a crucial facet of the self-determination of peoples such as Indigenous nations and communities is the responsibility and the right to make plans for the future using planning processes that are inclusive, well-informed, culturally relevant, and respectful of human interdependence with nonhumans and the environment (Walker et al., 2013). For Indigenous peoples, the United Nations Declaration on the Rights of Indigenous Peoples (UNDRIP) affirms key aspects of *the right* to make plans. UNDRIP's Article 3 states that by virtue of the right to self-determination, Indigenous peoples "freely determine their political status and freely pursue their economic, social and cultural development" (United Nations General Assembly, 2007). Moreover, UNDRIP's Preamble affirms that "control by indigenous peoples over developments affecting them and their lands, territories, and resources will enable them to maintain and strengthen their institutions, cultures and traditions, and to promote their development in accordance with their aspirations and needs." The Preamble also recognizes "that respect for indigenous knowledge, cultures and traditional practices contributes to sustainable and equitable development and proper management of the environment."

As Anishinaabe people (Ojibwe, Odawa, Potawatomi), planning figures prominently in our societies as a responsibility and not just a right, as is true in distinct respects for many other Indigenous peoples (see Jojola, 2001). We have a widely respected core philosophy, shared by many Indigenous peoples and often inspired by the Haudenosaunee, requiring us to consider the broader impacts of what we do now for the seven generations to follow. Depending on the context, this philosophy can refer to three generations prior (i.e., our ancestors), the present generation, and three generations into the future (i.e., our descendants); or it can refer to the long-term planning horizon of seven generations into the future (Benton-Benai, 2010; Walker et al., 2013). And when we consider broader impacts, it is common to look at the world as interrelated in ways that some people outside the Anishinaabe world do not always grasp, such as the complex interrelation of human health; storytelling; gendered and intergenerational relationships; cultural and ceremonial life; the intimacy of human relations with plants, animals and entities (e.g., water); and the moral responsibilities that come with family, clan, and band memberships (Borrows, 1997; Kimmerer, 2013; McGregor, 2009). One of the concepts Anishinaabek often use to describe this integrated conception of life is *bimaadizi* (verb) or "living in a good and respectful way" (Mitchel, 2013: 21; see also Gross, 2002). Though Anishinaabe language is made up mostly of verbs, some people also use the noun form, *bimaadiziwin*, in English written language, since the noun form may be perceived as flowing better in English grammar and style (Lyons, 2010).[1]

---

[1] I tried to use English spellings of words in Anishinaabemowin (the language of the Anishinaabek) that can be identified by diverse Ojibwe, Potawatomi, and Odawa people and people who work in relation to this language. I recognize that there are many accents and spelling systems, that I have mixed a few, and that some of the spellings I am using

Anishinaabe ways of life also stress the importance of future planning in order to live adaptively throughout the year, given metascale forces such as seasonal changes and shifting ecological trends that affect economies and trade, the availability of first foods and medicinal plants, and the timing of ceremonies (Clifton, 1986). Anishinaabe and other Indigenous peoples have built knowledges of how to live adaptively with nonhumans and the environment, lessons that are shared and imparted most often through oral and performative means, including stories, ceremonies, and intergenerational and family activities (e.g., hunting; Reo and Whyte, 2012). These knowledges represent valuable capacities for adaptation planning because they are community-based and, perhaps for that reason, are trustworthy (Scheman, 2012; Werkheiser, 2015). They also contain insights, conservation and environmental governance strategies, methods of analysis, and decision-making processes that arise from hundreds of years of collective memories, experiences, and trial and error in adapting to metascale forces, from historic climate change to the transatlantic fur trade.

Though Indigenous peoples have rights and responsibilities to plan, and useful knowledges for doing so, in the context of US and Canadian settler states, long-term planning for sustainability issues such as climate destabilization is challenging to put in practice for Ojibwe, Odawa, and Potawatomi peoples and other Indigenous nations and communities sharing the region and beyond. As settler states are here to stay, they have instantiated and enforce laws, economic policies, and practices of cultural and political domination that leave Indigenous peoples with little space to plan both creatively and practically about what to do in the future. Consider just a few examples. Settler states are often firm in their legal and policy commitment to enforce Indigenous jurisdictions as fixed and inflexible, such as treaty areas, reservation boundaries, and subnational (e.g., state or provincial) borders and transnational boundaries (e.g., US/ Canada; Marino, 2012; Theriault, 2013; Whyte, 2014). One consequence in some cases is that Indigenous peoples cannot practically plan to shift their seasonal subsistence and economic activities if a valuable plant's or animal's habitat moves outside of a treaty area or crosses a transnational border, because settler states would oppose such plans as "illegal" even when the plans are within Indigenous ancestral territories; flow from

are in some ways the least similar to how members of my tribe (Potawatomi) engage in English language spelling. Given that I use these terms every day with family, friends, and colleagues, I just tried to impart spellings people would recognize.

established Indigenous commercial, subsistence, and cultural practices; and are consistent with Indigenous interpretations of the purpose of treaties (Stark, 2010) or with the fact that some Indigenous peoples never consented in the first place to the instantiation of a transnational border bisecting their territories.

Or consider other planning issues stemming from how the weakening of Indigenous subsistence economies and trade networks creates incentives for Indigenous governments to engage with industries that they do not trust or feel are unsustainable. In one story I recently read from outside the Great Lakes, a former Iñupiat mayor of the North Slope Borough in the Arctic describes the dilemma he faced when he ended up supporting an Arctic offshore drilling program, which he and his community believed posed unacceptable environmental risks to their waters and food system. He said he was torn on what plans to make because, as the article states, 95 percent of the borough's taxes come from oil and gas. Moreover, the production in oilfields typically relied on for revenue was in decline. According to the mayor, "My biggest responsibility was maintaining the economic well-being of the borough and that largely has to do with maintaining oil in the pipeline" (Birger, 2012).

Finally, the political and cultural domination of settler states affects internal affairs in Indigenous governments. Consider tribes in the United States. Many tribal officials often feel pressure from their electoral constituencies to focus on pressing issues such as unemployment, sexual violence, and diabetes, among other challenges. Governmental units, from environmental services agencies to cultural preservation departments, are often siloed. That is, the units do not communicate or coordinate with one another even though they are responsible for addressing deeply interrelated issues, such as the health and cultural preservation, when, for example, a subsistence and ceremonially valuable fish population is contaminated with hazardous chemicals. These units are usually severely underfunded and employ staff whose time gets spread thin as workers juggle multiple projects. Unnecessary divisions can also separate tribal lawmakers, bureaucrats, and staff from elders, traditional and subsistence harvesters, gatherers, and spiritual and cultural leaders. For example, tribal staff often have to find ways to satisfy federal grant requirements and metrics that may conflict with cultural and subsistence values held by elders, harvesters, and spiritual leaders (Ranco et al., 2011).

The observations in the last few paragraphs arise from my work on climate change adaptation and sustainability planning with Indigenous nations and communities sharing the Great Lakes region, as well as my learning from Indigenous peoples in other regions about the challenges they are facing and how they are responding. This work ranges from facilitating the development of future climate change scenarios to writing and reviewing Indigenous adaptation plans to organizing dialogues connecting Indigenous governmental regulators, harvesters, and community members with scientists and engineers of other nations and heritages. I also convene or contribute to projects that put forward ethical principles and guidelines for cooperation between Indigenous parties and parties of other nations and heritages on climate change adaptation, large-landscape conservation, and environmental justice. As a Potawatomi person, I aim to support the planning efforts of Anishinaabek and other Indigenous peoples sharing the region on behalf of our continuance and resurgence as distinct and self-determining communities and nations. It is also my responsibility to share with and learn from others outside the Great Lakes region.

This brings me to the central topic of the essay: knowledge. A good planning process for any nation or community requires access to the most reliable and trustworthy sources of knowledge available for thinking about future scenarios and situations. Regarding climate change, for example, an array of different knowledges are needed: from variations in lake levels or shifts in the location of tree species in forests, to indicators tribes should be monitoring to track climate change trends, to health risks that are likely to be faced by tribal members if they lose access to culturally and economically important inland wildlife, to how tribal urban infrastructure, such as storm water management systems, will react to more intense precipitation events. Knowledges are needed of the different adaptation strategies that specific Indigenous communities or nations developed historically to shift to with the dynamics of ecosystems (e.g., knowledge of different varieties of plants suitable to different habitats), as well as the strategies that must be developed collaboratively and diplomatically with neighboring counties, towns, cities, states, and federal agencies (Grossman and Parker, 2012). For the purpose of planning, many Indigenous peoples rely on their own knowledges of how to live adaptively with nonhumans and the environment and how to build strong relationships with neighboring societies. Yet the work being done in a range of climate, sustainability, and environmental sciences is also valuable for Indigenous planning. Many Indigenous peoples and organizations already employ their own scientific staff and use the research of federal agencies and academic institutions to learn how to improve and evaluate environmental protection, conservation, and climate-change planning.

For some time, tribes have considered the benefits of using different sciences to improve their approaches to planning. It is also the case that climate, environmental, and sustainability scientists – and Indigenous persons who engage these fields – have been writing about the value of Indigenous knowledges to help improve scientists' research and capacity to support the decisions of leaders and public officials. Indeed, some Indigenous persons and many persons of other nations and heritages have created quite a buzz concerning the value of exchange with Indigenous knowledge systems, which they refer to under a number of names, including Indigenous knowledge (IK), traditional knowledge (TK), Indigenous knowledge of the environment (IKE), traditional ecological knowledge (TEK), and Native Science (Agrawal, 1995; Berkes, 1999; Burkett, 2013; Cajete, 1999). Here, I refer to all such English-language concepts as *Indigenous knowledges*, which is short for Indigenous knowledge systems. For the people in these fields, knowledge exchange is important because Indigenous knowledges possess lessons, principles, and practices that can teach peoples of other heritages and nations about living sustainably – the seven generations philosophy (Nelson, 2008). Indigenous peoples have local knowledges of the properties or behavior of particular plants and animals (Turner et al., 2011), ecosystem services (Alessa et al., 2010), or local environmental change (Reidlinger and Berkes, 2001) that scientists typically do not consider or have access to when they engage in their studies. The United Nations' report, *Our Common Future*, states that Indigenous peoples "are the repositories of vast accumulations of traditional knowledge and experience," and that "larger society... could learn a great deal from their traditional skills in sustainably managing very complex ecological systems" (World Commission on Environment and Development, 1987: 114–15). In many science fields, a story has been unfolding about the importance of Indigenous knowledges for research.

In this essay, I want to share another story – a story I began to tell earlier in this introduction – but one that is often not discussed in detail in science literatures on Indigenous knowledges: the value of Indigenous knowledges for us, the members of Indigenous communities, for our own planning, especially in relation to *today's* climate destabilization ordeal that is entangled with the problems we have with settler states and other colonial and corporate powers. I have found that scientists often appreciate what I will call here the *supplemental value* of Indigenous knowledges – the value of Indigenous knowledges as inputs for adding (i.e., supplementing) data that scientific methods do not normally track. In the domain of supplemental value, Indigenous peoples' planning processes will improve, in turn, by having access to the supplemented and, hence, improved science. But it is also the case that Indigenous knowledges have *governance value*. That is, they serve as irreplaceable sources of guidance for Indigenous resurgence and nation building. Scientists should appreciate governance value because it suggests that for some Indigenous peoples in knowledge exchange situations, we need to be assured that the flourishing of our knowledges is respected and protected. I hope to make the case for why it is important for scientists who work with Indigenous peoples to appreciate governance value so this understanding will improve their approaches to knowledge exchange with Indigenous peoples.

Supplemental Value and Indigenous Knowledges

Articles in climate, environmental, and sustainability sciences literatures tend to articulate concepts of Indigenous knowledges in ways that stress the value for supplementing scientific methods, or supplemental value. Consider just a few examples (of many available) mostly from climate and sustainability sciences. In 2012, the United Nations Educational, Scientific and Cultural Organization (UNESCO) and the United Nations University published *Weathering Uncertainty: Traditional Knowledge for Climate Change Assessment and Adaptation* (Nakashima et al., 2012). The report states, "Indigenous observations and interpretations of meteorological phenomena have guided seasonal and inter-annual activities of local communities for millennia. This knowledge contributes to climate science by offering observations and interpretations at a much finer spatial scale with considerable temporal depth and by highlighting elements that may not be considered by climate scientists" (Nakashima et al., 2012: 8; see also Reidlinger and Berkes, 2001). The value of Indigenous knowledges rests on their capacities to fill in gaps in certain scientific methods, such as a lack of local or historical data.

The report also mentions that Indigenous knowledges can expand the methods and findings that scientists consider in their research methods. For example, Weatherhead et al. (2010) describe work in Clyde River, Nunavut, in the Arctic. Inuit hunters claimed that it was becoming harder to predict the wind from day to day (i.e., wind persistence). The hunters' observations considered a number of features, including changes in the formation of seasonal ice crusts, animal behavior, sea-ice conditions, and snow forms. Climate scientists disagreed with the hunters. The weather station only observed changes in wind direction or wind persistence in northeast winds. Some of the difference, it turns out, was attributable to the fact that the weather station was in a stationary, flat area; hunters, instead, were traveling far and wide, within complex landscapes, and were paying close attention to certain snow and ice features as a matter of safety. This spurred the scientists to add more weather stations across the landscape, especially in hunting areas, and to engage in constant comparison between weather station data and Inuit hunters' observations. The collaboration has improved the information that hunters have access to about shifting conditions that matter to their subsistence hunting and safety, which certainly helps to improve their capacity to plan.

Examples such as *Weathering Uncertainty* and the story documented by Weatherhead et al. describe Indigenous knowledges in ways that most climate and other scientists can digest and connect to their research. Yet Indigenous knowledges originate in completely different cultural-linguistic contexts than those that many scientists are used to. Indigenous peoples may report their observations in language that is not empirically useful or acceptable to scientists because the language ascribes agency or spirituality to animals and plants, elements or entities such as water, and landscapes or ecosystem functions. Or Indigenous peoples may be perceived as embedding and enacting their observations within stories, ceremonies, or prophesies that scientists do not understand.

In Chie Sakakabira's collaboration with Iñupiat communities in the Arctic, she describes how many members discuss their knowledge of climate change and adaptive strategies through stories encoded in their languages, cosmologies, and kinship, as well as their spiritual relationships to nonhuman beings and spirits. In the case of the individuals with whom Sakakabira worked, some of their observations of climate change and adaptation are expressed through supernatural stories about changes in the dwellings of shape-shifters and ancestral spirits. The Iñupiat communities live according to relationships of moral reciprocity with whales, an animal they depend on economically, culturally, and for health – a connection so deep Sakakabira calls it *cetaceousnes* (whale consciousness). Climate change is experienced through changes in the availability of the whale tissue used for traditional drum membranes. Whereas historically drum ceremonies expressed the whales' invitations to bring people together, climate-induced disruptions in whale cycles have been associated with a resurgence in drumming ceremonies in some communities that now express humans' invitation for whales to come back to reciprocal relations (with humans). Iñupiat literally describes their relation to whales not as the whale cycle, which is digestible by many scientists, but as *kia-vallakkikput agviq*, or "standing by the whale," which is still an inadequate translation (Sakakabira, 2010: 1007; see also Sakakabira, 2017).

Writing on this issue of the expression of knowledges, Preston Hardison describes how Indigenous peoples may use English-language terms such as "good mind, guardianship, customary law, cosmovision, reciprocity, obligations and relations" to represent aspects of reality that scientists would describe using totally different concepts, such as "information, economics, intellectual property, common heritage, public domain, secular knowledge and open knowledge" (Hardison, 2014). Sometimes scientists see little value when Indigenous knowledges are expressed in ways that are less akin to how scientists already describe the world. The Arctic Climate Impact Assessment (2004), for example, is clear in its admission that "Indigenous knowledge is far more than a collection of facts. It is an understanding of the world and of the human place in the world ... The emphasis on the cultural aspects of indigenous knowledge in this assessment is not intended to detract from the great utility it has in ecological and environmental research and management." In the 2004 Assessment, then, certain aspects of Indigenous knowledges are filtered out as valuable for science.

Yet others working in climate science more broadly have emphasized that the linguistic-cultural contexts and expressions of Indigenous knowledges are precisely what scientists should value, especially those working on scientific approaches to planning, management, and policy making in relation to climate change, sustainability/resilience, and conservation. Maxine Burkett offers the following observations on what she refers to as "Indigenous environmental knowledge (IEK)."

The foundational worldview that forms the specific management tools prescribed in IEK are more relevant to the complex and ever-changing natural system that we have so deeply disturbed. In addition, IEK was oriented toward resilience for present and future generations. Instead of looking at the specific management tools, investigating and advancing the worldviews that spawned those tools and methods would be the most effective approach to the law and policy of climate change adaptation. Indeed, drawing on both the management practices and the knowledge and worldview on which they are based – while understanding the governance mechanisms behind them – may speed up the process of designing alternative resource management systems. (Burkett, 2013: 118)

For Burkett, it is precisely the culture that generates the value of Indigenous knowledges for scientific approaches to planning, management, and policy. The value of Indigenous knowledges here concerns lessons about "governance mechanisms." This value is discussed by many Indigenous scholars, including Ronald Trosper. In his work, he shows how taking seriously the cultural expressions of the potlatch ceremony of some Indigenous peoples in the Pacific Northwest of North America can yield key governance principles that ultimately should be intelligible to sustainability scientists interested in resilience, such as "high grading is not allowed, consumption has an upper bound, and there is always concern that ecosystem health should be maintained" (Trosper, 1995: 72). Trosper argues that while the cultural aspects of the potlatch ceremony may be initially difficult to comprehend by many scientists, it is nonetheless plausible that these cultural expressions create innovative ways for the societies to buffer, self-organize, and learn in response to environmental issues (Trosper, 2009). These cultural expressions can also be seen in Sakakabira's work, where society is organized to cultivate reciprocal moral relationships between people and whales – relationships that motivate an environmental stewardship ethic that is lacking in many societies. Such forms of expression from Indigenous knowledges offer climate, environmental, and sustainability sciences touchstones for thinking outside of the laws and economic policies of settler states such as the United States or New Zealand.

All the examples discussed in this section express a story that characterizes Indigenous knowledges as having a *supplemental-value* for scientists. Indigenous knowledges are often seen as associated with particular members of a community, such as hunters or ceremonialists, whose activities generate data and insights that can be used by scientists to improve scientific research. Additionally, from a policy perspective, Indigenous peoples are perceived to have knowledges that mimic sustainable ecological processes, and this is seen as useful and *supplemental*. The predominance of supplemental value in the literature helps to frame scientists' expectations about what will happen when they reach out to work with Indigenous peoples. It makes interactions an issue of research ethics. That is, scientists should make sure if they interview elders or access Indigenous peoples' archives that they do not impose risks on the individuals interviewed or the people affected by public release of archives. Here, Indigenous persons or archives of Indigenous knowledges are sources of information. Climate, environmental, and sustainability scientists usually argue that Indigenous peoples today can benefit from such knowledge exchange because Indigenous peoples will gain access to the improved information and research for use in their own Indigenous planning processes. The story of supplemental value, then, involves scientists finally embracing Indigenous knowledges that their predecessors ignored, while moving toward ethical processes for obtaining these knowledges from Indigenous peoples.

Indigenous Knowledges and Governance Value

There is another story about climate, environmental, and sustainability sciences, and Indigenous knowledges with which I am far more familiar. For many Indigenous peoples this conversation supports planning that helps them prepare for sustainability issues, such as today's climate destabilization (Walker et al., 2013). In these cases, Indigenous peoples believe Indigenous knowledges have an irreplaceable value as guides for structuring how they will prepare for, adapt to, and mitigate future sustainability challenges. I will discuss some examples that represent a wide range of Indigenous peoples. Before moving on to these examples, I will describe what I mean by Indigenous peoples' governance today. In the space I have here, I can only give a brief and rather abstract glimpse of how I understand governance, but enough to give readers a sense of where I am coming from when I return to Indigenous knowledges later in this section. Though my initial treatment of governance may seem abstract to some, I will provide multiple examples to illustrate the relationship between knowledge and governance.

I understand Indigenous governance according to two related conceptual constellations: *resurgence* and *collective continuance*, both of which are expressions of *collective self-determination*. Collective self-determination refers to a group's ability to provide the cultural, social, economic, and political relations needed for its members to pursue good lives. In my understanding, resurgence involves thinking about collective self-determination while grasping the full impact of systems (or structures) of settler colonialism on Indigenous lives today and into the future. The impacts of settler colonialism and the idea of resurgence have long been covered in Indigenous scholarship and advocacy, especially Indigenous writings on gender, feminism, and women's advocacy (Allen, 1992; Calhoun et al., 2007; Chrystos, 1995; Goeman, 2013; LaDuke, 1999; Maracle, 1996; Ross, 1998; Smith, 2005). Mishuana Goeman and Jennifer Denetdate, reflecting on the legacies of Indigenous feminist work, write that "the structures of our lives as Native women and men are shaped by racism, sexism, and discrimination. We strive to recover our former selves and push toward creating better future selves by reclaiming Native values, which have seen us through multiple traumas, including land dispossession and the loss of our freedoms" (Goeman and Denetdale, 2009: 9). Jeff Corntassel, in dialogue with Taiaiake Alfred, claims that "When considering how colonization systematically deprives us of our experiences and confidence as Indigenous peoples, the linkages between colonialism, cultural harm, and the disintegration of community health and well-being become clearer. Furthermore, this is a spiritual crisis just as much as it is a political, social, and economic one" (Corntassel, 2012: 88). Resurgence, then, concerns acting in ways that "reclaim and regenerate one's relational, place-based existence by challenging the ongoing, destructive forces of colonization" (88). Leanne Simpson claims that "Resurgence happens *within* Indigenous bodies and through the connections we make to each other and our land. That's how we strengthen ourselves within Nishnaabeg intelligence" (Simpson and Coulthard, 2014).

Place-based, embodied existence is important in the theory of resurgence because it points to ways of life in which Indigenous peoples do not depend in morally problematic or unjust ways on the resources and recognition of surrounding settler states. That is, such existence unburdens Indigenous peoples from having to trust the supply chains of settler states to provide healthy and safe food for Indigenous children, to rely on settler legal and juridical frameworks for equal representation and protection against violence, such as sexual violence against Indigenous women and two-spirit persons, and to depend on settler notions of citizenship that ultimately work to erase Indigenous political, cultural, and experiential differences, among other oppressive forms of dependence (Coulthard, 2007, 2014; Goeman, 2013; LaDuke, 1999). Governance can therefore be seen as a resurgence of Indigenous peoples' self-determination using "on the ground strategies" that establish a range of capacities for land-based collective self-determination, from greater economic independence to psychological (spiritual) awakening. These strategies are guided by philosophies flowing from Indigenous peoples' own knowledges, resources, and heritages, as wellsprings of practical forms of collective self-determination (Coulthard, 2006; Napoleon, 2013; Simpson, 2004; see also a related account of "heritage" in Figueroa, 2001).

Resurgence, for me, is in dialogue with the goal of collective continuance, which I have used to discuss Indigenous adaptation to climate change. I developed this concept by thinking through the role of Anishinaabe/Neshnabé seasonal calendars, which organize society to adapt to the dynamics of ecosystems. Collective continuance is an

Indigenous community's capacity to adapt in ways sufficient for its members' livelihoods to flourish into the future. Adaptation refers to "adjustments that populations take in response to current or predicted change" (Nelson et al., 2007: 397). The flourishing of livelihoods refers to Indigenous conceptions of (1) how to contest hardships imposed by settler colonial and other oppressive social structures and build good diplomatic relationships with parties who do not have oppressive intentions, (2) how to pursue comprehensive aims of robust living in response to the inevitability of change, like building cohesive societies, vibrant cultures, trustworthy sources of useful knowledge, strong subsistence, place-based and commercial economies, and peaceful relations with neighbors of other nations and heritages, and (3) how to make difficult decisions when circumstances require trade-offs, such as having to choose whether to put limited resources into job creation through the coal industry or invest instead in the environmental and cultural protection required for rekindling place-based supply chains for food and medicines. Given (1), (2), and (3), Indigenous collective continuance is a way of understanding Indigenous governance as a community's aptitude for making adjustments to current or predicted change in ways that contest settler-imposed hardships and other oppressions, establish quality diplomatic relationships, bolster robust living in the face of change, and observe balanced decision-making processes capable of dealing with difficult trade-offs (Whyte, 2013). Indigenous conceptions (1), (2), and (3) can be achieved when societies exhibit strong relationships in which the parties to the relationships (i.e., the relatives) see themselves as having reciprocal responsibilities to one another.

Together, resurgence and collective continuance create a rendition in broad strokes of what Indigenous governance means to me. Governance refers to the sphere in which we discuss community-based institutional means, strategies, and processes that are needed for Indigenous peoples to plan for climate destabilization and the dominance of settler states. Both conceptual constellations refer to the importance of collective capacities belonging to and stemming from Indigenous peoples. Collective capacities include land-based practices and vibrant cultures, among others. Both concepts also acknowledge that Indigenous peoples continue to adapt in relation to settler colonialism by adopting emerging means, strategies, processes, and other planning tools. So Indigenous collective capacities are always in dialogue with emerging practices that address today's challenges. For example, land-based practices may be guided by an Indigenous people's traditional knowledge of plant habitat that is rooted in traditions going back hundreds of years, but, at the same time, use "Western" scientific tools to monitor the impacts of pollution or warming on plant populations. Readers might recognize aspects of Gerald Vizenor's concept of survivance here. For Vizenor, "survivance is an active sense of presence, the continuance of native stories, not a mere reaction, or a survivable name. Native survivance stories are renunciations of dominance, tragedy, and victimry" (Vizenor, 1994: vii). One commentator interprets survivance as "renewal and continuity into the future rather than memorializing the past" (Kroeber, 2008: 25).

I now return to the topic of Indigenous knowledges. The theories of resurgence and collective continuance suggest that Indigenous knowledges are collective capacities that can provide trustworthy and useful wisdom for planning that supports collective self-determination in the face of change. That is, Indigenous knowledges are capacities Indigenous peoples can use to facilitate their own governance. Indigenous knowledges are not backward-looking repositories of information that are about historic or waning ways of life. Instead, they have a special value in Indigenous planning efforts that is different from the supplemental value of Indigenous knowledges for scientists described in the previous section. In what follows, I will consider some examples of how Indigenous knowledges are being used in planning processes by Indigenous peoples and organizations today to deal with sustainability challenges. Exchanges with different sciences figure prominently in each case.

The first example of Indigenous knowledges and governance is from the Karuk Tribe in North America, in what is referred to by most people as California. Karuk heritage involves longstanding relationships of interdependence with a range of foods, from deer to huckleberry to salmon. Historically, these foods were enhanced through intentional, systematic fire regimes that embodied complex ecological knowledge. In one study, about three quarters of the species Karuk people used for food or cultural practices were enriched in some way by fire (Norgaard). The Karuk also cultivated careful knowledges about how to steward the ecological conditions needed to maintain healthy fish populations, especially salmon, which figures importantly in Karuk diets. Yet earlier in the twentieth century, US government agencies, such as the Forest Service, banned Karuk burning and paved the way for the damming of the rivers, which presented an immediate challenge to the continuance of the Karuk food system. Ron Reed (Karuk) claims that "Criminalization of cultural practices matters for sovereignty because it directly prohibits the enactment of practices needed for the generation of knowledge" (Norgaard, 2014: 22). Kari Norgaard, in her work with Reed and Van Horn, says:

> The exclusion of fire from the ecosystem has a host of interrelated ecological and social impacts including impacts to cultural practice, political sovereignty, social relations, subsistence activities, and the mental and physical health of individual tribal members. In addition, Karuk tribal members are negatively impacted by the effects of catastrophic fires and intensive firefighting activities that in turn result from fire exclusion. (Norgaard et al., 2011: 73)

In response to these challenges, the Karuk have recently engaged in a project funded by the North Pacific Landscape Conservation Cooperative to rekindle their own burning practices and salmon stewardship, in order to stimulate the Karuk economy, address nutritional, health, and other food/dietary related problems, and adapt to climate change impacts that threaten to further weaken Karuk access to their foods (see ITEP, 2014).

Importantly, the project, which is focused on Karuk *knowledge sovereignty*, outlines a system for expanding the use of Karuk knowledge that was curtailed by settler colonialism. The plan involves establishing practices that will strengthen the transmission of Karuk knowledge within the tribe (such as improving intergenerational relationships and increasing youth involvement in environmental management), remove external policy and jurisdictional roadblocks to putting this knowledge in practice on Karuk ancestral lands, and ensure that external policies of the US settler state are favorable. For the Karuk, knowledge sovereignty is not just a knowledge exchange between the Karuk and outside scientists. It involves first strengthening the use and transmission of knowledge within the tribe, the capacity to use Karuk knowledge in as many parts of the landscape as needed, and the assurance that US settlers cannot threaten the flourishing of Karuk knowledges. Any scientist working with the Karuk must understand how scientific work fits into the larger idea of Karuk resurgence and collective continuance, which can be considered a value of Indigenous knowledge for the sake of governance (Norgaard, 2014; Norgaard et al., 2011; Wotkyns, 2013).

Lake sturgeon is an important subsistence species of the Little River Band of Ottawa Indians in what is now referred to as Michigan, yet in the twentieth century the lake sturgeon population was basically eliminated through settler overharvesting, dams, stocking rivers with non-native fish species for sport fishing, and environmental change. By the early 2000s, fewer than 40 to 50 fish per year spawned in one of the major rivers, the Manistee. The tribe believes that restoring certain native species, such as lake sturgeon, is important for strengthening the resilience of the region to withstand climate destabilization – not just in the sense that native species are tied to ecological resilience, which can be questioned on various scientific grounds, but because some native species also have existence value that can motivate people to be better stewards. For the Little River Band, resilience is connected to the tribe's philosophy of *bimaadizi* ("living in a good and respectful way") described in Mitchell. With this goal in mind, the tribe used its own knowledge of how people lived with sturgeon, sturgeon life cycles, and the genetic make-up of sturgeon in relation to families and clans to engage with biologists, tribal members, and others living within the watershed to restore lake sturgeon and bring together the entire watershed around the goal of sustainability (Holtgren, 2013; Holtgren et al., 2014).

One key development was the tribe's new cultural context group, which was made up of a diverse range of tribal members and biologists, who developed goals and objectives for restoration. Biologist Marty Holtgren describes the cultural context group as facilitating "a voice [that] was an amalgamation of cultural, biological, political, and social elements, all being important and often indistinguishable" (2013:135). Holtgren discusses how the goal was to "restore the harmony and connectivity between [lake sturgeon] and the Anishinaabek and bring them both back to the river." According to Holtgren, "Bringing the sturgeon back to the river has an obvious biological element; however, restoring harmony and connectively between sturgeon and people was steeped in the cultural and social realm. Each meeting began with a ceremony, and the conversation was held over a feast" (Holtgren, 2013: 136). Ultimately, the tribe established a riverside rearing system to protect young sturgeon before they can be released each fall. The sturgeon release involves a public ceremony in which up to 600 people now participate, of all nations and heritages in the region, to learn about the importance of sturgeon for the watershed. The program is based on relationships with government, nonprofit, and community partners in the watershed, as well as the integration of scientific and Indigenous knowledges of sturgeon. Ottawa knowledges, then, played an enormous role in structuring the scientifically informed pursuit of the tribe's governance in the region (Holtgren, 2013; Holtgren et al., 2014).

The Confederated Tribes of the Umatilla Indian Reservation (CTUIR, 2010), in what is now referred to by most as Oregon, has developed a "First Foods" framework for guiding their governance of climate change adaptation. CTUIR has a traditional knowledge system that they refer to as "food associated culture," which is a complex web of stewarding, harvesting, storing, and sharing a range of foods in connection with social, cultural, political, and economic life. The system, which is part of their larger philosophy called *Tamanwit*, is concretized through a number of practices, such as the order in which foods are served during feasts, which corresponds to the tribe's origin and other stories. Additionally, the CTUIR are addressing the importance of gendered knowledge when it comes to traditional foods. The tribe's comprehensive plan includes a foods category referred to as "Women's Foods," which include berries and roots over which some tribal women take on stewardship responsibilities. One elder, Marie "Butch" Dick, pointed out to the natural resources staff, "You're always talking about the men's foods. Who's going to take care of the women's foods?" (*Confederated Umatilla Journal*, 2008; CTUIR, 2010). To address the gap, the tribe has carried out women's food assessments, where the women lead by asserting their knowledge to support sound management decisions (Quaempts, 2012; Shippentower, 2014). Importantly, Indigenous women are not restricted to stereotypical roles; they have a right and responsibility to participate in planning, and they do so by respecting the genuine knowledge keepers who are on the land stewarding, harvesting, and sharing local foods (Quaempts, 2012; Shippentower, 2014).

In one presentation, I heard how women's Indigenous knowledges of plants guide how the Umatilla tribe structures climate change adaptation planning (Shippentower, 2014). The presentation described this knowledge as a "cultural, economic, and sovereign benefit of the CTUIR." In the planning process, it is precisely the women's knowledge that structures scientific research that seeks to learn more about "population and habitat management" and the effectiveness of what Shippentower calls "natural resource policies and regulatory mechanisms." An interesting example involved the tribe using ArcGIS in conjunction with and guided by women's knowledge "to develop a landscape level model that combines derived geographic information with field inventory data to identify habitat that support 5 food plants; preserve, manage and restore gathering, locations throughout the Ceded lands for Tribal Members ... and provide direct knowledge for assessing climate change," as well as determining "climate change strategies" (Shippentower, 2014).

The Climate and Traditional Knowledges Workgroup (CTKW, 2014) formed several years ago and is made up of Indigenous persons, Indigenous government staff, and experts in sensitive issues involving the sharing of Indigenous knowledges. The CTKW developed a set of guidelines through a collaborative effort with funding support from individual Indigenous governments and several US agencies. The group came together to respond to problems associated with the fact that Indigenous peoples who seek to use their knowledges in the ways described earlier do not have adequate protections for doing so. For example, in the case of copyright (a grant of a temporary monopoly by a government to provide economic incentives to individuals or firms for innovation), the law is key in defining what counts as public domain. Unfortunately, Indigenous knowledges are too often considered part of the public domain because they are judged to be too old to protect, and because they are often not written down. Because of a Supreme Court decision in 2001 (*Department of Interior v. Klamath Water Users Protective Assn*), Indigenous peoples are unable to share sensitive knowledge or information privately with the United States on a government-to-government basis. Any exchanges are subject to Freedom of Information Act (FOIA) requests (see Williams and Hardison, 2013). Another issue concerns the idea of "The Common Heritage of Mankind," which claims that some knowledges are so valuable to all of humanity that this value overrides any particular value they may have to the nations and communities who created them.

These regulations pose problems for tribes because sharing Indigenous knowledges with scientists can disclose risks to Indigenous governance. For example, telling scientists about Karuk fire management or Umatilla root harvesting may disclose the location of sacred sites and medicinal plants or the locations of fish, animals, and plants that people outside the tribe may wish to plunder. Deborah Parker of the Tulalip Tribe, for example, states, "Protecting cultural knowledge is an ongoing challenge, on many levels" (Wotkyns, 2013). Parker relates a local issue that illustrates one part of the problem: "We have a place where people like to go fishing. It's a place where human remains have been found. The tribe has put up signs – 'Private Area, for Tribal Members Only' – but others come in and constantly tear down the signs. It's really been a battle. They have no idea of sacred areas, places that need to remain untouched" (Wotkyns, 2013).

The Guidelines for Considering Traditional Knowledges in Climate Change Initiatives (NOAA 2014) seeks, among other things, to provide guidance for scientists. The guidelines emphasize that governance means Indigenous peoples get to define what Indigenous knowledge is for them in the course of collaboration. Moreover, Indigenous peoples, as collectives, set the rules for sharing Indigenous knowledges, including what knowledge can be shared and who is authorized to share it and in what form. The guidelines also reference important strategies for ensuring that scientists especially can collaborate with tribes in ways that do not pose risks of knowledge exchange. The guidelines are geared to ensure that Indigenous knowledge is protected because of its value for Indigenous governance, from resurgence to nation building.

In these examples, Indigenous knowledges have what I would call *governance value* for Indigenous peoples. Governance includes a range of planning pursuits of Indigenous collective self-determination involving research development, knowledge transmission, environmental regulation, and building education and awareness. Indigenous knowledges can serve to organize governance at all levels as capacities supporting resurgence and collective continuance. Indigenous knowledges are also a unique form of wisdom that can be disrupted if they are no longer practiced. Many of the projects just described seek to protect the practice of Indigenous knowledges within Indigenous communities and nations. Here, then, Indigenous knowledges are irreplaceable capacities that can guide Indigenous governance to adapt to forces including settler colonialism and environmental change. The idea of sharing or exchanging Indigenous knowledges with scientists should not be separated from the processes Indigenous peoples are undertaking to strengthen their knowledge systems. This is not to say that Indigenous knowledges are the only capacities of Indigenous peoples, but that they are special capacities in that they are tailored to particular places and peoples and are trustworthy from a community standpoint. Indigenous peoples living in metropolitan areas, often diverse in membership, guide their own planning through Indigenous knowledges (Bang et al., 2014; Goeman, 2013).

What Do Indigenous Knowledges Do for Indigenous Peoples? Supplemental Value and Governance Value

The question posed by the title of this section (and essay) is an important one for scientists in fields oriented toward sustainability, climate change, and other planning areas to ask. In the discussion of supplemental value, we do not know what Indigenous knowledges do for Indigenous peoples beyond how improved science can be used by Indigenous peoples in a trickle-down sense. But governance value is different, first because the knowledges are associated with Indigenous capacities for resurgence and collective continuance. Therefore, their primary value is tied to the well-being of current and future Indigenous persons, families, communities, and nations. Sometimes Indigenous well-being conflicts with scientific aspirations to add to the public domain of global scientific knowledge. Second, in governance value, Indigenous peoples are concerned about protecting their own internal capacity to cultivate, transmit, remember, and exercise Indigenous knowledges, despite what persons and organizations of other heritages and nations do. That is, we need to have *knowledge sovereignty* regardless of what scenarios the settler society throws at us. Third, Indigenous knowledges can actually guide scientific research; it does not have to be the other way around. That is, Indigenous knowledge is not only something people apply in order to generate information useful as a scientific byproduct. Indigenous knowledges are about governance in the form of resurgence and collective continuance that can organize scientific studies on behalf of sustainability. Fourth, Indigenous peoples determine, in a given case, how Indigenous knowledges should be defined and how they should be shared.

Assuming they agree with some of my points, climate, environmental, and sustainability scientists may take from this essay that it is important for them to learn about Indigenous governance value if they are going to engage in appropriate forms of knowledge exchange with Indigenous peoples. That is, scientists need to understand how they may or may not fit into emerging Indigenous governance in terms of resurgence and collective continuance. This is part of my truth here. From my perspective, scientists first need to understand their own positions in relation to Indigenous peoples. For example, when scientists, working for an institution, government agency, or university, approach an Indigenous nation, they must represent themselves as participating in the interests of the United States, a school, or the corporations who donated research money. While the scientists themselves may not agree with the agendas or ideologies of the settler sovereigns or business interests, they are inextricably acting on their behalf *in some way* according to the perspectives of many Indigenous peoples. So, for example, if a scientist treats Indigenous peoples as primarily interview subjects, that may completely ignore what the Indigenous peoples are trying to do in their own right, such as the Karuk Tribe's approach to knowledge sovereignty or the Umatilla Tribe's women's food assessment initiative. Such treatment reflects the scientists' privileging of their own governance agenda without showing respect for Indigenous governance. To be more respectful, scientists would have to ensure that Indigenous peoples have the time and space to be able to strengthen their internal knowledge systems, protect key aspects of their knowledge from going public, and influence the design of scientific research to suit the guidance they receive under their Indigenous knowledges. In theory, but also in some of my experiences, all of these considerations can very much change the approach, structure, and outcomes of cooperation between scientists and Indigenous peoples on long-term planning projects.

So, what do Indigenous knowledges do for Indigenous peoples? Indigenous knowledges have governance value for Indigenous peoples as an integral part of how our nations and communities plan for the future. The responsibility and right to plan for the future is a key component of collective self-determination and enshrined by important documents such as UNDRIP. Whereas many scientists and people of other heritages and nations value Indigenous knowledges for their own research – or supplemental-value – they also need to reflect on how acknowledging the governance value of Indigenous knowledges for Indigenous peoples may impact their approaches to knowledge exchange. Such acknowledgement should lead scientists to consider how Indigenous peoples interpret the governance value of the scientists' own goals and research approaches.

WORKS CITED

Abate, Randal, and Elizabeth Kronk, Eds. *Climate Change and Indigenous Peoples: The Search for Legal Remed itedies.* Cheltenham, UK: Edward Elgar Publishing, 2013, 96–118.

Agrawal, Arun. "Dismantling the Divide Between Indigenous and Scientific Knowledge." *Development and Change,* 26 (3), 1995, 413–39.

Alessa, Lilian, Andrew Kliskey, and Paula Williams. "Forgetting Freshwater: Technology, Values, and Distancing in Remote Arctic Communities." *Society & Natural Resources,* 23 (3), 2010, 254–68.

Allen, Paula Gunn. *The Sacred Hoop: Recovering the Feminine in American Indian Traditions.* Boston: Beacon Press, 1992.

Arctic Climate Impact Assessment. *Impacts of a Warming Arctic-Arctic Climate Impact Assessment.* Cambridge, UK: Cambridge University Press, 2004.

Bang, M., L. Curley, A. Kessel, A. Marin, and E. Suzokovich. "Muskrat Theories, Tobacco in the Streets, and Living Chicago as Indigenous Lands." *Environmental Education Research* 19 (1), 2014, 37–55.

Benton-Banai, Edward. *The Mishomis Book: The Voice of the Ojibway.* Minneapolis: University of Minnesota Press, 2010.

Berkes, Fikret. *Sacred Ecology: Traditional Ecological Knowledge and Resource Management.* Milton Park, Abington, UK: Taylor & Francis, 1999.

Birger, Jon. "Why Shell is Betting Billions To Drill for Oil in Alaska." *Fortune,* 165 (8), 2012. [online] URL: http://features.blogs.fortune.cnn.com/2012/05/24/oil-shell-alaska-drilling/

Burkett, Maxine. "Indigenous Environmental Knowledge and Climate Change Adaptation." *Climate Change and Indigenous Peoples: The Search for Legal Remedies,* edited by Randall S. Abate and Elizabeth Ann Kronk. Cheltenham, UK: Edward Elgar, 2013.

Borrows, J. "Living Between Water and Rocks: First Nations, Environmental Planning and Democracy." *University of Toronto Law Journal* 47 (4), 1997, 417–468.

Cajete, Gregory. *Native Science: Natural Laws of Interdependence*. Santa Fe: Clear Light, 1999.

Calhoun, Anne, Mishuana Goeman, and Monica Tsethlikai. "Achieving Gender Equity for American Indians." *Handbook for Achieving Gender Equity through Education*, edited by Susan S. Klein, Barbara Richardson, Dolores A. Grayson, Lynn H. Fox, Cheris Kramarae, Diane S. Pollard, and Carol Ann Dwyer. New York: Routledge, 2007.

Chrystos. *Fire Power*. Vancouver, BC: Press Gang Publishers, 1995.

Clifton, James A. *People of the Three Fires: The Ottawa, Potawatomi, and Ojibway of Michigan*. Grand Rapids, MI: Grand Rapids Inter-Tribal Council, 1986.

Climate and Traditional Knowledges Workshop (CTKW). Guidelines for Considering Traditional Knowledges in Climate Change Initiatives. URL: https://climatetkw.wordpress.com (accessed 3-5-15)

Confederated Umatilla Journal Staff. "Putting First Foods First." *Confederated Umatilla Journal*, XI (3), 2008, 1, 22.

Corntassel, Jeff. "Re-envisioning Resurgence: Indigenous Pathways to Decolonization and Sustainable Self-determination." *Decolonization: Indigeneity, Education & Society*, 1 (1), 2012, 86–101.

Coulthard, Glen S. "Indigenous Peoples and the 'Politics of Recognition'." *The New Socialist*, 58, 2006, 9–12.

"Subjects of Empire: Indigenous Peoples and the 'Politics of Recognition' in Canada." *Contemporary Political Theory*, 6 (4), 2007, 437–60.

Red Skin, White Masks: Rejecting the Colonial Politics of Recognition. Minneapolis: University of Minnesota Press, 2014.

[CTUIR], Confederated Tribes of the Umatilla Indian Reservation. *Comprehensive Plan*, 2010. [online] URL: http://ctuir.org/2010-comprehensive-plan

[CTKW], Climate and Traditional Knowledges Workgroup. *Guidelines for Considering Traditional Knowledges in Climate Change Initiatives*, 2014. [online] URL: https://climatetkw.wordpress.com

Figueroa, Robert Melchior. "Other Faces: Latinos and Environmental Justice." *Faces of Environmental Racism: Confronting Issues of Global Justice*, edited by Laura Westra and Bill E. Lawson. Boston: Rowman & Littlefield, 2001, 167–86.

Goeman, Mishuana. *Mark My Words: Native Women Mapping Our Nations*. Minneapolis: University of Minnesota Press, 2013.

Goeman, Mishuana and Jennifer Nez Denetdale. "Native Feminisms: Legacies, Interventions, and Indigenous Sovereignties." *Wicazo Sa Review*, 24 (2), 2009, 9–13.

Gross, L. "Bimaadiziwin, or the Good Life, as a Unifying Concept of Anishinaabe Religion." *American Indian Culture and Research Journal*, 26 (1), 2002, 15–32.

Grossman, Zoltan and Alan Parker, Eds. *Asserting Native Resilience: Pacific Rim Indigenous Nations Face the Climate Crisis*. Corvallis, OR: Oregon State University Press, 2012.

Hardison, Preston. "Safeguarding the Living Breath of Life." *Tribal Climate Change Webinar Series on Climate Change Impacts, Traditional Knowledge and Communication.* Hosted by the Institute for Tribal Environmental Professionals, June 16, 2014.

Holtgren, Marty. "Bringing Us Back to the River." *The Great Lake Sturgeon,* edited by Nancy Auer and Dave Dempsey. East Lansing: Michigan State University Press, 2013, 133–47.

Holtgren, Marty, Stephanie Ogren, and Kyle Whyte. "Renewing Relatives: Nmé Stewardship in a Shared Watershed." *Tales of Hope and Caution in Environmental Justice,* 2014. [online] URL: https://ssrn.com/abstract=2770100

[ITEP] Institute for Tribal Environmental Professionals. "Indigenous Peoples and Northwest Climate Initiatives: Exploring the Role of Traditional Ecological Knowledge in Resource Management," 2014. [online] URL: www.nau.edu/tribalclimatechange/tribes/tdk_nplcc.asp

Jojola, Ted S. "Indigenous Planning and Resource Management." *Trusteeship in Change: Toward Tribal Autonomy in Resource Management,* edited by Richmond L. Clow and Imre Sutton. Boulder: University Press of Colorado, 2001.

Kimmerer, Robin Wall. *Braiding Sweetgrass: Indigenous Wisdom, Scientific Knowledge and the Teachings of Plants.* Minneapolis, MN: Milkweed Editions, 2013.

Kroeber, Karl. "Why It's A Good Thing Gerald Vizenor Is Not an Indian." *Survivance: Narratives of Native Presence,* edited by G. Vizenor. Lincoln: University of Nebraska Press, 2008, 25–37.

LaDuke, Winona. *All Our Relations: Native Struggles for Land and Life.* Cambridge, MA: South End Press, 1999.

Lyons, Scott Richard. *X-Marks: Native Signatures of Assent.* Minneapolis: University of Minnesota Press, 2010.

Maracle, Lee. *I Am Woman: A Native Perspective on Sociology and Feminism.* Vancouver, BC: Press Gang Publishers, 1996.

Marino, Elizabeth. "The Long History of Environmental Migration: Assessing Vulnerability Construction and Obstacles to Successful Relocation in Shishmaref, Alaska." *Global Environmental Change,* 22 (2), 2012, 374–81.

McGregor, Douglas. "Honouring our Relations: An Anishinaabe Perspective." *Speaking for Ourselves: Environmental Justice in Canada,* edited by J. Agyeman, P. Cole, and R. Haluza-Delay. Vancouver: University of British Columbia Press, 2009, 27–41.

Mitchell, Jimmie. "N'me." *The Great Lake Sturgeon,* edited by Nancy Auer and Dave Dempsey. East Lansing: Michigan State University Press, 2013, 21–26.

Nakashima, Douglas. Kirsty Galloway McLean, Hans Thulstrup, Ameyali Ramos Castillo, and Jennifer Rubis. *Weathering Uncertainty: Traditional Knowledge for Climate Change Assessment and Adaptation.* Paris: UNESCO and Darwin, UNU, 2012.

Napoleon, Val. *Thinking About Indigenous Legal Orders.* Dordrecht, Netherlands: Springer, 2013.

National Oceanic and Atmospheric Administration (NOAA). "Guidelines for Considering Traditional Knowledges in Climate Change." U.S. Climate Resilience Toolkit, 2014; https://toolkit.climate.gov/tool/guidelines-considering-traditional-knowledges-climate-change-initiatives

Nelson, Melissa K., Ed. *Original Instructions: Indigenous Teachings for a Sustainable Future*. Rochester, VT: Bear & Company, 2008.

Nelson, D. R., W. N. Adger, and K. Brown. "Adaptation to Environmental Change: Contributions of a Resilience Framework." *Annual Reviews: Environment and Resources*, 32, 2007, 395–419.

Norgaard, Kari Marie. "The Politics of Fire and the Social Impacts of Fire Exclusion on the Klamath." *Humboldt Journal of Social Relations*, 36, 2014, 73–97.

Norgaard, Kari Marie, Ron Reed, and Carolina Van Horn. "A Continuing Legacy: Institutional Racism, Hunger and Nutritional Justice on the Klamath." *Cultivating Food Justice: Race, Class, and Sustainability*, edited by Alison Hope Alkon and Julian Agyeman. Cambridge, MA: MIT Press, 2011, 23–46.

Quaempts, E. "First Foods: An Obligation to Take Care of the Foods that Take Care of Us." Future of Our Salmon Conference. Columbia River Inter-Tribal Fish Commission, 2012.

Ranco, Darren J., Catherine A. O'Neill, Jamie Donatuto, and Barbara L. Harper. "Environmental Justice, American Indians and the Cultural Dilemma: Developing Environmental Management for Tribal Health and Well-being." *Environmental Justice*, 4 (4), 2011, 221–30.

Reidlinger, Dyanna, and Fikret Berkes. "Contributions of Traditional Knowledge to Understanding Climate Change in the Canadian Arctic." *Polar Record*, 37 (203), 2001, 315–28.

Reo, Nicholas James and Kyle Powys Whyte. "Hunting and Morality as Elements of Traditional Ecological Knowledge." *Human Ecology*, 40 (1), 2012, 15–27.

Ross, Luana. *Inventing the Savage: The Social Construction of Native American Criminality*. Austin: University of Texas Press, 1998.

Sakakabira, C. "Kiavallakkikput Agviq (Into the Whaling Cycle): Cetaceousness and Climate Change Among the Iñupiat of Arctic Alaska." *Annals of the Association of American Geographers* 100 (4), 2010, 1003–1012.

"People of the Whales: Climate Change and Cultural Resilience Among Iñuit of Arctic Alaska." *Geographical Review* 107 (1), 2017, 159–184.

Scheman, Naomi. "Toward a Sustainable Epistemology." *Social Epistemology*, 26 (3–4), 2012, 471–89.

Shippentower, Cheryl. "Women's Food and Climate Change." Presentation at the Tribal Foods Summit. Portland, OR, January 9, 2014.

Simpson, Leanne and Glen Coulthard. "Leanne Simpson and Glen Coulthard on Dechinta Bush University, Indigenous Land-based Education and Embodied Resurgence." *Decolonization: Indigeneity, Education & Society*, edited by Eric Ritskes, November 26, 2014. [online] URL: decolonization.wordpress.com/2014/11/26/leanne-simpson-and-glen-coulthard-on-dechinta-bush-university-indigenous-land-based-education-and-embodied-resurgence/

Simpson, Leanne R. "Anticolonial Strategies for the Recovery and Maintenance of Indigenous Knowledge." *The American Indian Quarterly*, 28 (3), 2004, 373–84.

Smith, Andrea. *Conquest: Sexual Violence and American Indian Genocide.* Cambridge, MA: South End Press, 2005.

Stark, Heidi Kiiwetinepinesiik. "Respect, Responsibility, and Renewal: The Foundations of Anishinaabe Treaty Making with the United States and Canada." *American Indian Culture and Research Journal*, 34 (2), 2010, 145–64.

Theriault, Sophie. "Canadian Indigenous Peoples and Climate Change: The Potential for Arctic Land Claims Agreements to Address Changing Environmental Conditions." *Climate Change and Indigenous Peoples: The Search for Legal Remedies*, edited by Randall S. Abate and Eliabeth Ann Kronk Warner. Cheltenham, UK: Edward Elgar, 2013, 243–62.

Treaty Indian Tribes in Western Washington. *Treaty Rights at Risk: Ongoing Habitat Loss, the Decline of the Salmon Resource, and Recommendations for Change*, 2011. [online] URL: www://nwifc.org/w/wp-content/uploads/downloads/2011/08/whitepaper628finalpdf.pdf

Trosper, Ronald L. "Traditional American Indian Economic Policy." *American Indian Culture and Research Journal*, 19 (1), 1995, 65–95.

Resilience, Reciprocity and Ecological Economics: Northwest Coast Sustainability. New York: Routledge, 2009.

Turner, Nancy J., Łukasz Jakub Łuczaj, Paola Migliorini, Andrea Pieroni, Angelo Leandro Dreon, Linda Enrica Sacchetti, and Maurizio G. Paoletti. "Edible and Tended Wild Plants, Traditional Ecological Knowledge and Agroecology." *Critical Reviews in Plant Sciences*, 30 (1), 2011, 198–225.

United Nations General Assembly. "United Nations Declaration on the Rights of Indigenous Peoples." New York: United Nations, 2007.

Vizenor, Gerald. *Manifest Manners: Narratives on Postindian Survivance.* Lincoln: University of Nebraska Press, 1994.

Walker, Ryan, Ted Jojola, and David Natcher, Eds. *Reclaiming Indigenous Planning.* Montreal: McGill-Queen's Press, 2013.

Weatherhead, Elizabeth C., Shari Fox Gearheard, and Roger Graham Barry. "Changes in Weather Persistence: Insight from Inuit Knowledge." *Global Environmental Change*, 20 (3), 2010, 523–28.

Werkheiser, Ian. "Community Epistemic Capacity." *Social Epistemology* 30 (1), 2015, 25–44.

Whyte, Kyle Powys. "Justice Forward: Tribes, Climate Adaptation and Responsibility." *Climatic Change*, 120 (3), 2013, 117–30.

"A Concern About Shifting Interactions between Indigenous and Nonindigenous Parties in U.S. Climate Adaptation Contexts." *Interdisciplinary Environmental Review*, 15 (2/3), 2014, 114–33.

Williams, Terry and Preston Hardison. "Culture, Law, Risk and Governance: Contexts of Traditional Knowledge in Climate Change Adaptation." *Climatic Change*, 120 (3), 2013, 531–44.

World Commission on Environment and Development. *Our Common Future.* Oxford, UK: Oxford University Press, 1987.

Wotkyns, Susan R. "Tribes and Climate Change." Institute for Tribal Environmental Professionals, 2013. [online] URL: www.nau.edu/tribalclimatechange/

PART II

BEDROCK

Toward a Kincentric Ethic

5

Indigenous Sustainability: Language, Community Wholeness, and Solidarity

Simon Ortiz

One of the powers of collaboration is brought to mind: meaning and comprehension are brought front and center creatively when different languages and cultures seemingly collide. – This thought came to mind at Qinghai Lake, China, August 2012

Language and Origins: Land, Culture, Community, and Wholeness

Srah-dzeh-nee-she maah meh gah-dzee'putee, eh maah meh khaimah-tse skuh-waa-tse'puuh. Our language is necessary and essential, and truly we need it. That is the meaning of the *Acqumeh* words in the Keres language with which I begin. Keres is the Indigenous *dzeh-nee*, or language, that *Aacqu*, or Acoma, and six other sister Pueblos in New Mexico speak. *Dzeh-nee*, therefore, is the traditional cultural language that bonds the seven Pueblo communities, while four additional languages are spoken there. Most important, Pueblo languages are the cultural foundation that secures for every Pueblo his or her place upon the *haatse*, or land.

There is no question that Pueblos belong physically within and upon the *haatse* as asserted in their Indigenous language. As Pueblos, they insist this belonging is a crucial matter, for it confirms their direct relationship with the land. This statement also assures that the nature of their human role is face-to-face as a people, or *hanoh*, or community that cannot be anything but essential, responsible, and obligatory since the land, or *haatse*, is seen and understood by them as the source of their origin.

This is very different from the way Western culture assigns its role to itself and to others, as well as the terms of control of the land that it purports to own. This assignment of role is the basis of US control and ownership of continental lands in general, especially those lands within its political and national boundaries. Necessarily, it is abstract but the United States assures the public and corporate world it has authority by virtue of government decree and constitutional rule of law. As a result, hegemonic rule is usually and ordinarily accepted since there is very little question that this is the assumed authority.

Indigenous peoples of the Pueblos simply say *Dai-sthee-stuutah-ah. Dai-stuh stuudeh-muuh. Dzah dzee-guwaah-eeskah-steeyuukai-eetyah.* "From here, we are. From here, we emerge." We do not have any other way of belief. The source of this narrative statement is the oral tradition of the Indigenous peoples of the Acoma Pueblo cultural community, but it is pretty much the same in all of the nineteen other Pueblos, as well as in most Indigenous American communities throughout the Americas. This statement is directly from the Indigenous narrative that is their worldview, literally. It cannot be expressed and comprehended any other way contextually except by referring to traditional knowledge that has its origin in the beginning of cultural formation and its role in assuring and defining the origin of Indigenous peoples of the Americas.

Indigenous origin and emergence from the land – for Pueblo peoples and other Indigenous cultures – is literal and not symbolic, although that is the way Western culture usually prefers to consider and comprehend it. *Dai-shtyuu-stuuh-deh-muh* is spoken quite often with a pointed hand or foot gently stamped to indicate that Earth is where the people originated. "From here – land-earth-ground – we arose and were given life." Literally? Yes. Mere symbol? No. Land-earth-ground is the material origin of people and all other forms of life and the living. This understanding includes not only living human societies and cultures but also the myriad items in all of Creation: animate and inanimate. From the center of this planet Earth to the farthest reaches of the universe. In all directions cardinal and otherwise, even those we do not indicate with usual, ordinary, and accepted Western scientific expression or articulation. Unfortunately, it has to be noted that Western cultural knowledge limits itself to proven scientific theory and practice and, heretofore, has disregarded Indigenous science by non-inclusion, neglect, ignorance, and discrimination, and the public is therefore limited by Western restriction.

Origin or Beginning is significant and primary to Indigenous consciousness. *Tsaiyah weh-meh uuyuugai'yee dzah.* I can hear an elder saying, "This is the first knowledge or understanding to have." To acknowledge origin or beginning from the land-earth is basic, vital, and essential.

Without the acknowledgement, there is no way to understand obligation and responsibility that is basic to the relationship our Indigenous human community has to the land. One can speak of it – and fully comprehend it – in personal terms such as, "We owe our lives to our mother because she gave us birth and sustenance at the beginning." An apparent understanding of that sort is obvious when Indigenous culture refers to planet Earth as the Mother Earth in articulations such as: "We must be thankful to Mother Earth for the food we share." Another understanding of that value is when the *Kahtzi-nah Shiwanah* bring gifts to children. The names of *Acqumeh waash-steechatra* are called at ceremonies, especially at midsummer. When a child hears her or his name, it is a summons to come forward and receive a gift: a basket or pottery bowl of fruit, nuts, breads, perhaps a doll or a bow with arrows. It is a gift from Earth brought by the *Kahtzinah Shiwanah*.

By receiving gifts, children are responding within this cultural dynamic. They are thankful, and they are bound in a cycle of reciprocity that they are a part of; the children must do likewise, then, to help the earth so that life may always be bountiful. Indeed, it is a response to the summons called forth by their origins or beginnings as it is delineated within cultural narratives of Indigenous world views. Human response to origins is very much an absolute part of the way land and culture are linked inextricably to community. Although seemingly separate conceptual entities, these elements are part of each other in terms of the role they have in wholeness. Land, culture, and community, together, are considered essential to wholeness and the struggle for wholeness.

In order to achieve and maintain Indigenous cultural continuity, active material activity has to be a commitment. When I was growing up in the Acoma Pueblo village of *Deetseyaamah*, our family had gardens, maize (corn), bean, hay fields, some apple, apricot, and peach trees, and pasture or grazing land to care for. Pueblo peoples were traditionally sedentary farmers, which was part of our upbringing: planting, hoeing, cultivating, irrigation, pulling weeds, and eventually harvesting corn, chili, pumpkins, melons, onions, beets, radishes, turnips, beans, apples, and peaches in the fall (obviously some of the cultivated foods were introduced by Europeans).

I used to think we were simply following the farming ways of white people – the *mericano hanoh* – until I learned from elders that a long, long time ago, way before the white people arrived, Indigenous peoples, especially Pueblos, had been farmers/sowers of plant seeds; they even had "developed" the corn plant into a food source from a wild grass plant.

They, like other Indigenous peoples, became a self-sufficient and self-sustaining community who took care of themselves very well. This ability to develop food sources derived from the cultural knowledge that was common to Indigenous peoples who lived thousands of years ago in the canyons, mesa lands, hills, and mountains that became our homeland in the Southwest, where we continue to live today.

The insistence on continuity is virtually a side effect of applied knowledge that is part of the interaction we as Indigenous cultural human beings have practiced within and with our natural environment, i.e., the semi-arid desert landscape where we Pueblo peoples live. Continuity derives from the relationship we had with our natural landscape, the desert lands with their mountains, canyons, and plateaus that became our domestic home. Continuity and its maintenance was an outgrowth of a philosophy stressing a relationship resulting from the constant and insistent awareness of our dependence on the lands that provided shelter, food, attire, tools – all fundamental elements that human beings need. Relationship was key, and it resulted in continuity because it turned into practical collaboration.

Continuity of collaboration or a constant association with the land and its natural features was a natural organic relationship; our ancestors interacted with the lands practically every instance – with every breath, every movement, every awareness – of their lives. They could not avoid or evade this relationship; their socioeconomic-spiritual relationship became, indeed, like living within the womb of a creator Being or Mother.

Soon – actually an awareness taking place over many, many, many countless generations – human beings realized they could only live beneficially when they interacted as collaborators. This, then, became a way of life, a cultural code; and eventually it became a philosophy of interactivity, one that was close and intimate. It was a worldview within which Indigenous peoples found succor; it became a definitive way of life. Human beings, living within a secure and protected place, provided for themselves by interacting with the environment that surrounded them – that, in fact, enclosed them. Their interaction resulted in the provision of resources that became their food, shelter, and clothing. This approach grew into a philosophical sense of cultural continuity because it was apparent that interactivity was not something that was coincidental but deliberate and intentional.

Community became apparent; it was evident as family, not only through offspring but its further manifestation as extended families that structured themselves as clans organized into intergenerational relationship systems. For example, I am of the Eagle Clan or *Dyaamih hanoh*. *Tse wahmuu, shruweh* Eagle or *Dyaamih hanoh stuudah*, because I am descended within a matrilineal line from a long ago *baabah*, grandmother, who was of the *Dyaami hanoh*, who gave birth to children, some of whom were female who birthed children, henceforth maintaining an ongoing clan lineage. Only females could pass on clan lineage, and eventually my mother birthed me as a *Dyaami* person. Thereafter, I was a child who was sustained generation upon generation by a principle and practice of familial and clan organization that was assured its continuity for the purpose of holistic support and self-sufficiency.

Systematically, intergenerational sustainability was established as an essential principle and practice of familial and clan organization that assured continuity and a system of holistic self-sufficiency. It was a tried-and-true and practical means of Indigenous sustainability perpetuated generation after generation. Although I could not, as an adult male, pass on Eagle clan lineage, my sisters and other female clan relatives would. This was the way it was for countless past generations, reaching back to epochs beyond the relatively recent time of Columbus's landfall on an island in the Caribbean Sea in AD 1492. This was the way it was even during that time when conflict became manifestly evident due to cultural outlooks and European worldviews, which clashed with the way Indigenous peoples regarded themselves and their cultural communities.

Land as Material and Spiritual Sustenance: Source of Indigenous Philosophy, Cultural Traditions, Religion, Knowledge Called "Science," and Moral/Ethical Behavior

With land as concept and located at the foundation of all things in Creation, it is possible to carry on. *Ehmee tse haatse neeyah heh-yah Ih-nee-yah kah-aiteetah eh shaapah-tse skuh-wow-teetah.* "Because of the land, it is possible for us to have existence and, therefore, to live sustainably." In fact, land is not only at the foundation of our living existence but it also carries the whole entity of what we know to be existence. *Ehmee tse haatse nee-yah heh-yah stuh-deh-eh.* "Because of the land, it is possible to live." Land is both a natural material resource and an abstract concept. Land is the source of food, water, medicine, and all nutritional needs for every living organism. So it makes sense for Keres-speaking Acoma people to say: *Dzee dzahnah haatse dzahnuh, dzah-dze guwaa*

Ih-nee-yah nuudah ghunuuh. "If there were ever be no more land, there would be no more existence."

Ehmee tse deekow-eh weh-meh neweetah'-wah-nah-shruu-stah, ai-haatse-shtyuu sraah-tsah-tseh-mah guumuustah. It is necessary to accept and understand that *haatse* is from where our origin arises. Our origin and the origin of all animate and inanimate life. Human, animal, insect, vegetal-plant life, minerals, all resources, all terrestrial landscapes. Everything big and little, everything in creation from the beginning of time to the present and into the future. Everything in creation is every-thing; nothing is excluded. Land is the context and the container or vessel of all. When the dancing *kahtzina* signal with hands and arms to all the horizons to indicate all of creation, it is an inclusive sign that nothing is left out: we and all life are together in existence. As said earlier, all things in life are enmeshed together; therefore sustainability is *Ih-nee-yah*, our existence.

The relationships we enjoy within the human community derive from the land also because it is pervasive and the most obvious context within which we find ourselves. The natural context of land, in a sense, encloses us, so that we are close to each other. Next to one another, physical land becomes as familiar to us as a relative. Skin to sand and stone. Skin to water, whether river, spring, rain, ocean. And grass and flowers to skin. Tumbleweeds, cactus, yucca to skin. Different looking, of course, from each other, but close in partnerships, relationships, and collaboration within desert and plateau land. Relationships are acts of nature, like ideas in motion in the plant world, and in the human community. Nature is our context, so we don't usually question it. We may not always be in agreement with it, but our relationship with it is unquestionable for the most part.

Shraa- dzeh-nee neeyah tse heh- yah sraayah shuutze. "With our language, we always welcome you." Language is more inclusive than that actually when it comes to relationships in the Indigenous community. Respect and regard are essential to strong relationships; so in terms of the relationship humans and land have to each other, reciprocity and inter-dependence are fundamental. This prominence is demonstrated by the vital connection to land shared by traditional Pueblo people who plant corn, bean, and squash seeds, and who cultivate and care for the plants once they sprout and begin to grow. Intense awareness of corn growing is expressed by the Hopi, for example, by songs sowers sing; the belief is that young cornstalks respond to the songs by growing. At Acoma, the *Shiwana Kah-tzina* have dancing songs that depict the growing corn, beans, and squash as happy, beautiful, and vigorous plants.

Demonstration of inclusivity is rhetorical obviously, but it is also expressed dynamically by the motions of dancing. When I was a little boy, I remember an old man came by our Acoma valley corn and pumpkin fields where my dad and I were pulling weeds among rows of corn. He was a lively and talkative man, my dad's friend, who said to me, *"Hah weh eemah, Naanah. Shrou-shee-tseh-tah-nah-tyu. Haweetrunee, shey-yah-yuu-tahneetyu."* "Come over here, Grandson. Let us dance. For the young growing plants, let us sing." And we did.

Haatse, in this case, is the instigator of language; in fact, language initiates and originates in the relationship we, as a human community, have with the land. Jeannette Armstrong, writer and linguist friend, who is an Okanagan tribal woman who used to be a Council Member of her tribal community in western Canada, says without hesitation that land is the originator and source of language. I will add that without language, there is no verbal acknowledgment of relationships possible since reciprocity, interdependence, responsibility, and obligation are rhetorical expressions of such. Further, this obligation extends to the ethical and moral responsibilities human beings have with plant, animal, and all other life forms of the earth. In return, in reciprocity, plant, animal, and all other life forms have physical, ethical, and moral responsibilities to human beings. *Ehguusheh ehmeh ehh Shranayahshi Iatiku skaiweeyah-ahnee.* Because that is the way our Mother Creator *Iatiku* allows us to be, to exist within Creation.

In a sense, this latter observation has a spiritual connotation and suggests an interesting parallel to Indigenous science as it relates to the dynamic of morals and ethics. Western scientific application, explanation, explication, and comprehension not only have to do with causes and effects but also with biological, chemical, and physical sequences and interactions between properties of substances interacting with one another that is crucial to a final outcome. Western hard science, we're told, has nothing to do with ordinary human whim or wile or superstition or passion that causes us to weep or love endlessly or even fruitlessly. Yet we, as Indigenous peoples who are human beings, need mechanisms and prophylactics to cope with the furious heat of Arizona and Mexican deserts or the frigid cold of Arctic storms in Alaska and northern Canada. We also need adequate remedies against unbearable physical pain, disease, and needless loss of life that often beset us. Do we believe scientific solutions fostered by Western science protect us? Many Indigenous peoples feel, think, and believe they cannot and do not.

On the other hand, moral and ethical dynamics and experiences seem to stem from or have to do with physical pain, severe disease, and needless loss of life often incomprehensible to human beings. Too often, moral and ethical complications and difficulties result in stasis that human social-cultural communities do not know what to do with, at least not immediately. However, there are options in the present era within our immediate and present locale that can be considered. I will present one in general terms that can be considered as viable, practical, positive, and relevant, especially to local Indigenous cultural communities and the large non-Indigenous population in Arizona.

Hohokam-O'odham Continuity: An Indigenous Canal and Irrigation System – Past, Present, Future

During the spring of 2013, I heard a presentation at Arizona State University by Kelly Washington, a member of the Salt River tribal community that is composed of O'odham and Pii Paash peoples, in which he focused on the cultural and social history of their tribal O'odham and Pii Paash community. A large portion of his presentation described the Hohokam-O'odham canal and irrigation system in the Phoenix valley and beyond. Without a doubt, it is one of the world's wonders of human achievement in the Americas. The canal and irrigation system spans the so-called "prehistorical era" – the time of pre-European culture in the Americas.

Mr. Washington called the Hohokam-O'odham irrigation system the largest ever built in North America or perhaps even in the whole world by any Indigenous cultural community. It was planned, designed, engineered, and constructed totally by Indigenous peoples before Euro-Americans came to the Americas. This fact is confirmed and verified by Dr. Jerry Howard, an archeologist who has researched and studied the Hohokam canal and irrigation system for the past 25 years. According to Dr. Howard, "These were the largest Indigenous gravity-feed irrigation systems in the New World, irrigating over 110,000 acres in a single valley at their peak." Without stating how large the Hohokam-O'odham systems were, Mr. Kelly Washington's estimation is far larger since he also spoke of ancestral O'odham communities farther to the south of Phoenix, including those in the areas of present-day Casa Grande and Florence, non-Indigenous towns along the Gila River.

As a descendant of an Indigenous traditional irrigation cultural community – namely, Acoma Pueblo in New Mexico – I am amazed at the size, sophistication, and achievement of the Hohokam-O'odham canal and irrigation system. I can only be convinced of the historical, cultural, environmental, and ecological interest such an achievement inspires. Previously, I had heard only a bit about the canal system via oral traditional stories told at my home of Acoma Pueblo. I had come across some Southwestern archeological and anthropological references to it, but enough to think of it as quite an accomplishment that benefitted human social-cultural civilization not only locally but also nationally and internationally. Obviously, the complexity and sophistication of such an endeavor was very impressive and awe-inspiring, something human civilization would have practical and optimal interest in.

When I came to be a professor at Arizona State University in 2007, I thought, and even expected, I would find Hohokam-O'odham Canal and Irrigation System Studies at the center of the university's large sustainability program, since one of its stated goals was the need for ecological systems that would benefit the present and future of Phoenix and the environs of Arizona. And since, along with making a traditional agricultural livelihood for themselves, those also were the environmental and ecological goals of the Hohokam-O'odham peoples who have lived for many, many generations in the arid lands of the Phoenix valley, I expected to find ongoing study and high interest in Indigenous knowledge of the Hohokam-O'odham canal and irrigation. That would, I thought, make absolute and appropriate sense, especially because I knew many universities were encouraging cultural and social diversities that were seen as strengths rather than burdens.

But, alas, such was not the case. I soon came to find that Hohokam-O'odham canal systems, as well as other Indigenous land-based accomplishments, were not featured. As far as occasional interest in traditional Indigenous – some may prefer the out-dated term "Indian" – environmental and ecological knowledge with reference to sustainability is concerned, I'm sure – or I assume – there is some reference to it in the academy. But there is little substantial interest in relevant knowledge that is definitively Indigenous American in origin in too many universities. This is a mystery of sorts presently: Why is Indigenous traditional or contemporary knowledge of sustainability not included in a major way at our centers of higher learning?

Major American research institutions can and should incorporate and collaborate with Indigenous American stewards of land, culture, and community by offering their faculties, curriculum programs, facilities, and resources to make sure Indigenous peoples have access, training, and research resources that will further benefit the responsibilities and obligations of sustainability. *Sharing tasks and duties – called reciprocity – that benefit not only us but the world around all of us is what we have to do.* We, as human beings, are people in terms of land, culture, and community. In other words, we can all be sustainable beings who are involved and engaged in sustainability. Certainly, it is up to us as scholars, writers, poets, artists, scientists, humanists, especially those of us who are of Indigenous heritage, to know we are bound by *shraa-haatse, shrou-yu-gai-yeshee, eh shra-ahsh-teetra.* Our land, culture, and community. Because that's who we are as sustainable beings.

6

A Single Strand: The *Nsyilxcin* Speaking People's *Tmix^w* Knowledge as a Model for Sustaining a Life-Force Place

Jeannette Armstrong

Based on both historical research and personal immersion, this chapter explores how Syilx ethics and governance are linked to land use and regenerative conservation of ecosystems. I present the perspective that the *nsyilxcin* speaking people's ecological knowledge represents a Syilx environmental ethic that is based in a knowledgeable land use connected to wisdom in Syilx governance traditions, which persists into contemporary practice. I show how this lived, Indigenous ethic can serve as a model for the type of "living in place" needed today for sustainability.

Research for my dissertation, *Constructing Indigeneity: Syilx Okanagan Oraliture and Tmix^wcentrism* (Armstrong, 2010), is central to the points raised in this chapter. This research focused on support for the theory that the Syilx people's ecological knowledge is the basis of everyday practice, which expresses an ethic that was not a form of mere intuitive morality toward their food source, or a practice of social anthropomorphism in the form of simplistic reverence for their relationships with their food sources, often linked to the terms *primitive* and *hunter-gatherers*.

I refer to the entirety of the *nsyilxcin* (those who speak Syilx language) groups as the *Syilx* to avoid local ethno-geographic reduction into separate groups speaking the same language, including Slocan, Lakes, Sanpoil, Southern Okanagan, Northern Okanagan, Similkameen, and the Kettle (Spier, 1938; Ray, 1939; Teit and Boas, 1975), and to avoid terms utilized to collect the ethno-geographic groupings into a one cultural profile among other Salishan speaking groups, including the use of the terms *Okanagan* (Ross, 1969) and *Colville-Okanagan* (Mattina, 1987; Kuipers, 2002).

95

The *nsyilxcin* speaking people, linguistically referred to as Colville-Okanagan, are associated with a large territory of occupation. In Canada, the *nsyilxcin* speaking people occupy a territory covering vast drainage areas of the Fraser and Columbia River systems between two major mountain ranges in inland British Columbia. In the United States, the *nsyilxcin* speaking people occupied vast areas of the Upper Columbia River system and its larger tributaries, the Okanagan, the Kettle, and the Sanpoil Rivers in eastern Washington State.

At contact, the Salishan language speaking peoples, of which the Syilx (*nsyilxcin* speaking) are one group, occupied a large territory covering vast areas of British Columbia reaching down to cover much of Washington State, much of northern Idaho, and part of northern Montana (Kuipers, 2002: viii).

The focus of my research was to study and confirm that the Syilx society embodies an ethic that maintains values and informs practices in land use and economy. My study concluded that the Syilx practiced a form of regenerative conservation of the lands they used over and over again, as the outcome of a society-wide environmental ethic based in *ecological knowledge*. An important feature of that practice is that the Syilx people were not nomadic or seminomadic. Even a cursory reading of ethnographical information demonstrates that the *nsyilxcin* peoples and indeed all Salishan peoples, whether coastal, riverine, or plateau, never simply wandered about following game, searching for food along the way. Central to the Syilx concept of sustainability, I confirmed that it was an egalitarian ethic that permeated their society and governance system and which included all local life forms. Research also confirms that the ecological knowledge required for securing sustenance, security, and the capacity to thrive is transferred from generation to generation, embedded in the language and in oral story, and in practices that produce social and environmental sustainability characterized by a one hundred percent land regenerative model.

The Syilx word *tmix^w* refers to the ecology of the land, including all life forms of a place, consisting of many relationships. The concept of *tmix^w* emanates from the Syilx language and is illuminated in the oral story tradition. The word allows access to the Syilx concept of the human duty to nature. Examining the word *tmix^w* allows us to perceive the depth of the Syilx knowledge of ecology; it is a way to see existence in that *tmix^w* is the life force of a place. Seeing the image in the word in the particular way that *nsyilxcin* as an Indigenous language carries nature images generates meaning, in that the word *tmix^w* literally displays many strands continually emanating and fanning outward from one source that is not visible. The image provides a dynamic view of what the ecology of the land actually does and refers, as an image, to every life form of a place, including the human, continuously emanating toward an invisible source. It is an Indigenous view. Nature is life force when seen as *tmix*^{w}. Each life form is a single strand of the life force of that place and requires others of that place to have existed and to continue to exist. In that way *tmix*^{w} captures the dynamics of the myriad relationships that make that place what it is. Syilx humans rightfully are seen as a single strand of that life force.

The view of Syilx being *tmix*^{w} themselves is a necessary element in their philosophy of egalitarianism toward all life forms. That view of *tmix*^{w} is a systems view and essential to understanding that a systems view is foundational to Syilx thought, and that it is constructed from a knowledgeable position based in the meaning of *tmix*^{w}. Syilx philosophy is centered on and based in an understanding that the ecology they are part of is *tmix*^{w}. Their philosophy is an Indigenous ethos specific to the meaning of *tmix*^{w} and should therefore be called a *tmix*^{w}-centric ethic. The meaning of the word *tmix*^{w} in the *nsyilxcin* language has retained the complexity of meaning throughout antiquity to the present in all aspects of daily life, governance, and formal religious practice. The Syilx philosophy can be appreciated as an alternative way of valuing nature in that it articulates the human moral duty to *tmix*^{w}. The Syilx social paradigm can be seen as constructed from the deep ecological knowledge of the human responsibility that must reside in each generation and must move continuously forward through language, practice, and oral story. Syilx knowledge can also be seen as a systems view, which is strongly expressed in their language, their stories, and their social construct.

The Syilx response to the moral issue of human utility of other life forms is also the foundation of an egalitarian type of governance the Syilx practiced, which was also extended outward in relations with other groups surrounding their territory. Syilx ecological knowledge can be seen in the judicious practices arising out of the wisdom that the ecology of their territory is a living whole system that requires human compliance with its regenerative requirements in order to interact with it in a non-destructive way. The Syilx social matrix reveals knowledge that whole-system regeneration is grounded in an ethic for which the fundamental requirement is nondestructive land use.

Syilx governance demonstrates a sophisticated insight that a devotion to full regenerative land use requires that the highest level of authority for resource guardianship has to be grounded in local knowledge, requiring a deep level of cooperation and solidarity among groups in the whole of the system. In that way the systems view can be seen as an essential element in the Syilx egalitarian approach to governance. A *tmix^w*-centric ethic requires governance that must socially ensure that the exercise of local authority is willingly supported by surrounding groups in a mutual concord of human interdependency to enjoy system-wide reciprocal benefits. The Syilx knowledge – that ethical conduct within nature is based in reciprocity – informs the active principles of collective reverence for the lives that nature gifts as sustenance as a return for participation in the continual regeneration of each life form.

Various ethnographical studies of the *nsyilxcin* groups, including Hill-Tout (1911), Ray (1939), Spier (1938), Teit (1975), and Bouchard (1998), reveal that the *nsyilxcin* maintained permanently specific resource areas where they lived, while village harvest areas in other locations were ready at different seasons. These locations were dwelling sites in their appropriate season, just as winter village sites located in the warmest areas of the valley floor were occupied about the same amount of time as each of the spring, summer, and fall sites. Walters in Spier (1938) reports that at all seasons of the year families lived away from the winter villages because single families moved throughout harvest zones, that villages along rivers had denser populations only in the winter, and that the chief of each village always knew the whereabouts of villagers because four or five sites were inhabited simultaneously by one band (Spier, 1938: 87). Winter dwelling sites seem to be categorized by the ethnographers as "permanent" only by the criterion of having immovable winter-appropriate structures. However, the fact that other dwellings were seasonally appropriate and transportable from one dwelling site to the next does not make other seasonal sites less permanently occupied or the people nomadic.

Immanently clear from the ethnographic reports and contemporary harvest practice is that people of each group and each village have knowledge of each site, including exactly when each is ready for occupation. As ethnobotanist Nancy Turner mentions, in any given village area the Okanagan-Colville had easy access to at least one, and more often two or three, major vegetation zones, as well as numerous habitats such as swamps, meadows, talus slopes, river banks, lakes, and rocky outcrops (Turner et al., 1980: 5). In Spier (1938), Post reports that each family went to the same vicinity each year for fishing, digging, and picking, and wintered at the sites, changing only if wood were scarce. He further explains that most families went to the same hunting ground every fall, and their sons continued to do so after their fathers died; also, women of a village gathered plant foods as a group and went to the same places year after year (Spier, 1938: 11–22). In a real sense, each village of the Nsyilxcin utilized and maintained, into the contemporary, permanent occupation and use of their land like a huge seasonal perma-garden. The "Syilx perma-garden" is a type of vertical ecological land-use system with vast natural areas for harvest beginning in the spring on the valley floor, in the summer moving up to the mountain foothills, and by fall up to the alpine forest levels. The Syilx then move back in the valley floor for the winter.

An undeniable fact in nsyilxcin territory is that plant foods have extremely short harvest windows as a result of the semi-arid interior summer heat. Exact ecological knowledge of weather effects on different locations, about when and at which altitudes the various harvests are ready, is an absolute essential. In the same way, knowledge of migrating bird and fish spawning cycles in different locations at different seasons in different weather is critical. The grazing, calving, and mating movement patterns of deer, moose, and elk, as well as the hibernating and life-cycles of food mammals, is crucial local knowledge. A long-term local basis of continued interaction with a specific area is the only way that level of knowledge could be held and transferred.

The Syilx environmental ethic is underpinned by socially and individually institutionalized practices of respect. Ethnographic studies of the Syilx reveal evidence, visible and recognizable to European eyes, of conservation practice and regulation exercised by fisheries and hunting chiefs and village subchiefs. Their regulatory powers were law. Chance refers to subchiefs as "subsistence governors." He highlights the specific example of the Kettle Falls Salmon Chief, who supervised the equal distributions of salmon to all tribes gathered during the salmon run from morning till sundown. He speculates that only then would the extent of the day's catch be known (Chance, 1973: 20).

Less visible than the chiefs were other regulators such as local head men and head women, who determined or regulated harvest takes and decided on which harvest areas were open for roots, berries, fresh fish, birds, and small mammals, as well as deciding which sites were to be left to another year. Spier (1938) says of the Southern Okanagan group that in every village, other than the village in which the chief is residing, there is a head man, not appointed by the chief, who directed the communal hunting and fishing of the village (98). Even a cursory search of oral and written records reveals similar common practices in every village and in every area of the Syilx. Invisible to external eyes are many best-practice schemes, harvest practices, and regulations still observed diligently into the contemporary. Such Syilx folk knowledge continues and resides in anecdotal information on plant harvesting methods and comprises a vast system of commonly known local regulatory practices.

The utmost respect for plants and plant communities is a core foundational element in all Syilx gathering practices. Turner (1980), who included my parents, an aunt, and two uncles among her expert informants in her research, *Ethnobotany of the Okanagan*, comments that all plants, particularly those important as foods and medicines, were regarded with the utmost respect and reverence. She reports that many Okanagan-Colville legends "refer to plants in their original state and describe the circumstances of their transformation to their present form." She reports that about 130 of the 260 species of plants known to the Okanagan-Colville were used as medicines (Turner et al., 1980: 152–53).

Personal observations and experience of best practices includes the knowledge expressed in common field harvest routines. In the same way that European gardening wisdom is more common-folk practice, Syilx field harvest practices are simply passed on in the field as the *best way* to do it. Some general best-practice methods observed informally for different plant harvests include: counting how many to take from within a measured standing radius; measuring distances between plants to harvest; determining what size they must be for harvest; measuring how big a patch must be left between patches or plots harvested; alternating one field, slope, or draw from year to year; fallowing sections by poking sporadic dig holes for seeds but not taking any plants; broadcast reseeding of discarded or damaged berries; ritual bush beating or shaking after harvest; seed pod beating ceremonially; protecting newly producing areas from harvest in order to strengthen growth; and selecting specific varieties and leaving other varieties of berries.

The long-term planning knowledge utilized in the practice of annual harvesting at specific dwelling sites, as well as the Indigenous form of perma-gardening practices at such sites, are definitely not features of nomadic or even seminomadic cultures following herds or crops over vast areas to gather by chance. The evidence of informal and formal knowledge practice for maintaining local sustainability concretely identifies the Syilx land-use ethic.

Animals, fish, roots, and berries were not simply gathered without regard to their own right to exist. One of the required social institutions was the observance of gratitude rituals. Ceremonial observances of gratitude maintained a system of society-wide ethical respect toward the lives of animals, fish, roots, and berries in their own right. Hill-Tout documents that the Okanagan observed first-fruits ceremonies through prayers offered to spirits who were supposed to preside over the operations of nature, and no one would think of picking a berry or digging a root until a feast was held (Hill-Tout, 1911: 134). Others report of the Southern Okanagan that first-fruit ceremonies were held after the first big gathering of camas, service berries, and bitterroot, with most of the band gathered at the chief's house where he stood and spoke (Spier, 1938: 32). Teit reports that the Northern Okanagan first-fruits ceremony was observed in every band before berries or roots were picked. He notes that the chief in the band made an offering on a bark tray (Teit and Boas, 1975: 291). In the first hunt, the first deer brought in by each man was distributed among the people of the camp, and this was an analog of the first-fruits rites for other products (Spier, 1938: 22). First-salmon ceremonies were carried on during the first four days each year that salmon were taken at a weir (Spier, 1938: 15).

Other more informal rituals of recognition, of relatedness, or of animals being on the same level as humans are common practices of the Syilx. Teit relates a story in the Similkameen of a hunting chief, who, taking off his cap, waved it toward the cliffs where the sheep were and spoke to them asking for their pity. He further reports that animals, especially large game, were treated with great respect, and spoken of differentially; when a bear was killed, a mourning song was sung, called the "bear song" (Teit and Boas, 1975: 291). Ethnobotanist Nancy Turner reports that medicines of all types are still treated with reverence and respect, and plants are spoken to and their help requested as they are being gathered and prepared (Turner et al., 1980: 150). While these practices might be attributed to an unsophisticated animistic belief system, the fact that they remain a prevailing, common, and contemporary practice of Syilx harvesters, hunters, and fishermen suggests that the practice was of a deeper social purpose than ancient mysticism.

Ethnographers in general agree, through information collected at different times, that the Salishan peoples of the Interior Plateau region, including the *nsyilxcin* speaking people, at early contact were peacefully organized. Ray, an ethnographer of the Sanpoil and Nespelem areas of the Syilx territory, in his study, *Cultural Relations in the Plateau of Northwestern America*, mentions that what is impressive and revealing is the pacifism that characterizes the groups of the central region (Ray, 1939: 35). He relates that Ross Cox, one of the earliest visitors to the

Syilx territory, said, "The historical stories of battle obtained are of occurrences in a past so distant that the accounts have a mythological flavor" (Ray, 1939: 79). Walters, in his study of the social structure of the Southern Okanagan Syilx territory, also points out that they evidently were a peaceful people for at least several centuries (Spier, 1938: 79).

Ethnographers disagree about how to characterize the political organization of the Salishan peoples. Ray offers that the political unit had to have been the village since no term existed for any larger political aggregation other than a term for the more inclusive dialectic division. He does note that units larger than the village did exist, but that they were social or linguistic in nature, identified by bonds of common habitat and common customs, values, religion, and language. He insists that the bonds were never political, although he observes that a striking feeling "of unity" existed among all speakers of one common Salishan dialect (Ray, 1939: 9). He notes that members of each village were subject only to their own chiefs and that the chief of one village never answered to the chief of any other village. Although collectives of villages acted together as bands, Ray maintains that these were like one large village and were unions of domestic and peacetime order (7–15). He presents a picture of what he terms the "atomistic nature of political organization" as having more than mere passive acceptance of village autonomy, in that autonomy was "strongly defended and is considered right and proper" (Ray, 1939: 4).

Studies by Spier in the Southern Okanagan area of *nsyilxcin* territory assert that each band was autonomous. The report ventures that the main factor in maintaining tribal unity must be blood relationship based on the constant intermarriage establishing blood relatives in each band. Individuals or families might fish, hunt, and establish themselves in any of the village sites belonging to an immediate or a friendly band (Spier, 1938: 73–87).

Likewise, Kroeber, in a larger study of many tribes along Pacific coastal areas of North America, observes that although there didn't appear to be a political unit other than the village, it is clear that villages existed in a state of neutrality toward one another, linked by peaceful trade, intermarriage, and participation in each other's ceremonies and festivals. He characterizes that linking of villages to be "like nations of the civilized world" (Kroeber, 1917: 396).

For the Salishan, peaceful interaction is facilitated by the different groups' language familiarity, as well as a similarity in customs and traditions. In fact, Hill-Tout, like other ethnographers, comments that careful inquiry reveals that the Salishan cultures followed so closely that of neighboring divisions that "a description of one is virtually a description of another" (Hill-Tout, 1911: 133). The continued practice of a pacifist social order over long periods also signifies intentional organizational methods to sustain a stable distributed system of economy and authority, particularly over such great geographical and cultural diversity.

Central to my view, as an insider of the culture and language, and my knowledge of *nsyilxcin* speaking people, is the nature of their political organization. It is clear that Salishan is a culture of peace and cooperation, and therefore the political structure does not require the hierarchical, centralized authority characteristic of and necessary to conquest or defense. Most political models available to ethnographers, and used as standards for comparison, would be those familiar to European social orders, and so political organization of another design would be invisible or at best misunderstood. An analysis of the same ethnographic information reveals the presence of a political structure maintaining a social order vastly different from the political order of conquest, defense, or capitalism.

The Salishan peoples enjoyed a peaceful political order in what may have been one of the largest collectives of local authorities operating as autonomous units of a political and economic aggregate encompassing over twenty-five Salishan language groups. The characteristic cultural interactions, in the intermarriages and inter-areal trade, should be viewed as the basis of the vast structural concord between member groups, which relied on chiefs facilitating peaceful lateral cooperation between culturally diverse and autonomous local units. This concord was reinforced by a great deal of inter-areal trade, intermarriage, and intercultural exchanges, which were observed by virtually every scholar of Salishan peoples. The groups enjoyed and achieved interdependent reciprocity, at the same time they continually reinforced the value of peaceful relations with each other, based on a strong practice of deference to the village chiefs' management of resource sites in their jurisdictions.

The leadership that had to evolve for this form of structural concord provides insight into the governance required for maintaining peace in such a large system of cooperating units. Ray reports, "Nowhere in the Plateau is chieftainship based upon wealth." He provides an insightful description of chieftainship among the Okanagan of the Sanpoil, in which it was clear that in the case of a vacancy, the village would assemble and select one of the eligible relatives of the chief by standards of honesty, sound judgment, temperament, and most importantly "skill in arbitration" (Ray, 1939: 19–20). Ray also provides solid evidence of women serving on the council or assembly among a number of central Plateau tribes, and that female chiefs are known to the Southern Okanagan and the Lakes *nsyilxcin* speaking groups. He comments, "[I]t is quite clear that female chieftainship is here a simple outgrowth of the principle of political and sexual equality" (24).

Chance, whose historical research focuses primarily on the Colville-Okanagan of Kettle Falls, demonstrates that chieftainship is the central authority associated with inter-areal peaceful resource allocations. He provides a chart from 1830 to 1831 of visiting tribes, which lists seven Salish tribes and two non-Salish Plateau tribes camped at Kettle Falls. He details the Salmon Chief's methods for equal distributions of salmon resources among his own and the many different tribes assembled in his jurisdiction at Kettle Falls (Chance, 1973: 18–19).

Anastasio, in his doctoral research, *Intergroup Relations in the Southern Plateau*, argues that such a level of peaceful relations relied on active inter-relations. He demonstrates that there were formal inter-tribal mechanisms that regulated intergroup relations that permitted the peaceful settlement of intertribal disputes, as well as the co-utilization of resource sites. He points out that it was the responsibility of the whole of the larger cooperating unit to guarantee the welfare of persons, which allowed property and gift exchange between groups and which extended kinship between them (Anastasio, 1955: 91). Anastasio's research established that the political structure "was not disorganized and understandable only in the perspective of each local group; rather … it had an areal organization which was flexible and shifting within a certain range of variability" from place to place (Anastasio, 1955: 4).

From that perspective, the political organization expressed was opposite the type of political organization required for an imperialistic intent. The highest level of authority and responsibility would have been found at the village level, to maintain peaceful cooperation with other autonomous villages or units of local authority, beginning with those in one language group and progressing outward to encompass surrounding Salishan groups. The result was a high level of local resource control and, therefore, sustainability, in terms of products and their exchange. Such a level of local resource control would have generated and required a wide spectrum of cultural and political diplomacy. Constant deference to local authority as the main level of governance would have created an intelligent structure, which relied on and placed a high value on specific local ecological knowledge. Reinforcement of absolute local authority, control, and management would have formed the basis of a strong political, economic, and social interchange culture between neighboring units. This structure would necessarily sustain an order in which no units compete for the same resources but must willingly cooperate in constant peaceful interchange and trade of goods so each can benefit reciprocally. Where resources are scarce and fragile, the tribes operate out of the *knowledge* that local autonomy is an absolute requirement for successful management to ensure full regeneration of local resources; further, it is critical to maintain autonomy in order to sustain the interdependent mutual needs and benefits of each unit as a part of a larger system of exchange reciprocity.

The languages, stories, and practices that differentiate one group from another are place-specific critical features that regenerate entire systems of knowledge. Specific and different knowledge embedded in language and stories central to their customs and practices reflects the requirements of the system for full regeneration. That ethnographic views are colored by conquest and land expansionist political structures does not change what studies of the Salishan peoples reveal. Making alliances and mutually supporting the equality of each autonomous unit in a knowledgeable concord of mutually interdependent cooperation requires knowledge of the underlying reasoning.

The Syilx construct, as well as all Plateau Salish cultures, requires a more informed definition that clearly differentiates them from agricultural, marine, nomadic, and seminomadic cultures, in order to describe their political organization. Key is the knowledge of a people who strongly defended local authority as a responsibility with unquestionable rights to steward the environment based on a strong adherence to environmental law, but which also provided opportunities for individual freedom in the philosophical expectations of self-imposed best practices that immerse every individual, family, community, and nation in the knowledge of why adherence is necessary. This personalized level of stewardship, resulting in the Syilx ethic reflected in social institutions and political leadership, is possible only through an accessible localized long-term knowledge of the requirements of every resource.

The long-term knowledge that connects the past to the present and the present to the future is a Syilx societal ethic, defined by the Syilx's relationship with the land. Long-term knowledge of the environment is framed and transferred in Syilx stories. The perspective of humans as being themselves *tmix*^{w} allows access to the Syilx view of human existence within nature as life-force. The Syilx knowledge of required codes of conduct toward each other utilizes story as a form of intergenerational discourse directed at human conduct in relation to the environment, and is expressed as the human responsibility of the inherited state of being *tmix*[w] themselves as life-force. It is based in the knowledge of having an established equilibrium within the dynamic interdependence that is nature, and is focused on the concept of the human being continuously bringing her/himself into equilibrium with the inhabitants of the life-force place. This equilibrium requires being continuously guided by a philosophy to re-constitute and engage as Indigenous to that place.

The Syilx social paradigm incorporates knowledge of life forms affected by the human as a part of everyday life. Indigeneity as a philosophy of sustaining a life-force place is aptly imaged in the Nsyilxcen language and is situated as a framework of good practice in terms of attitude, lifestyle, and land use directed toward full regeneration of the whole life-force place as a functioning order. To be Syilx is to continuously sustain a unity of existence within the generation-to-generation, year-to-year, and season-to-season cycle of the life-force place. As one of many strands, being Syilx means one is continuously being bound in that expectation with others on the land to form one strong thread. This strong thread, which says that humans must learn to move forward together, is a social moral imperative. This concept is the fundamental meaning of being Indigenous. It is the fundamental meaning of being Syilx. The science involved in acquiring that level of knowledge is based in long-term careful observation and transferred through a portable documentation method in the language and stories, continuously reflecting the desired relationships within the local ecology.

Clearly allying with Indigenous peoples currently living their Indigeneity *in-situ* and the fostering of those peoples re-indigenizing themselves through local customs, laws, and languages in a contemporary context, is fundamental to the reinstatement of a contemporary form of *Indigeneity*. This requires radical changes in social processes and new approaches to governance. It would produce a transformative shift from a framework of control and domination to one of collaboration that in so doing would institute new ways of being. The shift toward constructing such mechanisms would be a pronouncement of environmental justice for all peoples. As the late John Mohawk said, "I think that when we talk about re-indigenization, we need a much larger, bigger umbrella to understand it. It's not necessarily about the Indigenous Peoples of a specific place; *it's about re-indigenizing the peoples of the planet*. It's about us looking at the whole thing in the broadest of possible ways" (Nelson, 2008: 259). Whether the concept of re-indigenization is integrated into scientific language, in terms of caring for the resilience of ecological forces specific to different places, or into a more local cultural idiom, it is an intrinsic part of a required environmental ethos. First steps toward re-indigenization require a dialogue about the questions that confront modern society – questions related to the global mobility of populations and the resultant global monoculturing and dislocation from knowledge of place. Re-indigenization in that sense is less about how long people have been in one place but more about embracing and fostering society-wide knowledge and ethics of the specific requirements of *tmix*^{w} in each place, while creating institutions at local levels to meet those requirements.

In conclusion, the model of the Syilx people is one that demonstrates how society might rethink itself. The Syilx are one group among a highly successful society of over twenty-five other Salishan speaking groups who coexisted next to each other. Together they held in place a vast intertribal level of knowledge intent on peacefully instituting required social codes to insure the land's regenerative capacity. The "indigenous" construct of intertribal mechanisms that interlocked the groups into a vast network operating like the different cells of a body provides a valuable vision of the environmental ethic now required in society.

In the Syilx perspective, humans must perceive how the *tmix*^{w} regenerate themselves and know, therefore, how humans can move forward in unity with the life-force of their place. We must know that human beings are intertwined and bound with the *tmix*^{w} as one strand of many that produces the regeneration of other strands. Sustaining, strengthening, and protecting each *tmix*^{w} in an equality of existence through the cycles of days, seasons, and years requires the knowledge that being human is a *tmix*^{w} responsibility.

WORKS CITED

Anastasio, Angelo. *Intergroup Relations in the Southern Plateau.* Unpublished PhD dissertation, University of Chicago, 1955.

Armstrong, Jeannette. *Constructing Indigeneity: Syilx Okanagan Oraliture and Tmixw centrism.* Electronic Publication. Greifswald, Germany: University of Greifswald, 2010.

Bouchard, Randy. "Northern Okanagan, Lakes and Colville." *Plateau, Handbook of North American Indians,* Vol. 12, edited by Deward E. Walker, Jr. Washington, DC: Smithsonian Institution, 1998, 238–50.

Chance, David H. *Influences of the Hudson's Bay Company on the Native Cultures of the Colville District. Northwest Anthropological Research Notes. Memoir No. 2,* edited by Roderick Sprague and Deward E. Walker. Moscow: University of Idaho, 1973.

Hill-Tout, Charles. "Report on the Ethnology of the Okanak'en of British Columbia, an Interior Division of the Salish Stock." *The Journal of the Royal Anthropological Institute of Great Britain and Ireland*, 41, 1911, 130–61.

Kroeber, A. L. "The Tribes of the Pacific Coast of North America." Proceeding, Nineteenth International Congress of Americanists, Washington, 1917, 385–401. Available at: www.lib.berkeley.edu

Kuipers, Aert H. *UM Occasional Papers in Linguistics No. 16, Salish Etymological Dictionary*. Missoula: University of Montana, 2002.

Mattina, Anthony. *Colville-Okanagan Dictionary*. Missoula: University of Montana, 1987.

Nelson, Melissa K., Ed. *Original Instructions: Indigenous Teachings for a Sustainable Future*. Rochester, VT: Bear & Company, 2008.

Ray, Verne F. *Cultural Relations in the Plateau of Eastern Washington and Northern Idaho*. Los Angeles: Southwest Museum Administrator of the Fund, 1939.

Ross, Alexander. *Adventure of the First Settlers on the Oregon or Columbia River*, edited by Milo Milton Quaife, 1849. New York: The Citadel Press, 1969.

Spier, Leslie, Ed. *The Sinkaitekw or Southern Okanagan of Washington*. Contributions from the Laboratory of Anthropology 2, General Series in Anthropology 6, Menasha, WI: George Banta, 1938.

Teit, James A. and Frans Boas. *The Salishan Tribes of the Western Plateaus: An Extract from the 45th B.A.E. Annual Report 1927–28*. Facsimile Reproduction 1973. Seattle: The Shorey Book Store, 1975.

Turner, Nancy J., Randy Bouchard, and Dorothy I. D. Kennedy. *Ethnobotany of the Okanagan-Colville Indians of British Columbia and Washington*. Occasional Papers of the BC Provincial Museum, No. 21, 1980.

7

Toward a Philosophical Understanding of TEK and Ecofeminism

Joan McGregor

Life on Earth as we know it is in trouble: global climate change, resource depletion, and biodiversity loss all threaten us. Searching for solutions to these problems, we should pay attention to Albert Einstein's famous advice: "We can't solve our problems with the same thinking we used when we created them." The global environmental crisis is arguably a result of the predominantly Western industrialized nations' distorted conception of nature and humans' relationship with the natural world. Western industrialized nations have conceptualized the natural world at least since the Scientific Revolution as a machine – the "other," lesser, inert commodity to be dominated by man [sic] and used for his purposes. One consequence is that the natural world has been exploited to the brink of destruction (Merchant, 1990: 100–05).

Not everyone shares the view of the natural world as a resource to be used and abused as a commodity. Indigenous peoples' conception and relationship to the natural world is antithetical to this exploitative oppressive conception. Looking for routes out of the environmental crisis, well-known environmentalist David Suzuki argues for "the power and relevance of their [Indigenous peoples'] knowledge and worldview in a time of imminent global ecocatastrophe" (Suzuki, 2001: xxxv). Traditional Ecological Knowledge (TEK) embodies "the culturally and spiritually based way in which indigenous peoples relate to their ecosystems" (LaDuke, 1994: 127). TEK is *not merely* descriptive knowledge about the natural environment, knowledge gained by experience in a place, but also prescriptive – that is, it provides an account of how people *ought to act* in relationship to nature. TEK is then a blend of science, spirituality, and ethics. In this way (and in many others), it differs from traditional Western scientific accounts of nature that merely describe nature (Mendelian genetics, for example) but say nothing about how we morally ought to treat nature (see Peirotti, 2010: 274–87).

Confronted with the problems of sustainability, Indigenous views of the proper relationship with the natural world are a rich source of knowledge that might help build a sustainability ethics. In order to understand the underlying theoretical and philosophical rationale of TEK, we will look to a philosophical school of thought called "ecofeminism," which has affinities with Indigenous views, sharing some assumptions about humans' relationship to the natural world. Ecofeminists reject Western industrial society's conceptual framework premised on the separation of humans *from* nature, and the domination of nature *by* humans. They argue that the domination of nature is connected to the domination of women by men and the colonization of nonwhites, both of which ecofeminists see as supported by what they call an "oppressive conceptual framework."

The philosophical literature on ecofeminism outlines a robust account of what is wrong with the dominant worldview about our relationship with nature, and provides a new worldview and practices, which are not premised on domination. I'll use ecofeminism to elucidate theoretical foundations similar to that of TEK and in particular consider TEK as a source of moral knowledge and prescription about our relationship with nature. TEK embodies important moral lessons that provide the larger society a path out of our sustainability crisis. The philosophical underpinnings of TEK, that is, the ontology, epistemology, and ethics, haven't been fully explored by non-Indigenous scholars. This chapter, through the lens of ecofeminisim, will attempt to explain the major theoretical commitments of TEK.

I will explore these two frameworks – ecofeminism and TEK – and their relationships to one another, as well as their mutual critique of the dominant Western industrial worldview. TEK has a long and rich history that can't be adequately explained in this short chapter (see the other chapters in this book for more background and examples). Nevertheless, even in this truncated account, exploring TEK through the lens of philosophical ecofeminism, the underlying theoretical structure will become more apparent. Furthermore, by explicating how TEK is different from and in opposition to, for example, Western Baconian science's approach to nature as mechanistic and dead, a critique which feminists highlight, TEK should become more understandable to a non-Native audience. The first and second sections briefly explicate TEK and ecofeminist frameworks.

In the remaining sections, I explore the concepts and approaches that are critical to both TEK and ecofeminism – namely, the conception of self, the approach to ethics, the role of the affections, how moral theorizing is done, the epistemological approach, and finally the role of power relationships.

Traditional Ecological Knowledge

One disclaimer must be made about Indigenous views of the natural world: there is no monolithic Indigenous belief system dictating the correct treatment of nature. Hundreds of tribes exist in the United States alone, not to mention the many Indigenous peoples around the globe, with their own views about their relationship to nature. It is dangerous to essentialize the "Indian view" about any subject matter (for an early version of the tensions between these views see Deloria, 1994: 31). Furthermore, I want to avoid the stereotypes of "American Indians as nature lovers" or as children of the wild who worship a Mother Earth goddess, which has its own pernicious implications. The "special relationship" that Native people have to the land is the subject of robust debate (see, for example, Booth and Jacob, 1990; Johnson, 1992; Kapashesit and Klippenstein, 1991; Tsosie, 1996). Nevertheless, some general similarities in worldviews, conceptions, values, and epistemic approaches in Native views about their relationships to the earth exist, and they can provide fruitful ways of thinking about humankind and nature. As Deborah McGregor notes in "Coming Full Circle: Indigenous Knowledge, Environment, and Our Future," there is a growing "recognition that Indigenous people all over the world developed sustainable environmental knowledge and practices that can be used to address problems that face global society" (McGregor, 2004: 28).

Many scholars are exploring Native American ideas about our relationship to nature and TEK in general, Ronald Trosper being one of them. After cautioning against a facile assumption of a monolithic Native American view, Trosper articulates a number of remarkable similarities among the frameworks of Native views. What he calls the model of "traditional Indian worldviews" is premised on four basic principles, which he argues support "an ethic of respect":

1) "Community: Human beings are part of a community that includes all beings; each has its proper role, and each has obligations to others. The sacred aspect of this assumption is that all beings have a spirit. The political aspect is that human-to-human relationships

are similar to human-to-animals and human-to-plant relationships. The economic aspect is that reciprocity in exchange must
exist" (Trosper, 1995: 67).

2) "Connectedness: While the idea of community provides sources of
responsibility and a guide to proper behavior, the idea of connectedness is a description of how the world is" (Trosper, 1995: 67).
This principle also cautions that we cannot treat entities in isolation, and that our actions have far-reaching consequences due to
nature's connectedness, much like the "butterfly effect" from chaos
theory.

3) "The Seventh Generation: Past human generations left a legacy
and we have a duty to pass on that legacy as far as the seventh generation" (Trosper, 1995: 67). In the Iroquois Nations
Constitution, for example, dating from AD 1000, they required
that "In every deliberation, we must consider the impact on the
seventh generation."

4) "Humility: Humility dictates that in taking action, humans should
be humble. The natural world is powerful and will be able to cause
trouble if not treated properly" (Trosper, 1995: 67). Nature is
intricately connected in complex relationships that we can't fully
understand, which argues for a culture of humility as opposed to
arrogance in the face of our limited knowledge.

These four principles describe TEK and provide a worldview or, using
the German word, a *Weltanschauung* – a philosophy of life based on
one's conception of the world. TEK is not only a body of knowledge
about an ecosystem that is known in a particular community after living in a place for millennia: "TEK is not just knowledge *about* the relationship with Creation, it *is* the relationship with Creation; it is the way
one relates" (McGregor, 2004: 394). Further, McGregor explains that
Indigenous people view "the people, the knowledge, and the land *as a
single, integrated whole*" (McGregor, 2004: 395). As opposed to Western
science, TEK is holistic and cannot be compartmentalized into different
types of knowledge (chemistry, biology, etc.). Also, it is inseparable from
the people. TEK is "a way of life, a relationship that requires *doing*"
(McGregor, 2004: 396). This underscores the ethical dimensions of TEK;
it is a good way of living life, what we might call the "virtuous life," and
not merely a body of knowledge about the natural world. Western science doesn't say anything about *how* we should live; it merely describes
the world. We see the divide playing out when climatologists author dire
reports about human-caused climate change, but their facts about the

world don't usually prescribe how people *ought* to behave in light of them – a divide between facts and values.

Ecofeminism

"Drawing on the insights of ecology, feminism, and socialism, ecofeminism's basic premise is that the ideology that authorizes oppression based on race, class, gender, sexuality, physical abilities, and species is the same ideology that sanctions the oppression of nature" (Gaard, 1993: 1). Ecofeminists argue that some conceptual frameworks are oppressive since they explain and attempt to justify relationships of domination and subordination (Warren, 1990: 125). The dominate Western conception of nature, for example, explains and justifies the use and destruction of the natural environment for human purposes on the basis of the superiority of humans to nature. This oppressive relationship emerges in European modernism, which sees nature as a machine to control rather than a living organism to nourish. Founders of modern science and philosophy – namely, Francis Bacon, William Harvey, René Descartes, Thomas Hobbes, and Isaac Newton, justify humans' role as the "masters and possessors of nature" (Merchant, 1990: 297) through the use of reason. Further, traditional philosophical and scientific work neglected women's experiences, perspectives, and ways of knowing, which were not thought "rational" (Jaggar, 1992: 363–64). Feminists objected to the disregard of women and nonwhite experiences, perspectives, and ways of knowing, including Indigenous perspectives. Even when women's and nonwhite experiences are acknowledged, they are treated as inferior and not sources of knowledge – referred to as "epistemic oppression" (Dotson, 2014: 115–38). Traditional Western philosophical ethics overvalues traits such as "independence, autonomy, intellect, will, wariness, hierarchy, domination, culture, transcendence, product, asceticism, war, and death," while it undervalues "interdependence, community, connection, sharing, emotion, body, trust, absence of hierarchy, nature, immanence, process, joy, peace, and life" (Jaggar, 1992: 364). (This is not to claim that every culture constructs these traits in these ways.) Finally, traditional Western ethics prioritizes what are thought to be "'male' ways of moral reasoning that emphasize rules, rights, universality, and impartiality over 'female' ways of moral reasoning that emphasize relationships, responsibilities, particularity, and partiality" (Jagger, 1992).

Ecofeminism is a family of theories, all of which reject the domination of women and nature. The ethics of ecofeminism involves a "shift from a conception of ethics as primarily a matter of rights, rules, or principles predetermined and applied in specific cases, to entities viewed as competitors in the contest of moral standing, to a conception of ethics grounded in what Jim Cheney calls 'defining relationships,' i.e., relationships conceived in some sense as defining who one is" (Warren, 1993: 267). *How* we are in relationships with others, humans and nonhumans, is centrally important – not merely that we *have* a relationship with the other (Warren, 1993: 267). Relationships form our identities, our communities with the human and nonhuman world. Storytelling and narrative are central to understanding ourselves and our relationships with others and nature.

Ecofeminism is "inclusivist"; it draws from the stories of women and men around the globe, including Indigenous stories, which recount the destruction of the earth fueled by a conception of nature as separate and dead. Ecofeminists reject the notion that they are providing an "objective" view of the world. Rather, they acknowledge that the "twin dominations of women and nature as social problems rooted both in very concrete, historical, socioeconomic circumstances and in oppressive patriarchal conceptual frameworks which maintain and sanction these circumstances" (Warren, 1993: 267).

The value of care is generally central to feminist ethics and so too in ecofeminism, which adds values important to relationships – those of love, friendship, trust, and reciprocity. The dispositions of care, empathy, and kindness are resurrected as central to the moral life. Feminist authors initially focused on relationships between humans, but ecofeminists expanded the concept to include caring relationships to animals and the rest of nature (see, for example, Donovan and Adams, 1996). Feminist scholars such as Stacy Aliamo and Susan Hekman (2008) are refocusing feminist thought on the human body, as well as the natural and material worlds, through a theoretical frame called "material feminisms." Gender-power differentials are systemic, as are racial ones, shaping our institutions, practices, and principles, and they need to be exposed and reformed for substantive moral change to occur.

Feminist theorists reject the traditional Western philosophical focus on universal principles, particularly the importance of justice and rights. Universal principles, whether utilitarian or deontological, generate obligations to any person similarly situated. These theories (for example, those of Immanuel Kant, Jeremy Bentham, and John Rawls) take what is claimed to be the impartial perspective. According to feminist ethicists, traditional philosophical ethical theories have not paid sufficient attention to the relationships people have as parents, children, spouses, friends, and workers, as well as how those relationships, including gendered and environmental ones, shape specific moral responsibilities. Often the responsibilities within those relationships, such as childcare in parenting relationships, are unequal, with women bearing a greater burden. Foregrounding relationships, particularly gendered ones, uncovers the inequalities of women's lives but also articulates a different picture of our moral lives. Not everyone has the same responsibilities; rather, individuals' responsibilities differ on the basis of the roles and relationships they inhabit. More often than not, the relationships and communities that we find ourselves in and are integral to who we are, and not ones that we choose to accept and thereby cast off if we desire. The notion of "self" differs for feminists, rejecting the traditional Western philosophical notion of the atomistic self and adopting relational conceptions of self.

These are general outlines of TEK and ecofeminism. The core philosophical concepts that elucidate TEK are: a relational conception of self, an ethic of responsibility, the role of care and affections in moral life, how moral theorizing is done (specifically the place of naturalistic epistemology in ethics and the role of narrative), and the role of domination and subordination in maintaining oppressive conceptual frameworks of nature.

Conception of the Self

Two dominant views of the self define the Western philosophical tradition: the Kantian view and the *homo economicus*. Both conceptions emphasize the individual as a free and rational chooser, an autonomous agent. There are, however, differences in emphasis:

> The Kantian ethical subject uses reason to transcend cultural norms and to discover absolute moral truth, whereas *homo economicus* uses reason to rank desires in a coherent order and to figure out how to maximize desire satisfaction. Whether the self is identified with pure abstract reason or with the instrumental rationality of the marketplace, though, these conceptions of the self isolate the individual from personal relationships and larger social forces. For the Kantian ethical subject, emotional bonds and social conventions imperil objectivity and undermine commitment to duty. For *homo economicus*, it makes no difference what social forces shape one's desires provided they do not result from coercion or fraud, and one's ties to other people are to be factored into one's calculations and planning along with the rest of one's desires. (Willet et al., 2014)

Both views of the self negate the role of context in which a person finds him or herself, as well as how that context shapes the conception of self. Both also negate the role that others – one's family, friends, and community – play in creating the conception of self. Both Western traditions believe we are fully autonomous in our creation of the self, views that have been problematic for feminist philosophers. For instance, Virginia Held writes that "[a]mong the characteristics of the ethics of care is its view of persons as relational and as interdependent" (Held, 2006: 156), unlike most dominant Western normative ethical perspectives, which view individuals as rational, isolated agents.

Emphasizing only the importance of reason, for example, Thomas Aquinas states, "the intellectual nature is alone requisite for its own sake in the universe" (Pegis, 1997: 220). Prioritizing rational thought creates a sharp divide between humans and nonhumans, with humans deemed superior because of their ability to reason. Historically, only white men were thought to exercise reason, while nonwhite men and women were thought not to be rational. Indians were considered to be "central feature of the wilderness [the uncivilized, irrational] … conquest of the wilderness entailed conquest of the Indian" (Utley, 1983: 34). This notion of the superiority of man over nature dates back to Plato and Aristotle's idea of "The Great Chain of Being," a worldview that justified sexist and racist beliefs, as well as oppressive systems of conquest and control.

The view of self that privileges reason over other capacities, such as the emotions, is problematic for feminist philosophers and many Indigenous peoples, but it explains the dominant theory that claims men are separate and superior to nature. The mind, the intellect, and reason are not material; they are separate and superior (in the Great Chain of Being) to the material world. Decontextualizing the self from the environment and others makes impossible the intimate connection with nature that is necessary for a deep moral understanding of the nonhuman world. Seeing oneself as self-created, not a product of one's physical and social conditions, alienates one from others and community. Indigenous peoples and ecofeminists reject the dualism of the reason/emotion divide and the mental/physical, arguing that humans have all of those characteristics. Ecofeminist theory conceives the self in connection to others, as do Indigenous conceptions. The self is defined in relation to one's tribe and family, as well as one's land or place; all are intrinsically connected, and one cannot understand oneself outside of those relationships. Those features are not accidental but essential to who one is, creating a strong "sense of place" in Indigenous communities. Those facts, including who is one's family and tribe and where one is from, are constitutive of an individual's self. The role that tribal affiliation plays in Native Americans attitudes about themselves, for example, bears this out. TEK is built upon this conception of the self in intimate connection to a place and knowledge of that natural community. As Annie Booth and Harvey Jacob elaborate in their work, "The Ties that Bind: Native American Beliefs as a Foundation for Environmental Consciousness," the land plays a significant role; it is "important in determining a perspective of self"; Indigenous people see themselves as "part of the land, they consider the land to be part of them" (Booth and Jacob, 1990: 521).

How Indigenous peoples conceive of themselves is significant and stands in contradistinction to widely accepted Western views. Conceiving oneself as part of a place, intimately connected with the place and the people, will shape one's moral attitudes about treatment of the land and animals in that place. By despoiling the place one lives, one destroys and damages oneself. The notion of the self as intimately connected to a place and a community of people with shared values can be seen in the different ways Native communities and Western governments define risk assessment for toxic substances. Mary Arquette et al. (2002) in "Holistic Risk-Based Environmental Decision Making: A Native Perspective," describe a project in Mohawk territory of Akwesasne where the community-defined model of health comprised of individual and community indicatives, and traditional cultural practices, recognizes vulnerable populations, including animals. Here "health" has a different understanding than the one used by the EPA guidelines for risk assessment.

Responsibility Ethics

Feminist ethicists argue that the overemphasis of traditional philosophical ethics concerning justice and rights, which goes hand in hand with the view of the atomistic self, excludes "communal values" such as care, responsibility, interdependence, and trust. Feminists have tended to develop an ethics of *responsibility* that is distinguished from, for example, what Margaret Walker calls a "theoretical-juridical model" (Walker, 1998: 18–19). The theoretical-juridical model focuses on universal rights, duties, and abstract principles of justice that transcend culture, history, and material conditions. As opposed to thinking of ethics in terms of impersonal, abstract moral principles (with right and wrong answers), feminists view ethics in terms of personal moral responsibilities, acknowledging the conflicts in those relationships that might need to be resolved to sustain ongoing interpersonal relationships. This form of ethics is based on care and a sense of responsibility as well as obligations to others.

Trying to understand the structure of responsibility, feminist ethicist Claudia Card (2002) distinguishes two perspectives: (1) the "backward looking" or evaluator's perspective, and (2) the "forward looking" or agent's perspective. The backward-looking perspective is the one articulated in most contemporary ethical and legal theory – looking back to some previous action in order to judge it. This perspective is concerned with attributions of praise and blame, punishment and reward, regret, excuses, and mitigation. The forward-looking perspective, on the other hand, "embodies a perspective of agency" (Card, 2002: 26). It involves taking on, or choosing, responsibility, "which can be for what has not yet occurred or has not yet been done" (Card, 2002: 25). Margaret Walker explains the structure of responsibility as follows: "[s]pecific moral claims on us arise from our contact or relationship with others whose interests are vulnerable to our actions and choices. We are obligated to respond to particular others when circumstances or ongoing relationships render them especially, conspicuously, or peculiarly dependent on us" (Walker, 1998: 107). Walker's account that we are obligated to respond to the particular claims of others embodies the forward-looking notion of responsibility. We must choose to take responsibility for those who are vulnerable. These two perspectives are not, of course, mutually exclusive, and one can suppose that both are important.

Responsibility ethics, based on caring for others and nature, accurately characterizes Native American ethics where, for instance, responsibility to care for the earth and community are central themes. Responsibility to community, which includes future generations of that community, is also basic to Native views. In *Other Destinies*, Louis Owens writes: "Native American writers are offering a way of looking at the world that is new to Western culture. It is a holistic, ecological perspective, one that places essential value upon the totality of existence, making humanity equal to all elements but superior to none and giving humankind crucial responsibility for the care of the world we inhabit" (Owens, 1994: 29). Native American writers such as N. Scott Momaday, in "An American Land Ethics," pay tribute to the responsibility ethic:

In Ko-sahn and in her people we have always had the example of a deep, ethical regard for the land. We had better learn from it. Surely that ethic is merely latent in ourselves. It must now be activated, I believe. We Americans must come again to a moral comprehension of the Earth and air. We must live according to the principle of a land ethic. The alternative is that we shall not live at all. (Momaday, 1997: 49)

McGregor points out that "Aboriginal people in Canada understood their relationship with Creation and assumed the responsibilities given to them by the Creator" (McGregor, 2004: 388–89). These are not ethics that conceptualize the land or animals as having rights granted by humans, for which we have abstract obligations or duties, but rather that we have a particular responsibility for taking care of them. Often Indigenous relationships with animals are thought of in terms of kinship, writes Bill Neidjie (1985) in *Kakadu Man,* where humans are not separate or superior to nonhuman persons such as animals, plants, or other natural elements, but are instead related to them.

Native American worldviews are generally focused on communal values, not individualistic ones. As discussed earlier, the Indigenous conception of self can't be understood in isolation from community; hence the community becomes an important locus of value and the source of responsibilities. We understand ourselves through the relationships we find ourselves embedded in, as family and as community members. Those relationships shape and define our moral responsibilities. TEK is something we "do" according to McGregor (McGregor, 2004: 391), not merely something we know; it is a "way of living" (Battiste and Henderson, 2000: 42). The "doing" is normative, shaped by what is proper or correct for *that* person to do. Different people have different responsibilities under TEK, and the "doing" is acting based on your responsibilities. Kyle Whyte's discussion of Indigenous women's view of their responsibilities illustrates how the responsibilities are specific to them, as well as how they are constitutive of those women's identities: "the specific responsibilities they perceive themselves to have within the systems of responsibilities that matter to their communities. Such responsibilities can range from acting as custodians and teachers of local ecological knowledge to serving as conveners of political movements promoting respectful coexistence with neighbors" (Whyte, 2014: 600). The knowledge is specific to a people and cannot "be separated from the people who hold and practice it, nor can it be separated from the land/environment/Creation" (McGregor, 2004: 38).

TEK does not appeal to abstract universal moral principles of justice or universal welfare for conclusions or prescriptions for action. Instead, it relies on an understanding of how the complex interdependent relationships we have with other human beings, animals, and the land (being connected and thereby in a community with them) generates a web of responsibilities to those entities. That knowledge has been developed over eons. Community has different scales and natures – namely, local and global, human and nonhuman, physical and metaphysical, temporal, past, current and future, and social and cultural; hence our responsibilities are varied and complex.

TEK understands that our relationship with the natural world needs to be reciprocal; the world is not just here for human purposes – we have responsibilities to the natural world. Shay Welch discusses the idea of "gifting" in Indigenous cultures as an analog to reciprocity in feminism. "The practice of gifting," Welch says, "mirrors the feminist practice of reciprocity since both generate and maintain relationships with others and engender responsibilities to them" (Welch, 2013: 213). Reciprocity and balance extends to relationships among humans, including future generations, and between humans and the natural world (see Kapashesit and Klippenstein, 1991). N. Scott Momaday describes "the necessary relationship as an act of reciprocal approbation, 'approbation in which man invest himself in the landscape, and at the same time incorporates the landscape into his own most fundamental experience'" (Momaday, 1976: 80). Not only do Native American and feminist views share the focus on responsibility and the interdependence of communal values, they also share the notion that the particularities of a specific context are relevant to moral responsibility: "Native American traditions ... are embedded in a particular context. The impact and meaning of a tradition stems from lifelong conditioning, preparation, and participation. It is built into the language, into the way life is lived and experienced, and within a specific physical/social context" (Booth and Jacob, 1990: 525). Responsibility is built from the particularities of the context in which one lives, not deduced from general abstract principles.

Care and the Role of Affections

Feminist theorists have drawn our attention to the role of care and feelings in moral relationships. Nell Nodding, for example, says that morality requires the "sentiment of natural caring. There can be no ethical sentiment without the initial, enabling sentiment" (Nodding, 1989: 79). Though not new to moral philosophy, over two centuries ago David Hume and Adam Smith argued for "social sentiments" to motivate morality. Today feminists bring the sentiments into morality in a concrete and particular fashion. For Nodding, caring for the well-being of others is "based on experience and encounter." The affections to the land and living things are not abstract and general as in Hume and Smith, but concrete and particular to embodied experiences of nature. Ecofeminism emphasizes concrete embodied experiences as "a source and a result of perceptive appreciation and greater receptivity to nature's wonders" (Norlock, 2011: 497). Those values of perceptivity and receptivity are central practices to the ethics of care.

Lived experiences in particular environments, a perceptive and visceral appreciation of land and receptivity to its nuances, are central to TEK and most Native American accounts of caring for nature. These views are illustrated in Native American literature, from Vine Deloria (1994), Louise Erdrich (1988), Linda Hogan (1996), and Simon Ortiz (1977), to Leslie Marmon Silko (1977) and many more. Having an acute, perceptive appreciation of and relationship to one's environment (one's place), as well as receptivity to the natural world, play an essential role in Native accounts of the moral connection to the land. The affections of care and love are central elements in Indigenous approaches to the treatment of land. Many have argued that the current environmental problems of Western industrialized societies are a result of not perceiving nature as a subject of our attention as moral beings – not caring for it and only treating it as property for economic ends. That attitude has resulted in the destruction and despoliation of nature. Ecofeminist approaches that find a central role for the *moral* attitude of care were thought revolutionary, but care has been central to the moral attitude of the Native land ethic for millennia: "Care and respect extended beyond the land to other living beings, a 'kinship' with other living beings" (Booth and Jacob, 1990: 522).

Another theme that characterizes Native views perceives the earth as an animate being; sometimes, as with the Nez Perce, the earth is described as a mother since the people come from her. Black Elk, a Lakota, said, "Is not the sky a father and the earth a mother and are not all live things with feet and wings or roots their children." The status of "mother" makes the earth worthy of respect, care, and love. You don't do things for your mother because she has a "right" to them; you do them out of respect, care, and love. It is because of an emotional connection that you treat your mother in a loving and respectful manner. The centrality of the affections of care and love for the earth position TEK in a vastly different relationship with nature than the approaches shaped by Western views. Western science and technology values nature as something to be used, a resource for human purposes, irrespective of its effects on nature. In Western science there are no affections to nature, only description, supposedly value-free, for the instrumental use of nature's resources.

How Moral Theorizing Is Done and Naturalistic Epistemology

Feminist theorists believed the methodology of ethics should be revolutionized, and their approach was to naturalize ethics. Alison Jaggar notes: "Naturalizing ethics requires that the development of ethical concepts, ideals, and prescriptions should occur in collaboration with empirical disciplines such as psychology, economics, and the social sciences" (Jaggar, 2000: 459). In seeking to transcend the whole of science and history, most Western philosophical ethical traditions have rejected naturalism for universal and timeless moral truths sought through reason. These so-called universal perspectives, feminists have pointed out, are often the perspectives of men in privileged positions who have endorsed and furthered the unequal status of women and nonwhite peoples, while, at the same time, denigrating their values. These "universal" perspectives also support the subjugation of nature and the colonization of so-called "primitive" cultures.

"Naturalized moral knowledge," writes Margaret Walker, "begins with the best of what we think we know, morally and otherwise, and proceeds by comparative and typically piecemeal justification in which we continue to help ourselves to moral understandings and other beliefs that have stood firm up to that point" (Walker, 1998: 264). According to Walker, moral change occurs when there is pressure and demands on old practices, or when they are applied to different people. This occurs within society and not in some abstract realm of moral truth. In Walker's account, ethics is a continuing negotiation among people, a practice of allotting, assessing, or deflecting responsibilities; and those responsibilities adjust based on our understanding of particular practices and pressures that force change.

Native conceptions of TEK and the moral understandings that frame it are developed from traditional knowledge (from generation to generation), empirical knowledge (gained by observation), and revealed knowledge (acquired though spiritual origins and recognized as a gift) (McGregor, 2004: 388). And all of this knowledge evolves over time. The way nature should be treated is a result of this complex mix of sources, creation stories, rituals, and experiences. TEK is not general and universal knowledge; it is specific to a place and known by the people in that place. Our moral understandings – how we should behave toward others, animals, and plants – are developed from experiences over time. It is a naturalized moral knowledge that can be valuable to non-Native populations attempting to understand sustainability in a particular place.

Ecofeminists have also been concerned about the sources of knowledge; for example, they argue that knowledge can originate from situated sources and that expertise comes in many forms, not merely from science and reason. Until recently, TEK wasn't acknowledged by non-Native groups as a source of knowledge about ecosystems and resource management because its "pedigree" wasn't the expertise of Western science. Feminist theorists have been championing the argument that knowledge "is that of a situated knower, and hence of situated knowledge: knowledge that reflects the particular perspectives of the subject" (Anderson, 2017). Expanding what counts as knowledge opens a space for the authority of TEK in the non-Native world. Indigenous peoples have been subjects of "epistemic oppression" – the "persistent epistemic exclusion that hinders one's contribution to knowledge production" (Dotson, 2014: 115). That epistemic exclusion is an "unwarranted infringement on the epistemic agency of knowers" (Dotson, 2014: 115). Indigenous peoples' ability to be epistemic agents participating with others in knowledge production has been undermined due to this oppression. Indigenous knowledge did not count as knowledge in the dominant society; rather, it was treated as inferior to the knowledge of Western science. Today, however, there is a growing recognition of the importance of local knowledge of ecosystems and resources management. Though the epistemology differs from Western beliefs, "Native Science," to use Gregory Cajete's (2000) term, provides a wealth of significant knowledge about environmental change that is necessary to ensure the sustainability of ecosystems and cultures (for example, see Ford and Martinez, 2000: 1249–50; Gómez-Baggethun et al., 2013: 72).

Both ecofeminists' and Native peoples' ethics, and TEK in particular, rely on the use of narratives to better understand morality. Explaining moral reasoning, Walker says it "takes the form of narratives, specifically narratives of identity, relationship, and value. It presents moral problems in terms of histories and relationships of the parties involved and their shared understandings of what is important" (Walker, 1998: 264). Native peoples tell stories – narrative accounts that describe relationships and responsibilities to other people, animals, and the land. Rather than start, as many philosophers have done, from ideal theory – abstract, universal norms such as those of Immanuel Kant or Jeremy Bentham – and "apply" them to problems, Native accounts, similar to feminist ones, start with historical, cultural, and empirical circumstances, a bottom-up approach to develop normative understandings. This approach evaluates and critically reflects moral understandings through narratives in order to determine whether the way we characterize moral understandings is intelligible and coherent. We tell our children and each other how we should behave in the world; for example, the responsibility for the seventh generation in decision-making prescribes a responsibility to future generations. Through narrative we understand what we can do to each other, what we can do to the land and animals, and what we must do, as well as who is responsible and who is not. Gregory Cajete in *Native Science* says:

> The metaphoric mind underpins the numerous ecological foundations of Native knowledge and has been specifically applied in creating the stories that form the foundation of the complex and elaborate forms of Native oral traditions. Realizing that the greatest source of metaphor comes from nature, these stories are filled with analogies, characters, representations drawn from nature, metaphors that more often than not refer back to the processes of nature from which they are drawn, or to human nature, which they attempt to reflect. Because Native science is thoroughly wrapped in a blanket of metaphor, expressed in story, art, community, dance, song, ritual, music, astronomical knowledge, and technologies such as hunting, fishing, farming, or healing, rationalistic scientists, its 'younger brothers,' have difficulty understanding its essence of creative participation with nature. (Cajete, 2000: 30–31)

Power Relationships, Particularly Domination and Submission

Ecofeminists have been centrally concerned with the oppressive conceptual framework that presumably justified the domination of women, Indigenous peoples and other colonized peoples, and nature. Those relationships of domination and submission have been supported by supposed empirical and moral differences between men and women, white men and nonwhite men, and humans and nature. Women were thought to be the intellectual and moral inferiors of men, thereby justifying structures of social and political systems where men dominate. The subordinated role was justified because women were associated with the physical, with nature, as were purported "primitive peoples," whereas men were associated with reason, the mental, and the mental was superior to the physical, as Thomas Aquinas and others stated. Nature was dominated by man and considered subordinate because it wasn't rational. But not all men qualified, notably Indigenous men: "Indians and their works did not qualify as human in the same sense as Spaniards or Englishmen" (Utley,

1983: 33). Further, "in the Indian, whites saw the lower order from which they themselves had progressed" (Utley, 1983: 34).

Domination of nature, conceiving nature as inferior, leads to a Western distorted, alienated relationship. The manner in which scientific research is practiced in America fuels this attitude, "almost exclusively [at] the creation and exercise of power" in seeking industrial and economic progress. According to Aldo Leopold, scientific research should be "the creation and exercise of wonder, of respect for [nature's] workmanship" (Leopold, 1940: 343). Rather than see ourselves as "conquerors" of nature, Leopold cautions that we should humbly acknowledge ourselves as another member of the "land community." Reconceptualizing the West's relationship with nature calls for a profound shift in our view of nature, from valuing it as property to be used as a commodity, something to dominate and subdue, to seeing ourselves as "fellow members" or kin of a community. This notion is integral to the Indigenous views embedded in TEK, which reject alienation from the natural world, and see humans as part of and dependent on nature. Moreover, TEK rejects the dualism that has been a predominant framework in Western thought, which considers nature as different, separate, and lesser than man. TEK appreciates that we are part of a particular environment.

Feminist theorists recognize the full range of power relationships – men over women, rich over poor, and first world nations over colonized nations. Feminists foreground power relationships, the particular identities and relationships in which individuals find themselves, and how those contexts and relationships of power shape moral relationships. Native peoples – along with their views, traditions, and knowledge of the environment – have been discounted or ignored by the dominant culture because Indigenous systems do not, for many reasons, fit the paradigm of Western mechanized science. Some critics claimed, and still claim, that Native environmental knowledge is not scientific, and therefore it is dismissed as not truly a source of expertise and knowledge. Foregrounding the role that power plays in marginalizing certain ways of knowing exposes this system of oppression and might lead to reforms in social and political systems where we share expertise and knowledge about particular places and, importantly, the proper way to treat them.

Conclusion

The values that define TEK have a long and successful history of supporting Indigenous peoples' relationship with particular ecosystems. This chapter outlines a philosophical understanding of TEK by drawing on the insights of ecofeminism. In so doing, the chapter exposes the meta-physical underpinnings of the nature of the self, the epistemology of TEK, how knowledge is gained and by whom, and value theory, in particular its focus on the affection of care and responsibilities to particular places, people (including future people), animals, and natural elements. Essential to both TEK and ecofeminism is a worldview that denies we are separate and superior to the natural world, replacing this view with one that sees humans as part of nature, which necessitates its care and respect. We should not dominate the world and treat nature solely instrumentally any more than we would dominate and commodify our family. TEK is a responsibility ethic; we have responsibilities to each other, the land, plants, and animals – for now and the future. Care and love are essential attitudes to help determine and shape our relationship to the earth. Both sets of theories find an important place for narratives to develop moral understandings of our responsibilities to specific ecosystems and communities. Feminist philosophers have developed the underlying philosophical foundation for many of these concepts, which can explain and provide a philosophical account of TEK. This is not to imply that TEK can be fully understood through the lens of ecofeminism; rather, some of these concepts have significant affinities and can mutually support one another. The globe is sorely in need of new frameworks and values to solve environmental and cultural problems. The world's peoples can learn about sustainable living from TEK since "Indian peoples, who traditionally interpreted their relationship with land and the future generations as holistic, cyclical, and permanent, sustainability was the natural result, if not the conscious goal of deeply rooted environmental ethics and traditional land-based economics" (Tsosie, 1996: 286–87). The rest of us need to learn those lessons.

WORKS CITED

Anderson, Elizabeth, "Feminist Epistemology and Philosophy of Science," *The Stanford Encyclopedia of Philosophy* (Spring 2017 Edition), edited by Edward N. Zalta. URL [online]: https://plato.stanford.edu/archives/spr2017/entries/feminism-epistemology

Arquette, Mary, Maxine Cole, Katsi Cook, Brenda LaFrance, Margaret Peters, James Ransom, Elvera Sargent, Vivian Smoke, and Arlene Stairs, "Holistic Risk-Based Environmental Decision Making: A Native Perspective." *Environmental Health Perspectives*, 110 (2), 2002, 259–64.

Battiste, Marie and James Henderson, *Protecting Indigenous Knowledge and Heritage*. Saskatoon, SK: Purich Publishing, 2000.

Booth, Anne and Harvey Jacob. "The Ties that Bind: Native American Beliefs as a Foundation for Environmental Consciousness." *Environmental Ethics*, 12 (1), 1990, 27–43.

Cajete, Gregory. *Native Science: Natural Laws of Interdependence*. Santa Fe, NM: Clear Light, 2000.

Card, Claudia. "Responsibility Ethics, Shared Understandings, and Moral Communities." *Hypatia*, 17 (1), Winter 2002, 141–55.

Deloria, Vine, Jr. *God Is Red: A Native View of Religion*. Golden, CO: North American Press, 1994.

Descartes, René. *Discourse on Method*, quoted in Merchant, "Ecofeminism and Feminist Theory," 297.

Donovan, Josephine and Carol J. Adams, Eds. *Beyond Animal Rights: A Feminist Caring Ethic for the Treatment of Animals*. London: Continuum International Publishing Group, 1996.

Dotson, Kristie. "Conceptualizing Epistemic Oppression." *Social Epistemology*, 28 (2), 2014, 115–38.

Erdrich, Louise. *Tracks*. New York: Henry Holt and Company, 1988.

Ford, Jesse and Dennis Martinez. "Traditional Ecological Knowledge, Ecosystem Science, and Environmental Management." *Ecological Applications*, 10 (5), 2000, 1249–50.

Gaard, Greta, Ed. *Ecofeminism*. Philadelphia: Temple University Press, 1993.

Gómez-Baggethun, Eric, Esteve Corbera, and Victoria Reyes-García. "Traditional Ecological Knowledge and Global Environmental Change: Research Findings and Policy Implications." *Ecology and Society*, 18 (4) 2013. [online] URL: http://dx.doi.org/10.5751/ES-06288-180472

Held, Virginia. *The Ethics of Care: Personal, Political, and Global*. Cambridge, UK: Oxford University Press, 2006.

Hogan, Linda. *Dwellings: A Spiritual History of the Living World*. New York: Touchstone, 1996.

Jaggar, Alison. "Ethics Naturalized: Feminism's Contribution to Moral Epistemology." *Metaphilosophy*, 31 (5), 2000, 459.

"Feminist Ethics." *Encyclopedia of Ethics*, edited by Lawrence C. Becker and Charlotte B. Becker. New York: Garland Press, 1992, 363–64.

Johnson, Martha. "Documenting Dene Traditional Environmental Knowledge." *Akwe:kon*, 9 (2), 1992, 72–79.

Kapashesit, Randy and Murray Klippenstein, "Aboriginal Group Rights and Environmental Protection," *McGill Law Journal*, 36, 1991, 921–61.

LaDuke, Winona. "Traditional Ecological Knowledge and Environmental Futures." *Colorado Journal of International Environmental Law and Policy*, 127, 1994, 127–48.

Leopold, Aldo. "The State of the Profession." *Journal of Wildlife Management*, 4 (3), 1940, 343–46.

McGregor, Deborah. "Coming Full Circle: Indigenous Knowledge, Environment, and Our Future." *American Indian Quarterly*, 28 (3–4), 2004, 385–410.

Merchant, Carolyn. "Ecofeminism and Feminist Theory." *Reweaving the World: The Emergence of Ecofeminism*, edited by Irene Diamond and Gloria Orenstein. San Francisco: Sierra Club Books, 1990, 100–05.

Momaday, F. Scott. *The Man Made of Words*. New York: St Martin's Press, 1997.
  The Way to Rainy Mountain. Albuquerque: University of New Mexico Press,
  1976.
Neidjie, Bill. *Kakadu Man*. Canberra: Mybrood, 1985.
Nodding, Nel. *Caring: A Relational Approach to Ethics and Moral Education*.
  Berkeley: University of California Press, 1989.
Norlock, Kathryn. "Beyond Receptivity: Leopold's Land Ethic and Critical
  Feminist Interpretation." *JSRNC*, 5 (4), 2011, 497–509.
Ortiz, Simon. *Woven Stone*. Tucson: University of Arizona Press, 1992.
Owens, Louis. *Other Destinies: Understanding the American Indian Novel*.
  Norman: University of Oklahoma Press, 1994.
Pegis, Anton, Ed. *Basic Writing of Thomas Aquinas*. Indianapolis: Hackett
  Publishing, 1997.
Peirotti, Raymond. "Sustainability of Natural Populations: Lessons from
  Indigenous Knowledge." *Human Dimensions of Wildlife*, 15, 2010, 274–87.
Silko, Leslie Marmon. *Ceremony*. New York: Penguin Books, 1977.
Suzuki, David. "A Personal Foreword: The Value of Native Ecologies." *Wisdom
  of the Elders*, edited by Peter Knudtson and David Suzuki. Toronto:
  Stoddart, 2001, xxi–xxxv.
Trosper, Ronald L. "Traditional American Indian Economic Policy." *American
  Indian Culture and Research Journal*, 19 (1), 1995, 65–95.
Tsosie, Rebecca. "Tribal Environmental Policy in an Era of Self-Determination: The
  Role of Ethics, Economics, and Traditional Ecological Knowledge." *Vermont
  Law Review*, 21 1996, 286–87.
Utley, Robert. *The Indian Frontier of the American West 1846–1890*. Albuquerque:
  New Mexico Press, 1983.
Walker, Margaret. *Moral Understanding*. New York: Routledge, 1998.
Warren, Karen. "Introduction to Ecofeminsim." *Environmental Philosophy: From
  Animal Rights to Radical Ecology*, edited by Michael E. Zimmerman, J. Baird
  Callicott, George Sessions, Karen J. Warren, and John Clark. Englewood
  Cliffs, NJ: Prentice-Hall, 1993, 253–67.
  "The Power and the Promise of Ecological Feminism." *Environmental Ethics*,
  12 (2), 1990, 125–46.
Welch, Shay. "Radical-cum-Relational: A Feminist Understanding of Native
  Individual Autonomy." *Philosophical Topics*, 41 (2), 2013, 203–22.
Whyte, Kyle Powys. "Indigenous Women Climate Change Impacts, and Collective
  Action." *Hypatia*, 29 (3), 2014, 599–616.
Willett, Cynthia, Ellie Anderson, and Diana Meyers. "Feminist Ethics." *Stanford
  Encyclopedia of Philosophy*, edited by Edward N. Zalta, 2014. [online]
  URL: http://plato.stanford.edu/archives/fall2014/entries/feminism-ethics/

8

Wolves and Ravens, Science and Ethics: Traditional Ecological Knowledge Meets Long-Term Ecological Research

Michael Paul Nelson and John A. Vucetich

After many years of studying the relationship between wolves and moose on Isle Royale we learned there is a special relationship between wolves and ravens. The presence of ravens influences the size of wolf packs: wolves living in larger packs each get more food because they lose less food to scavenging ravens. They do this by eating a moose so quickly that ravens have little time to scavenge. The details are fantastically complicated, and while wolves in larger packs must share their food among their brothers and sisters, parents and offspring, that sharing is not so costly as losing food to scavengers. So ravens have something to do with explaining why wolves live such intensely social lives – a trait otherwise rare among carnivores. What an astonishing connection. The value of a connection like this lies in its ability to generate wonderment and care for nature. When we decide that the purpose of science is to generate wonder about nature, rather than to control nature, we will not be far from a relationship with nature that can flourish for all time and generations.

Adapted from Vucetich, 2010

Similar to other academic disciplines, philosophy is divided into subdisciplines, specialties. Epistemology is the study of the nature of knowledge, the various ways we might come to know something, and the explanations for why some bit of information might be true or false. Metaphysics is the study of the nature of being and our assumptions about what humans are in relationship to nature, as well as what nature is in relationship to humans (for example, are humans and nature one and the same, related, distinct, something else – and why?). Ethics focuses on questions of value, proper conduct, right and wrong, good and bad, arguments about what we ought to do, how we ought to live, who or what possesses direct moral standing, and what constitutes a good life.

When we combine all three of these elements we use the term *worldview* to refer to that package of beliefs. Our interactions with the world are a reflection of that worldview. A change in worldview, therefore, pulls a thread connected to our interactions with the world.

Scholarship on Traditional Ecological Knowledge (TEK) often seems focused on the epistemological dimension of philosophy. This scholarship often posits that Native peoples have special ways of knowing, not because they possess some extra sensory organ, but because of their long tenure in, and attention to, a given landscape (e.g., Menzies, 2006). This scholarship also attempts to demonstrate how those different epistemologies, or ways of knowing, lead to different information and different assumptions about the ecological systems we study.

But do we sometimes fail to have the full conversation about TEK? That is, is our interest in TEK merely an epistemological interest, merely an inward-looking and fairly obtuse discussion about the possible plurality of ways of knowing, or is there really something more important at stake here, something this conversation, at times, alludes to, but fails to specify? Given how excited undergraduates in our Philosophy of Ecology classes are about discussing TEK, and given how bored they tend to be in our epistemology courses, it seems unlikely that interest in TEK is merely an interest in comparative epistemology.

Interest in TEK likely has far less to do with epistemology and even metaphysics, and far more to do with perceptions about an ethical shift or the overall worldview we believe is necessary for healing our relationship with nature. Romanticized or not, many people glimpse – and admire – in TEK the ethically inclusive worldview that seems to flow naturally from prolonged land tenure, persistent observation, and a set of virtues, including respect, humility, empathy, and care. Moreover, these people see in Native traditions and worldviews the possibility of an inclusive environmental ethic. By "inclusive environmental ethics" we mean what modern environmental philosophers refer to as the attribution of intrinsic value or direct moral standing to the more-than-human world. This nonanthropocentric moral system signals a fundamental challenge to our current dominate Western relationship with nature.

A fear exists, however, that Western Scientific Ecological Knowledge (SEK) and the Western worldview are so fundamentally different from TEK and a Native worldview that the emergence of an inclusive environmental ethic from within the traditional Western worldview is all but impossible. This concern is illustrated, for example, when TEK is defined in stark contrast to SEK (e.g., Cleveland, 2009). One origin of this concern might have to do with the perceived lack of ability within Western culture to extend direct moral standing to the nonhuman world. While the centrality of the direct moral standing, or personhood, of the nonhuman world is obvious in Native American ethics (see Callicott and Nelson, 2004), it is certainly far less obvious in Western ethical and cultural traditions. Western ethics and culture, however, leave plenty of room to assign personhood to at least some nonhumans. This possibility manifests itself not only in contemporary theories in environmental ethics – from the zoocentric to the ecocentric – but also in contemporary legal conversations asserting the personhood of at least certain nonhuman animals (Siebert, 2014), and even in contemporary writing by ecologists (see, for example, an essay on the personification of wolves by Vucetich, 2013).

Another source for the belief that TEK and SEK are fundamentally distinct, and that an inclusive ethic cannot evolve within Western culture, might be the perceived purpose of science in each tradition. In 1605, an architect of Western science, Francis Bacon, famously claimed in his *The Advancement of Learning* that the purpose of science was "for the glory of the Creator and the relief of man's estate." While the motivations of Western science have become considerably more secular since Bacon, the central focus of SEK is taken to be that knowledge is valuable for its own sake and for manipulating the world around us for the purpose of material gain for humans. That purpose is so taken for granted that we no longer even recognize it as an answer to the question, What is the purpose of science? This situation is problematic because the most important difference between TEK and SEK might be the answer to that question. To understand the purpose of SEK one must first understand his or her metaphysical beliefs, which include the belief that many things in the nonhuman world are persons, relatives, and community members. With that metaphysic, the purpose of TEK is to better understand those persons so that they can be related to in a manner that honors concern for the interests of those nonhuman persons.

By analogy, the purpose of TEK is akin to the purpose of the courtship a couple might go through on their way to becoming marriage partners, i.e., to better understand those persons so that they know how best to care for each other, not how to sustainably extract the most out of each other. Pierotti and Wildcat, for example, discuss the purpose of ecological science from an American Indian perspective, especially when

Native peoples are asked, "What good is the work that you do?" The authors write,

> This question contains the hidden assumption that if what we do does not directly benefit human beings in some way it is without value. We often answer that our work teaches us more about the other members of our community and how to live with them, but most people of Western heritage appear confused by this answer, and do not understand this point. In contrast, if we give this answer to Native American elders, they are completely satisfied, for they understand implicitly what we are trying to accomplish, and its significance to humans. (Pierotti and Wildcat, 2000: 1339)

The attribution of personhood to the land or to nature might be challenging for the Western mind, though we see it evolving. In the following sections, we comment on what might occur within the Western tradition if the nature of personhood were to change.

Connections Between SEK and TEK

One point of connection between SEK and TEK that might seem obvious turns out to be false. That false point of connection suggests itself by first recognizing that the Indigenous and Western worldviews (at least recent ecologically informed Western worldviews) both believe we should relate to nature properly because human well-being is intimately connected to nature's well-being. Moreover, much research in the SEK framework is intent on, motivated by, and successful at understanding those connections. However, it would be incomplete, inaccurate, and likely insulting to limit the value of TEK to this value only, or to suggest this as the main point of ethical connection between TEK and SEK. This would be akin to citing the ability to perform household chores or the benefit of an income tax write-off as the sole, or even main, value of one's children.

For the interest in ecological connections to be a genuine point of connection between SEK and TEK, those connections would have to be sought not only for the purpose of maintaining human welfare, but also for maintaining the welfare of nature – i.e., for the sake of nature – itself. The importance of connections is captured, we believe, in the paragraph that opens this essay, describing the amazing connection between ravens and wolves.

A second genuine point of connection between SEK and TEK may be found in the ethical virtue of humility. In TEK, humility is necessary for relating to nonhuman persons – necessary because they *are* persons. Humility is also important for Indigenous cultures because they view nature as not only personified, but also as powerful and unpredictable. SEK, in certain modes, also recognizes that nature is powerful and unpredictable. That idea is well captured by ecologists' appreciation for ecological surprises (Doak et al., 2008), tipping points (Dakos and Hastings, 2013), and synergistic interaction (Valiente-Banuet and Verdú, 2013). Some members of the SEK scientific community understand that those conditions require, and even inspire, a sense of humility. As Doak et al. (2008) point out with regard to ecological surprises, "[T]he extent and frequency of major 'surprises' in ecological systems argue for substantial humility about our predictive abilities" (953).

That the natural world is complex and inherently unpredictable is not a new idea in the history of Western science. In his classic book *On Growth and Form*, the father of mathematical biology, Sir D'Arcy Thompson (1917), wrote: "It is the principle involved, and not its ultimate and very complex results, that we can alone attempt to grapple with" (643). While that sentiment has been embraced by many (though certainly not all) scientists, it has not been consistently highlighted in our relationship with nature, especially by those who apply scientific knowledge to decisions about how we relate to nature.

Connections Between TEK and LTER

> Our relationship with land cannot heal until we hear its stories. But who will tell them?
>
> Robin Wall Kimmerer (2013)

The most basic epistemological difference between TEK and SEK may be that TEK is premised upon knowledge born through long tenure in a place, while SEK tends to be largely focused on short-term observations. Within SEK we mainly think in limited time spans. In 1994, ecologist Robert May summarized the obsession with the short-term within modern Western ecology. Of some 308 ecological studies reviewed, the mean duration was only 2.5 years. Of 749 studies published in the journal *Ecology* in the 1980s, only 1.7 percent lasted more than five years.

Even in SEK, however, there are exceptions to this short-sightedness. The US National Science Foundation sponsors two programs of relevance here. Both the Long-Term Ecological Research (LTER) network, which consists of twenty-four designated sites around the country, and the various forms of LTER in the Long-Term Research in Environmental Biology program, recognize the unique value of LTER. Both LTER and

TEK at least appear similar for being place-based and committed to the long-term. But LTER also has an unmet potential to reflect an ethical outlook like that glimpsed in TEK.

While SEK is certainly capable of demonstrating connections and humility, LTER is especially valuable for highlighting the importance of connections and the need for humility. Perhaps the most important point of connection between TEK and SEK is manifest in LTER. In particular, one of the most important features of TEK is the assignment of personhood to the landscape and many denizens of the landscape. It is the notion of nonhuman personhood that seems so difficult for many Westerners to grasp, and therefore for SEK to embody. An idea, however, born of the Western mind, might be critical for understanding that kind of personhood. That idea is "sense of place" (SOP), a concept that has been developed by scholars such as Tim Cresswell and Yi-Fu Tuan, among others. Moreover, sense of place is also a powerful (though too often implicit) foundation of LTER. An SOP is formed when the natural history, culture, and geography of a place commingle in our minds and form the stories – lyrical stories and scientific stories – that define a place. Connections between TEK and SEK might be found through SOP. Within SEK, LTER seems a particularly reliable way to discover SOP. Making these connections, however, would require a larger community of scholars to become familiar with existing ideas pertaining to SOP and to further solidify those ideas in a way that would facilitate SOP's connection to ecological science and environmental ethics.

Though LTER is not typical within SEK, it can be seen as a critical means for helping us discover an SOP by revealing the connections that allow for the story of a place to be told, to be wondrous, to spark the appropriate ethical attitude toward a place. While it is certainly true that good scientific knowledge is important for developing a "healthy" relationship with the land, a relationship leading to the flourishing of humans and the land also requires a proper ethical "attitude" toward both humans and the land. We should recognize that science in general (and LTER in particular) can contribute something important to both necessary elements for flourishing. Since an important part of SOP is storytelling, and since places usually only share their stories over long periods of time, it takes time to get to know a place in order to tell its story. Among SEK, perhaps only LTER can provide this unique contribution to sense of place and hence provide an ethical parallel to TEK within the Western cultural tradition.

In the fall of 1936 (and again in 1937–1938), ecologist and ethicist Aldo Leopold (who worked squarely within the SEK framework) traveled to the Rio Gavilan in northern Mexico. During this trip, Leopold glimpsed land that was "a picture of ecological health"; that experience complicated his Western perception of land dominated by, he now saw, sick soil and impoverished biota; and that crystallized his ethical focus on the preservation of the "integrity, stability, and beauty of the biotic community." This experience forever altered Leopold's sense of place – both those familiar places now understood as less healthy than they could be, and places like the Rio Gavilan. LTER is likewise primed to develop and deliver those stories of connections, images of harmed or healthy land, a revised sense of place, and to therefore contribute to an inclusive ethic.

In an essay, "Song of the Gavilan," inspired by that episode, Leopold wonderfully articulated an expression of how a Western scientist can understand the importance of sense of place.

The song of the waters is audible to every ear, but there is other music in these hills, by no means audible to all. To hear even a few notes of it you must first live here for a long time, and then you must know the speech of hills and rivers. Then on a still night, when the campfire is low and the Pleiades have climbed over rimrocks, sit quietly and listen for a wolf to howl, and think hard of everything you have seen and tried to understand. Then you may hear it – a vast pulsing harmony – its score inscribed on a thousand hills, its notes the lives and deaths of plants and animals, its rhythms spanning the seconds and the centuries. (Leopold, 1966: 158)

WORKS CITED

Callicott, J. Baird, and Michael P. Nelson. *American Indian Environmental Ethics: An Ojibwa Case Study*. Englewood Cliffs, NJ: Prentice Hall, 2004.

Cleveland, David A. "Traditional Ecological Knowledge." *Encyclopedia of Environmental Ethics and Philosophy*, edited by J. Baird Callicott and Robert Frodeman. Detroit: Gale Cengage Learning, 2009, 318–22.

Dakos, Vasilis and Alan Hastings. "Editorial: Special Issue on Regime Shifts and Tipping Points in Ecology." *Theoretical Ecology*, 6 (3), 2013, 253–54.

Doak, Daniel F., James A. Estes, Benjamin S. Halpern, Ute Jacob, and David R. Lindberg. "Understanding and Predicting Ecological Dynamics: Are Major Surprises Inevitable?" *Ecology*, 89, 2008, 952–61.

Kimmerer, Robin Wall. *Braiding Sweetgrass: Indigenous Wisdom, Scientific Knowledge, and the Teachings of Plants*. Minneapolis: Milkweed Editions, 2013.

Leopold, Aldo. *A Sand County Almanac: With Essays on Conservation from Round River*. New York: Ballantine Books, 1966.

May, Robert. "The Effects of Spatial Scale on Ecological Questions and Answers." *Large-Scale Ecology and Conservation Biology*, edited by P. J. Edwards, R. M. May, and N. R. Webb. London: Blackwell, 1994, 1–17.

Menzies, Charles R., Ed. *Traditional Ecological Knowledge and Natural Resource Management*. Lincoln: University of Nebraska Press, 2006.

Pierotti, Ramond and Daniel Wildcat. "Traditional Ecological Knowledge: The Third Alternative (Commentary)." *Ecological Applications*, 10 (5), 2000, 1333–40.

Siebert, Charles. "Should a Chimp Be Able to Sue its Owner?" *New York Times Magazine*, April 23, 2014.

Thompson, D'Arcy. *On Growth and Form*. Cambridge: Cambridge University Press, 1917.

Valiente-Banuet, Alfonso and Miguel Verdú. "Human Impacts on Multiple Ecological Networks Act Aynergistically to Drive Ecosystem Collapse." *Frontiers in Ecology and the Environment*, 11 (8), 2013, 408–13.

Vucetich, John A. "Introduction." *Wild Wolves We Have Known: Stories of Wolf Biologists' Favorite Wolves*, edited by Richard P. Thiel, Allison C. Thiel, and Marianne Strozewski. Ely, MN: International Wolf Center, 2013.

"Wolves, Ravens, and a New Purpose for Science." *Moral Ground: Ethical Action for a Planet in Peril*, edited by Kathleen Dean Moore and Michael P. Nelson. San Antonio: Trinity University Press, 2010, 337–42.

PART III

EXTENDED WEB

*Land-Care Practices and Plant and Animal
Relationships*

9

Redefining Sustainability through Kincentric Ecology: Reclaiming Indigenous Lands, Knowledge, and Ethics

Dennis Martinez

Over the years that I have been engaged as a cultural survival advocate and ecocultural restoration consultant in partnership with Indigenous communities in various parts of the globe, I've sadly had to witness the destruction or degradation of cultures and homelands as well as irreparable harm to our plant and animal relations and their habitats. The more I have traveled, researched, and listened to the stories of Indigenous victims of forced evictions and relocations to make way for conservation reserves, parks, or state-private land development schemes, I've come to realize that there is a developing and imminent crisis, unrecognized by most as such, of an order of magnitude that will affect the ability of humanity to live sustainably on Earth. The very survival of the relationship between humans and the natural world – an increasingly fragile relationship that is as critical to the future well-being of life on Earth as it has been for the whole of human existence – is at risk.

I use the term *Indigenous* to refer not only to present-day land-based tribal cultures and some closely related traditional peasant/pastoralist/ fisher cultures but also to the Pleistocene ancestors of all humanity. Modern traditional Indigenous peoples still hold the human evolutionary biological heritage (like all of us) as well as, to some degree, the evolutionary *cultural* heritage of all persons living today. That cultural legacy is still with us, but it is hanging by only a few strands that were once part of a robust life-web animated by the co-evolution of humans with the natural world. Traditional Indigenous cultures and traditional ecological (environmental) knowledge (TEK), including Indigenous stories, dance, songs, and languages, depend for their continued existence on the ancestral lands in which Indigenous culture and knowledge is rooted, and without which its cultural flowering will wilt and die – with ominous consequences for not only Indigenous peoples but for all humanity. For those who scoff and say, as we so frequently hear today, that we cannot return to the past, anthropologist Paul Shephard answers: "We can go back to the Pleistocene because, as a species, we never left. We can go back to nature ... because we never left it" (Shephard and Shephard, 1998: 170) – ten thousand years of civilization against at least a quarter of a million years of evolution.

By "evolutionary cultural heritage" I mean an ancient way of being with nature, not only with plants and animals, but with the primal natural forces of fire, water, wind, and the earth – a way of relating respectfully to all life as kin and the earth as a nurturing mother. I call this familial relationship "kincentricity," and Indigenous cultural land-care practices "kincentric ecology" (Martinez in Salmon, 2000: 1328). I coined the term "kincentricity" in a 1995 Karuk tribal report to the United States Forest Service (Martinez, 1995: 1–30). Kincentricity refers to the reciprocal relationships contained in Indigenous stories of an "Original Compact" made between the animals and humans. Animals would offer their lives to humans provided that humans would take care of the plants and animals by asking for permission to harvest – leaving gifts in exchange for lives taken, not taking more than is needed, showing respect for their bodily remains after they were killed and butchered for food, and not failing to regularly care for their habitats and relations. If humans failed to honor this compact, the plants and animals would refuse to offer their lives for human sustenance and would cause harm or misfortune to the hunter or gatherer, his or her family, and even future generations of their community. This kincentric relationship has evolved over time into what modern Western peoples call ethics: a code, model, or standard that guides or regulates our behavior with the natural world. Because Indigenous ethics regulate cultural land-care practices that provide protection, sustenance, and well-being for the people, it could be called an ethical-economic model. Since this ethical-economic code informed the daily activities of men and women working together to survive on the land, it had to work well over long periods of time or people would not have continued to survive. This model enabled millions of our ancestors to survive – sustainably – through a gauntlet of environmental adversities. Some societies, favored by a bountiful land-base, were even able to maintain an affluent subsistence lifestyle, spending relatively little time on the tasks of subsistence and more time on socializing, creating art, playing games, music, teaching, and so on.

My aim in this chapter is to give "sustainability" a concrete and specific meaning from the perspective of a very different ethical-economic model than the present globally dominant one. I will contrast traditional Indigenous and modern Western ethical-economic philosophies and their very different effects on the environment and on sustainability. Neoliberal capitalism, the current economic system of choice for the West (sometimes referred to as the "North," with less developed countries termed the "South"), claims its own environmental solutions. The problem with its so-called solutions to environmental degradation, especially climate destabilization and global warming via "green" capital investments and innovative technology, is that it runs head-on into a significant conundrum: The framing of their solutions to sustainability problems involves the very economic forces and belief systems that have caused the problems in the first place.

The British mathematician and philosopher, Alfred North Whitehead (1933), used the term "misplaced concreteness" to describe the thinking of people who believe in something in spite of overwhelming evidence to the contrary, i.e., today's defenders of the inevitable and necessary triumph of science and technology when the evidence tells us that every "success" is followed just as inevitably by previously unforeseen new problems (all too common examples today include viruses and antibiotic resistance or pesticides and resistant targeted organisms over time), while continuing to deplete the world's scarce resources. The track record of Indigenous environmental sustainability offers a proven alternative that we will visit later in the chapter. Without the reclaiming of Indigenous homelands, knowledge, and the ethical competence that continue to be lost, the world will also lose a well-tested and successful ethical-economic model that may be the last good option for environmental sustainability.

A key objective of this chapter is to make the case for the *modern relevance* of traditional Indigenous ethical economics and Traditional Ecological Knowledge (TEK), as well as the relevance of traditional Indigenous peoples as an alternative modernity (Gaonkar, 2001: 1–23) – a way of knowing that has proven capable of adapting to change over millennia and continues to do so in the present. TEK is a way of knowing that is informed by environmental wisdom and adaptation that have survived and even prospered through environmental events of extraordinary lengths and extremes in some of the most difficult places to live on Earth. Indigenous peoples provide a model of how to live on the earth that has been tested and then tested again and again – often with relatively high populations and with technology that, in the hands of others less experienced and exercising less restraint – was capable of wreaking destruction on the environment. Those who made serious mistakes, of course, did not survive.

I see the loss of this model as a crisis not only for Indigenous and other vulnerable peoples of the world, but its already manifest effects may well spring what noted geographer and historian Charles Mann calls the "Malthusian Trap" on the rest of humanity (Malthus, 1992; Mann 2011: 229–31). As the promises of the Industrial and Scientific Revolutions for world prosperity through perpetual economic growth and technological progress continue to fall short of expectations, and the environment collapses under the weight of unsustainable levels of economic production and consumption worsen, this trap appears to be upon us. This will happen even if world population stabilizes because environmental degradation is already well advanced at even present population levels. Thomas Malthus, the first professional British economist and author of *Essay on Population* in 1798, had quite reasonably predicted starvation from unrestrained population growth but failed to anticipate the technologically driven high levels of food production finally achieved in the late twentieth century. These achievements have so far forestalled his prediction of global mass starvation due to populations increasing faster than technological progress can supply people with sufficient food. But the very production "miracles" like the Green Revolution, beginning in the 1960s that have until now postponed starvation, are likely to lead to the same dismal result that Malthus foresaw.

In what way could Malthus' dire prediction of mass starvation in our own time come true? Not exactly in the way Malthus was thinking, or at least Malthus did not balance his attention to the likelihood of human starvation with the greater likelihood of the exhaustion of food-producing English soils due to the shift from their traditional local subsistence agriculture to international commodities markets requiring maximum output achieved through industrial monocultures and intensive farming methods of even marginal land (Foster et al., 2010: 280). In keeping with Malthus' class bias, he naturally favored increasing agricultural production by wealthy landowners while reducing the population of the poor and increasing middle and upper class production-consumption (Mann, 2011: 228–31). Today, global neoliberal capitalism continues to emphasize population reduction of the poor in developing countries while increasing production-consumption in richer developed counties. Today, capitalism's increased tempo of production is destroying the environmental basis for food production even as technologically driven greater efficiency in agricultural output is feeding more and more people. However, productivity has already begun to level off, with organic methods increasingly out-performing the conventional chemically driven agribusiness methods of the Green Revolution. Until organic methods are more generally adopted and, especially, Indigenous kincentric ethics/ecology are better understood and then successively implemented by local people in local places, ecological collapse will begin to reverse agricultural production to the point people will begin to starve – regardless of population size. This is what is meant by the "Malthusian Trap" or "Paradox."

Another prescient thinker, living in China in the eighteenth century and virtually unknown today, did manage to put his finger on our own probable economic and environmental future. Author of the eye-opening 2005 book *1491*, Charles C. Mann brought this midlevel but influential member of the Qing (Manchu) dynasty to our attention in his subsequent book, *1493: Uncovering The New World Columbus Discovered* (Mann, 2011). His name was Hong Liangji, who, like Malthus, understood that sooner or later farm-grown food would fail to keep up with population growth and starvation would ensue. But Hong went further. Not only would people starve, the land itself would turn on the people, as he accurately predicted well before the Sichuan agricultural boom, fueled by newly introduced Native American crops like tobacco, maize, and potatoes, ended in calamity; Hong states: "Heaven-and-Earth's way of making adjustments lies in flood, drought, and plague" (De Bary, Lufrano: 174). Although Hong has been all but forgotten by the world, he foresaw "Heaven-and-Earth's way of making adjustments" for any age and for any society when people abuse the land.

In Hong's time and place, a massive internal migration pushed farming into marginal forested hill country, leading to deforestation, flooding, disease, social chaos, and eventual starvation. The land never recovered its former healthy state (Mann, 2011: 227–31). What does "Heaven-and-Earth" have in store for the twenty-first century? All available evidence tells us that the Malthusian Trap is going to spring, probably sooner than later. A faith-based economic system that believes continuous technological innovations and smart green capital investments will allow continuously increasing production without serious environmental consequences will set the world back, not forward, undoing the Industrial (and the Green) Revolution's promise of perpetual progress and prosperity. Stabilizing population levels, usually beneficial only in the short term, will not matter when the environment gives out due to an economic system guided by an ethical code lacking in respect for the earth and its peoples.

The Roots and Impacts of Modern Neo-Liberal Capitalism and Development

In the twenty-first century, the evidence for a new kind of development in speculative capitalism is becoming increasingly visible, a qualitative turn of events in the way global lands (especially farm lands) and resources are being practically given away by national governments to an international crop of state and private entrepreneurs of every conceivable variety, mostly in developing countries. Africa, in particular, has been targeted (especially by China) and is called by some "the last agricultural frontier" on a continent in which only 10 percent of the land has secure tenure (Magdoff, 2015: 9). This assault is also happening in Asia, especially South and Southeast Asia; Mexico, Central, and South America; Eastern Europe, especially Ukraine and Western Russia; and Australia. Areas rich in wildlife are sometimes closed to local people so that friends of real estate speculators or obliging government elites can hunt and establish tourist lodges that service the rich. Forests are closed to locals to serve the needs of investors in the global carbon market, including state takeovers of forests used by Indigenous subsistence cultures (Martinez, 2010: 12; Pearce, 2012: ix, x). Investigative journalist Fred Pearce quotes British private equity consultant Graham Davies, who notes that in Africa, "the vast majority" of investors are "only interested in commercial Western-style agriculture, largely ignoring the continent's 60 million small farms that produce 80 percent of sub-Saharan Africa's farm produce" (Pearce, 2012: ix).

Between 32 and 82 million hectares (80 to 200 million acres) of "empty" global farmland, according to soil and plant scientist Fred Magdoff, have been "brought under foreign control ... as of May 2012 ... with the amount constantly increasing" (Magdoff, 2015: 9). Other estimates vary from 120 million to 560 million acres. Many large deals are made in secret, so the acreage is probably closer to the higher estimate. In any case, the figure seems to be substantial both in size and in its effects on Indigenous peoples inhabiting these "empty lands" – and it is growing rapidly (Pearce, 2012: vii, ix). Along with the sudden substantial jump in food prices in the 2008 World Food Crisis, there is increasing food insecurity, creating a severe burden on the world's two billion poor, especially when so much former cropland is going into biofuels (Altieri and

Toledo, 2011: 590). Increasingly, climate change is causing more severe and longer droughts that are also responsible for much water loss and the subsequent shortage of food crops.

It is a tragic state of affairs when we have to witness the utter disregard by twenty-first-century vandals (and the corrupt governments that facilitate their acts of piracy) for the poor, Indigenous, and closely related peasant/pastoralist communities who occupy so-called "empty lands," and who are falling prey to the greatest peacetime land grab in world history (Altieri and Toledo, 2011: 590; Pearce, 1993: 291–301, 303). Who are these land pirates and resource poachers and how is this happening? Their acts are well documented by investigative and environmental journalists (See Dowie, 2011 and Pearce, 1993 for more detailed information). These "bio-pirates" include logging and mining concessions, North American evangelicals, hedge-fund managers, Chinese and other state corporations, narco-terrorists, Goldman Sachs and a variety of other commodity traders, biodiversity funders, corrupt national elites, Russian oligarchs, Western mega-agricultural capitalists, microchip billionaires, and individual financiers and speculators (Pearce, 2012: vii).

Other losses of land, particularly for Indigenous peoples, are attributable to big international nongovernmental organizations (BINGOS), which are either directly or indirectly causing the evictions and relocations of Native communities on every continent, but particularly in Africa, South/Southeast Asia (including Indonesia and Papua New Guinea), and Latin America. Standing behind these tragic occurrences are a number of Western scientists, especially economists, wildlife biologists, ecologists, and conservation biologists with the best of intentions. There are notable exceptions, but most activists supporting the conservation of "wilderness" without people have little knowledge of Indigenous cultural landcare practices or environmental history, although they carry enormous authority with the global environmental community. In my experience as a participant in environmental conferences and other related activities over many years, I often hear the phrase "good" or "sound science," as in "our environmental work is based on good science." BINGOS do not usually evict Indigenous peoples directly; rather they pressure government leaders to steal the land in the name of "good science," cashing in on the nearly universal credibility carried by the West in science and other weighty progressive matters. I examine this issue in detail later when I compare the methodologies of TEK and Western science in terms of the comparative efficacy and efficiency of Indigenous and Western conservation endeavors. Many readers will be surprised to learn how much more effective and efficient Indigenous conservation practices are compared to Western models while, perhaps most surprising of all, performing conservation at a fraction of the cost of BINGOS.

Before I turn to a fuller discussion of how the Indigenous ethical-economic code informs and guides Indigenous cultural land-care practices, and how it was instrumental in achieving high levels of sustainability, let's examine the historical origins, philosophical bases, and leading characteristics of the dominant Western ethical-economic model of neoliberal capitalism. This model is exemplified in the economic dominance of modern transnational corporations facilitated by corrupt government elites who are discouraging beneficial Indigenous land-care practices by removing communities from their homelands and/or imposing restrictions on their customary land-use practices. Their disregard for the environment, seen especially in the industrial land management methods that are exacerbating climate change through *unanticipated* harmful cascading ecological events such as increases in the intensities and frequencies of forest fires, decreases in the availability of ground water, habitat destruction, the loss of ecological function, and a plethora of other environmental degradations, may have already crossed some of the nine essential life-sustaining environmental thresholds of no return (Foster et al., 2010: 13–19).

Brief History of Capitalism

Modern capitalism derives historically from the great sixteenth-century European transformation of the Christian separation of God and Heaven from the material world that, in the process of its metamorphosis, became modern "Dualism," or the separation of mind or spirit from matter (made famous by René Descartes and called "Cartesian Dualism"). It was only a short step historically and philosophically to the notion of an impersonal nature or, in modern philosopher and ecofeminist Carolyn Merchant's words, "the death of nature" (Merchant, 1983: 1–6).

It was the sixteenth-century British natural philosopher Frances Bacon who took materialism to its logical conclusion: empirically based knowledge of nature became the gateway to power *over* nature. Building on the biblical injunction to exercise dominion over the earth and all creation therein, Bacon preached the *religious duty* to dominate and control nature through the use of empirical methods in order to make the earth yield her long-held secrets. Christianity, a rigidly dutiful belief system sweetened with the opportunity for adherents to achieve a future reward in heaven, also led believers to seek a Kingdom of Heaven on Earth, eventually preaching a progressive message that natural philosophers, including Bacon, used to encourage the improvement of society by controlling and improving nature (Tarnas, 1991: 272–77).

Western capitalist economics is very much like faith-based religions with respect to its unbounded optimism and blind belief in never-ending future progress. Modern philosopher Richard Tarnas sums up Bacon's progressive "visionary ideal" as "the scientific conquest of nature for man's welfare and God's glory" (Tarnas, 1991: 275; Marx in Foster et al., 2015: 285–86; Foster and Yates, 2014: 7–8). Paradoxically, while the fruits of the sixteenth- and seventeenth-century Early Modern Intellectual Renaissance and Enlightenment, Protestant Reformation, and Scientific Revolution of unparalleled material wealth, technological progress, and secular triumph over religion continue to grow unabated into the twenty-first century, the ancient world of religious faith in God's providence also continues in the guise of the Western belief in heaven on Earth or eternal progress whatever the costs. And the costs are very high indeed.

Balancing economic development and resource conservation by avoiding resource depletion and ecological collapse, while simultaneously satisfying the material requirements for human well-being – the nearly universal definition of sustainability – is not possible in our present economic environment dominated by individualistic free-market capitalism that must expand continuously in order to survive. Constant growth requires a constant supply of raw materials regardless of their known or unknown rates of depletion, as well as a strong faith that either resource substitutions and/or more efficient future technological "fixes" will save us. Capitalism is inherently and blindly optimistic and could correctly be described as faith-based economics. Capitalism cannot do otherwise, cannot slow its rate of resource consumption and still be capitalism, since it must give satisfactory financial returns to capital investors and, *as required by law*, shareholders (Foster and Yates, 2014: 7–8; Saito, 2015: 26). Steady-state economics is also not an option for society, however attractive that alternative is to some optimistic economists. If the economy is not going forward, not accumulating ever more material from nature to convert into more consumer products, however blind its supposed guiding market hand and however green or noble its objectives, it is going backward (Foster and Yates, 2014: 1–24; Georgescu-Roegen, 1971: 19). Growth is the mantra we hear daily in media financial reports when they "do the numbers" for NASDAQ or the Dow. It is what keeps investors in a permanent state of anxiety and sends the market into repeated cycles of bearish crashes and bullish upswings.

Technological innovations or improvements in efficiency, as for example a reduction in greenhouse gas emissions (GHGs) through *more* fuel-efficient vehicles, will not mitigate capitalism's constant need to increase production of green goods (e.g., more fuel-efficient vehicles). This is due to an economic phenomenon known as the "rebound effect": the greater the efficiency of production, the more products will be developed, the cheaper and more plentiful the products due to increased efficiency, the more products will be consumed (and wasted). It is a perfect positive feedback loop. The sixteenth-century Baconian belief in the inevitability of continued future progress based on science and technology no matter the odds against it, as well as the quasi-religious duty to resolutely break through the existing boundaries of knowledge and technology, continue to inspire the best minds of the twenty-first century. The irony here is that many supposed science-based endeavors are not based solely on scientific or empirical evidence. For example, many natural resource or environmental management practices are based (unconsciously of course) on the inherited sixteenth-century Baconian belief in Christianity's responsibility to control and improve nature for human use and benefit. Nature is assumed to be wildly inefficient and wasteful and therefore in need of human control, much like re-engineering or fine-tuning an inefficient piece of equipment. This worldview is, of course, the classic Western machine metaphor that is now in the process of becoming a digital/systems metaphor.

British environmental economist David Pearce sums it up correctly: "[S]ustainable economic development (is) fairly simply defined. It is continuously rising ... consumption per capita or GNP (Gross National Product), or whatever the greed indication of development is" (Pearce in Foster et al., 2010: 41, 113). Capitalism requires a constant and perpetual supply of consumers for its products. There is an eventual and inexorable limit, of course, to material supplies but not necessarily to consumers. The classic economic textbook curve used to illustrate consumer demand graphically (think Economics 101) is "elastic" and, according to capitalist theory ("Says Law"), demand will either recede when consumer incomes drop or increase when incomes rise. In reality, however, there will not necessarily be any increase in buying when incomes rise. Consumers often hold on to their money or pay back debt – thus the need for the creation of market demand through corporate manipulation of consumer needs and desires. Consumerism in turn drives capitalist production. Modern consumer culture is built on consumer dissatisfaction, an endless litany of "needs" generated by media advertising (among many other cultural means) and unbelievably vast hidden (and legal) networks of digital deception that are accumulating a seemingly inexhaustible amount of biographical and demographic information about everyone of us (called "Big Data" in recent years). These developments can only happen in an individualistic culture that has failed to provide sufficient meaning for people who are constantly in pursuit of their identities outside the circle of the rest of humanity and the natural world. This individualistically centered culture fails to place enough value on gratitude and too much value on getting as much material goods as possible for as little as possible (aptly captured by the "Black Friday" phenomenon), consequently leaving societies vulnerable to the manipulation of existential dissatisfaction by predatory commercial interests in hot pursuit of customers.

Neoclassical capitalism bases its future prospects and its self-serving belief in its rightful place in the *natural* order of things on the hollow assurances of a self-serving ahistorical ideology. University of Oregon professor and author John Bellamy Foster and his colleague Michael Yates note that capitalism asserts that "*left to itself* [it] generates full employment" (my italics) as if it were governed by a natural law that holds that capitalism *never* fails to return to its former state of "full-employment equilibrium" following any (especially government) interference (Foster and Yates, 2014: 9). French economist Thomas Piketty, in his newly released and controversial *Capital in the Twenty-First Century*, challenges capitalism's claim to a natural tendency to remain in equilibrium unless disturbed by government intervention (Piketty in Foster and Yates, 2014: 1–24; Piketty, 2014: 7). Nobel Prize winner and Princeton professor of economics and international affairs, Paul Krugman, explains Piketty's critique of capitalism in terms of a new economic hypothesis called "secular stagnation," which offers a more realistic characterization of capitalism: "If the secular stagnationists are right, advanced economies now suffer from persistently inadequate demand, so that *depression is their normal state, except when spending is supported by bubbles ... they prop up demand. Unfortunately, they're not sustainable ...*" (my italics) (Krugman, 2014: 42).

The evidence for secular stagnation as the prime dynamic in the perpetual recession/depression cycles of capitalism is compelling. It seems that the main cause of economic growth is not "natural law" (an old Theist term that corresponds to "Divine Law"), but excessive debt coupled with speculation-driven bubbles – until they burst and growth sinks as consumer demand shrinks and recedes into a recession, and the bubble begins again through speculation-driven debt and so on, again and again. It should be noted that wars also contribute to economic upswings, which explains the great and growing disparity in wealth in advanced economies, especially the United States. Present neoclassical capitalism could not be more incapable of sustainability.

Also, the global environmental community cannot depend on foundation funding for operating conservation reserves and parks, as the capitalist money that keeps foundations afloat is fickle and may become less dependable in the future. This is a very important reason for allowing Indigenous peoples to perform the primary conservation work in their own homelands. *Recent documentation shows that Indigenous peoples can do conservation at a fraction of the cost of BINGOs* (First Peoples Worldwide, 2011; Martinez, 2010; Poole, personal communication, January 30, 2012).

Indigenous Peoples as Canaries in the Mine

Although the vast majority of the Indigenous peoples of the world, subject to more than 500 years of brutal colonial policies, have few illusions about their prospects in the myriad of development schemes and crusades of whatever stripe (evangelical Christianity and Western conservation being two of the more recent of the White Man's Burdens), they continue to experience the effects of global capitalism more acutely than others. They are the world's canaries in the mine, harbingers for the rest of us, experiencing the first and most direct impress of environmental assault by market-based land grabs and fossil-fuel-dependent development. Indigenous subsistence cultures are particularly vulnerable because most inhabit fragile biomes, such as the arctic, deserts, and tropics; they are also the most vulnerable to climate extremes and global warming, giving cause for concern to Indigenous peoples who have the most to lose (Martinez, 2010: 1).

Taking the broad view into the not so distant future, economists and other social scientists, including Piketty (2014), Krugman (2014), and Foster (2015), show us rather convincingly the probable end-game of the perpetual booms and busts of capitalism's "secular stagnation." This "system" offers repeated cycles of growing prosperity for the world's infinitesimally small percentage of the wealthy and powerful, the so-called "Masters of the Universe" or "one percenters" (actually, *one tenth* of one percenters), while the rest of us continue to descend into ever-deepening debt and despair – giving new meaning to the terms "economic *depression*" and "*natural* economic laws."

Indigenous peoples – some still holding onto their homelands and resisting calls for their removal, still possessing the knowledge and practical ecological know-how inherent in their subsistence-based lifeways, as well as the ethical competence to survive well enough (and hopefully, long enough) – can serve as an ethical-economic model for the world when it most needs it. This is the fundamental choice held out to the rest of the world, which raises a fundamental question: *How can the core sustainable economic-environmental ethics of this traditional Indigenous model be adapted to modern environmental and politico-economic changes?* The remainder of the chapter attempts to answer this question so that, over the next few generations, there is at least the opportunity to consider a different option for a sustainable relationship with each other and the natural world, an intelligent and urgently needed response to the present developing crisis.

I do not think it is an overstatement to say that the earth's remaining undeveloped lands, including the ancestral homelands, knowledge, and cultures of the still viable traditional Indigenous and peasant/pastoralist peoples, may well become the final victims in the last act of the eighteenth- and nineteenth-century Industrial Revolution. We see the weakening of the ancient co-evolutionary link between humans and the natural world and the final great enclosure of the global commons by powerful land-grabbing corporate and state interests, not to mention big Western environmental NGOs. Investigative journalist Fred Pearce has called this blatant land and resource robbery "a last round-up on the global commons" and asks, "Is this the inevitable cost of feeding the world and protecting its surviving wildlife?" (Pearce, 2012: x).

Award-winning environmental journalist Mark Dowie, addressing the rapid acceleration of evictions of Indigenous peoples from their ancestral homelands, writes: "… the future of land rights in the world is that most of the Earth's remaining natural resources and most of its high biodiversity ecosystems are currently occupied by people, most of whom are Indigenous" (Dowie, 2011: 199). In Dowie's study of Native cultural groups, he found that "whether the [land] conflict is with an extractive transnational, the World Bank, a BINGO, or the … military; the end result is pretty much the same – loss of livelihood, food security, freedom, and culture" (Dowie, 2011: 199).

As tragic as this loss of Indigenous livelihoods, cultures, and (inevitably) identity is when viewed at the human scale, why should it concern those who are addressing global climate change, environmental degradation, species losses, and other immediate and challenging *modern* problems? And even more perplexing for many is how the loss of the homelands of a mere 7 or 8 percent of the world population (including the 4 percent Indigenous population combined with the 3 or 4 percent still mostly traditional smallholder peasant, pastoralist, and fisher populations) poses an obstacle to the global achievement of environmental and economic sustainability? I plan to answer these seemingly reasonable questions by showing how and why relatively small Indigenous and peasant populations, the lands they occupy, and the knowledge they still possess are important to the development of a sustainable ethical-economic model far out of proportion to their low population numbers.

But we first need to know who Indigenous peoples are and why fisher, peasant, and pastoralist societies are included in a book about *Indigenous* knowledge and sustainability. An often used definition of "Indigenous" or "tribal" comes from the International Labor Organization's (ILO, 2011) Convention 169, Article 14: "tribal peoples in independent countries whose social, cultural and economic conditions distinguish them from other sections of the national community, and whose status is regulated wholly or partially by their own customs or traditions or by special laws or regulations" (Dowie, 2011: xii). But not all governments recognize "tribal," as for example in Africa. Also, as Dowie points out, "there is no legal definition of Indigenous peoples, partly because there is no legal definition of the word peoples" (Dowie, 2011: xii). It took more than two decades of effort at the global level to gain acceptance in the United Nations of the term "peoples" following the word "Indigenous," although there is still no recognized *legal* definition. It is important from a global Indigenous point of view that an apostrophe, when the word is used in the possessive case, be placed after "people", i.e., "peoples'." This may seem trivial, but it is not a small matter to Indigenous representatives in high-level international negotiations, because it reflects the relatively recent recognition of the pan-Indigenous or collective nature of the world's Indigenous nations, united in their struggle for recognition of their common *Indigeneity*. My preferred definition follows that of the ILO (except for "tribes," a term invented by anthropologists for their own convenience), but I also follow Dowie in his more inclusive emphasis on traditional peasant and pastoralist cultural groups, especially nomadic pastoralists who cross national boundaries with their flocks or herds, e.g., Másai cattle or Sámi reindeer (Dowie, 2011: xii).

Mexican ethnoecologist Victor Toledo, explaining the difficulties of drawing a distinct boundary between "Indigenous" and "peasant" (which also includes pastoralists), shares his expert opinion: "Large numbers of indigenous peoples are ... peasant producers (smallholders typically farming one or two hectares) and therefore can be indistinguishable from the non-indigenous peoples living nearby ... [M]any mestizo peasants (persons in Mexico who are speaking Spanish regularly by eight or nine years of age even if of predominantly Indigenous blood) are direct descendants of the indigenous peoples living nearby and retain most of their cultural traits ... by considering other characteristics than languages it is possible to enlarge the number of indigenous peoples in the contemporary world" (Toledo, 1999: 2). Here Toledo puts as much importance on culture (except for language) as on blood. Most *mestizos* in Mexico carry some Indigenous blood, but when they are identified by this term, they are in effect culturally *Méxicano* and no longer culturally *Indio*. Toledo estimates that there are 300 to 350 million Indigenous peoples, based primarily on language, while an additional 300 million or so are culturally related peasant people. Conservatively, this totals 600 to 650 million people who Toledo includes in the category of "Indigenous" and who collectively share in cultural "Indigeneity" (Toledo, 1999: 1–10).

I am convinced that the population estimates by Toledo and others, often based on government estimates, are conservative because, in the long and turbulent conflicts between nation-states and Indigenous peoples, it has always been in the interest of states to underestimate Indigenous populations since lower estimates bring states closer to their objective of complete national assimilation and resource exploitation. Probably more importantly, these population underestimates bring nation-states closer to complete access to and control of the natural resources on Indigenous lands – the first step in the enrichment of national treasuries with hard currency in return for facilitating the appropriation of Indigenous lands and resources by transnational corporations and other speculative capitalist enterprises. For similar reasons, the United States has historically favored high blood quantum requirements (sometimes as high as 50 percent) for federal recognition of Native Americans and Native Hawaiians.

The estimated 600 to 650 million Indigenous persons (including "peasant" and "pastoralist" peoples) live in 75 of the world's approximately 200 countries and speak 4,000 to 5,000 of the world's 7,000 spoken languages. While comprising only 7 or 8 percent of the global population, Indigenous peoples comprise 80 to 90 percent of the world's cultural diversity; further, according to The Worldwide Fund for Nature (WWFN,

2008), 80 percent of the earth's "biodiversity hotspots" are located on Indigenous territories (WWFN, 2008: 4). The term "hotspot" refers not only to areas with exceptional biodiversity but also places where bio-diversity is under threat of immediate development. This startling fact underscores the ecological weight carried by such a small number of Indigenous people, who are the only ones still standing in the way of economic development and possible species extinctions in those places. Moreover, approximately half of the world's 3,000 Indigenous cultural groups are found in 80 percent of all terrestrial ecosystems, with most of the earth's biodiversity in the tropics located within Indigenous territo-ries and occupying most of the protected areas of Latin America (Alcorn, 1993: 424–26; Toledo, 1999: 1–10).

With 80 percent of the earth's biodiversity hotspots located on Indigenous lands, Indigenous peoples are clearly ecologically important far out of proportion to their small populations. This striking corre-spondence between their lengthy tenure (probably measured in tens of thousands of years) and the survival of biodiversity in lands they still occupy strongly suggest that they *have been environmentally sustainable on about 20 percent of the terrestrial surface of the earth for a very long time.* Toledo concludes that Indigenous peoples have the "lowest ecolog-ical impact" of the world's diverse cultures (Toledo, 1999: 4). What did Toledo mean by the *"lowest ecological impact"* of the world's diverse cultures? Was it a small Indigenous population with primitive technology living off nature's benevolent bounty in an American Garden of Eden, leaving only footprints and taking only low-hanging fruit? The evidence suggests otherwise: While Indigenous peoples had the *least damaging* ecological impact when compared with other cultures, *they were also enhancing or improving it with their cultural land-care practices.* I know enough about Toledo's understanding of Indigenous land-care practices to believe he would agree that Native people were enriching the biodiversity of their environments, especially through frequent low-intensity burning using *traditional* swidden ("slash-and-burn") agroecology. Toledo partic-ularly emphasizes "habitat patchiness and biological as well as generical variation" – a result primarily of the use of fire (Toledo, 1999, 6). Suffice it to say that scientific documentation, coupled with Indigenous oral tra-ditions, supports the case for biodiversity enhancement.

Surprisingly, Western scientists do not hold this view. Typically, they are skeptical of the value of Indigenous land-care practices in con-serving species and maintaining ecological health, primarily because of three widespread myths: (1) Nature was so bountiful that little or no effort was required by Indigenous peoples to survive reasonably well; (2) Indigenous populations were so low that they could not have made much of a difference in the structure and composition of the landscape even if they had wanted to; and (3) their technology was too primitive to have had any significant effect on the environment.

Science, as scientists never tire of telling us, is self-correcting. Indigenous population estimates are an instructive example of self-correcting science. American Indian population estimating began with ethnographer James Mooney in 1928. He arrived at a tally of 1.15 million inhabitants in North America at the time of discovery. Famous anthropologist Alfred Kroeber cut back Mooney's population estimate to 900,000 with only 8.4 million for the entire Western hemisphere. Later, with more sophisticated demographic tools at the scientists' disposal, and with the availability of new research, it became clear that there were population losses of up to 95 percent due to introduced European diseases that Native people had no immunity to in the 180 years following first contact, and population estimates abruptly began to climb. By 1983, Henry Dobyns, drawing from his own research and that of others from the 1960s and 1970s, published *Their Number Became Thinned*, which estimated a population of between 90 and 112 million for the entire hemisphere and 10 million for North America. Indeed, Indigenous population densities in central Mexico were estimated to be higher than anywhere else in the world, with more than twice the number of persons per square kilometer than either China or India. Great European cities such as London, Paris, and Rome had significantly lower populations than some Indigenous cities in Mexico and South America (Mann, 2005: 101–03, 108).

Opposition to this bold population estimate was immediate and ferocious, and it continues by some in the academy. Why is it so difficult for scholars to accept these high population numbers? Of course, the demographic research could be argued or even rejected outright. But I think the primary reason for this rejection was accurately captured by ethnologist Lenore Stiffarm: "It's perfectly acceptable to move into unoccupied land. And land with only a few 'savages' is the next best thing" (Mann, 2005: 104).

"Empty lands" has always been the colonizers' most convenient and expedient excuse for land expropriation. Or, if Native numbers were too great to be so gratuitously dismissed, the rationalization was always (and still is) that the inhabitants were "unproductive," not willing or able to bring the lands in their care into production in the manner of "civilized" peoples such as Europeans who express their domination of nature after the fashion of Bacon, by *forcing* the earth to reveal her secrets and yield to what they want or need in the way that is the most efficient for the producer (farmer). This production was thought to be orderly and rational, which practically anyone could see in the rectilinear structure of European farms with their repeating straight rows of crops, together, of course, with their initially very high *short-term* productivity. Surely, no rational being could, upon viewing what the White Man had done to the land compared with what the Native seems *not* to have done (leaving "wilderness" as it is still called), fail to see the obvious difference. This is the heart of the matter. Europeans (and others later) simply were not able to *see* what it was that nonfarming Indigenous cultures, and to some extent even those more sedentary societies whose subsistence farms or gardens were perceived as chaotic or messy, as for example the Maya *milpa*, were really doing. Or why they were "destroying" the land with the widespread use of repeated burning.

The Indigenous presence on the land was misunderstood by the invaders in the same way that Indigenous spirituality without churches or theological texts was misunderstood. "They have no religion" was as commonly voiced as "they have no agriculture," and sometimes by extension, "they have no culture." The conquering, killing, and removal of Indigenous peoples (obviously subhuman "savages") was not wrong because they clearly were standing in the way of civilization and progress. Colonists simply could not grasp that the extraordinary productivity of these new unknown lands was partly (and, in some places, the greater part) the *result* of thousands of years of Indigenous cultural land-care practices that were informed by a highly adaptive system of learned ecological and biological knowledge – *Traditional Ecological Knowledge (TEK)* – growing cumulatively in particular locales over generations and changing as environments changed. Viewed from the perspective of "self-correcting" Western science where virtually all scientific knowledge is provisional – theories are the state of knowledge only until a better or more inclusive theory replaces it – TEK can also be described as provisional in the sense of its environmental adaptability, contradicting the widespread myth of the "static" nature of traditional knowledge. Yet TEK is also cumulative in ways that Western science is not. Instead of "revolutions" occurring in science every two or three generations, especially in theoretical physics and other "hard" sciences, or in sciences like academic or theoretical ecology that historically have held more than one major theoretical position at any given time, TEK is place-adaptive: Change in local environmental knowledge normally occurs very slowly in any particular place and is more cyclic than revolutionary in a linear sense. For example, while much of Western scientific theoretical reasoning is based to a varying extent on past knowledge accumulation, some so-called hard sciences can change their theoretical framework within a generation when factual "anomalies" do not fit the framework and are reformulated into a new theory. TEK, on the other hand, is situated in slow, "stable" environmental change that repeats itself over generations, e.g., plant flowering times that indicate other ecological changes such as the arrival of salmon or the time to harvest sea weed, which have been stable over long stretches of time. Generation after generation this happens – until an event like climate change begins to change it all. But nothing is then "overthrown"; the new changes in indicator plants are simply added to the rest of knowledge and adjustments are made in community behavior. TEK is thus rooted in place-based knowledge, while Western science is far more speculative and theoretical, partly because it is less place-specific and more generalized, less historical and contextual, i.e., more theoretical.

Thus, over long periods of time, more understanding occurs as cycles repeat in local places and more wisdom is cumulatively learned through an intergenerational chain of knowledge – remembering environmental events and changes as told in stories over generations. As in societies in general, some intelligent and experienced individual knowledge holders and specialists became reliable community guides from generation to generation, often holding knowledge that other members of the community lacked. This is somewhat similar to secret Indigenous spiritual societies that keep intergenerational knowledge and rituals for the community's spiritual benefit without allowing it out of the care of a select few.

The contrast between the Western and the Indigenous ethical-economic models could not be greater. The Indigenous kincentric model is based on a gifting ethic, an ethic where gifts cannot be owned but have to be passed on to others in the community. They are part of a "cycle of obligatory returns," to use the words of fisheries historian and researcher Jim Lichatowich, referring to how Pacific North American Indians were able to sustainably manage salmon without an individualistic free-for-all competitive market (Lichatowich, 1999:33–37). The situation of salmon fisheries provides an excellent example of what can happen when the Indigenous ethical-economic model and responsible community-based resource use is replaced by the Western industrial-mechanistic free market model where short-term industrial efficiency trumps long-term sustainability – demonstrating the *ethical incompetence* of the dominant economic model.

Case Study: Salmon and Hatcheries

Lichatowich is an experienced natural resource manager in the US Pacific Northwest. He has documented the sorry story of the virtually unrestrained exploitation of salmon in the US Northwest, British Columbia, and Alaska from the time Indian elders say the salmon were so numerous a person could practically walk across streams and pools on their backs, to the present, when annual salmon runs are counted in the hundreds instead of the tens of thousands, and fishing has been dramatically curtailed or prohibited altogether. The reasons for this calamitous decline are many and complicated, including changing ocean conditions (much of it a direct result of global warming, including warming waters and ocean acidification), loss of quality riverine and estuarine habitat, ocean overfishing, blockage of salmon runs returning to their natal streams to spawn by dams lacking fish "ladders," unscreened irrigation diversions, sloppy logging practices, and more. But one of the primary reasons for the decline is the emphasis put on fish hatcheries instead of habitat restoration and, until recently, the lack of adequate fishing regulations and limits. Wild fish (nonhatchery) stocks have nearly disappeared, dropping in most rivers south of Alaska and British Columbia to five percent or less of the total salmon population.

The salmon industry's almost exclusive reliance on hatcheries highlights the essential differences between the Indigenous and Western industrial-capitalist models. Remember Francis Bacon's famous sixteenth-century dictum: Unlock nature's secrets through science's empirical methods and gain the ability to dominate and control nature for human benefit – hence the term *resource*, meaning for the benefit of humans alone. This still dominant philosophy views nature through the prism of the classic Western machine metaphor. As successful as this mechanistic orientation has been in the hard sciences of physics, chemistry, and engineering, with stunning triumphs in space exploration, industrial production, digital breakthroughs, medical technology, and pharmaceuticals (based originally on Indigenous herbal knowledge), it is still susceptible to what Lichatowich calls "dogma," e.g., "nature is wasteful and profligate, ... humans know better, ...we should manage nature for the benefit of our own species, and ... we can tinker with it as one might adjust an engine or a wind-up-clock" (Lichatowich and

Zuckerman, 2003: 17–31). Hatcheries were built to artificially increase salmon production, of course, but this method also meant taking salmon out of their natural habitats, where salmon co-evolved for 55 to 100 million years, swimming in the same waters where dinosaurs once waded. Inferior hatchery-reared salmon have diluted the genes of wild stocks, leading to poor adaptation to perilous river and especially ocean conditions due to lower disease resistance and compromised health and vigor. The far more populous hatchery salmon populations have declined in the US south of Alaska's Copper River to unsustainable levels. Their decline is not because hatcheries don't do an adequate job of rearing and releasing salmon. Hatcheries put out millions of juvenile salmon, but too many do not survive, especially in the first two to five years in the ocean. The tinkering by salmon managers was clearly not working. Hatcheries could not replace natural regeneration. It was all about efficiency: simplifying nature by reducing her to easily managed components in order to maximize material benefits for society. But unlike machines, salmon (or any other species or natural entity) cannot be "reduced" to interchangeable units; wild salmon *belong* to particular birthing streams for biological and ecological reasons – including geological features (stream pool availability and depth; structural diversity such as boulders and large down wood); water ph, depth, and flow speed (beaver ponds moderate flow while providing benefits to juvenile salmon's growth and survival); appropriate aggregate size for spawning; and water temperatures and oxygen levels. Either positive or negative effects can occur based on the length of time from egg laying to emergence from gravel in salmon nests or "Redds" – to ensure a longer period of protection from predation *while gaining maximum sustenance from the yolk in their egg sacks, increasing the odds of ocean survival* – a service not provided by hatcheries when juveniles or "fry" are regularly released too early. Other factors include riparian vegetation type and cover, food (insect) availability, disease resistance, and more. Hatcheries cannot duplicate most of these ecological conditions, let alone the co-evolution of specific life-history events. Moreover, salmon have survived frequent and even cataclysmic environmental events, including droughts, floods, fires, and hundreds of feet of lava, sediment, and ice (Lichatowich, 1999: 5). Think again of Whitehead's "misplaced concreteness": fishery scientists know this principle but many continue to ignore it and rear salmon in hatcheries instead of promoting natural regeneration by restoring quality fish habitat and, for most of the past, *inappropriately* enforcing appropriate fishing regulations (Lichatowich, 1999: 5).

What I have written about salmon could be said about any number of other commercially important species under industrial management. Although some recognition of the *unsustainability* of these practices now exists, not much has changed. Why is this? The phenomenon of "misplaced concreteness" is part of the answer. So is the quasi-religious certainty that science and technology will always, in the end, offer innovative solutions. After all, human progress for people living in developed countries is experienced daily in the seemingly endless breakthroughs and improvements in science and technology. But the believers are still not seeing the forest for the trees. While scientists and natural resource managers know well the empirical evidence suggesting the failure of hatchery-reared salmon, they continue a practice, by default, that is at the heart of the industrial ethos that bears the deepest responsibility for the failure of Western society to achieve even a small measure of environmental sustainability. *Indeed, the capitalist-industrial/ethical-economic model that has ruined a once sustainable salmon fishery is also precluding any rational solutions to climate destabilization and global warming or any number of other environmental challenges.* It would be instructive to examine historic Native salmon-care cultural practices in order to contrast them with the Western industrial practices I have already described. We can find some of the essentials of TEK in actual historic, and to some extent, present cultural practices in a variety of terrestrial, ocean, estuary, river, lake, and stream habitats. Western scientists and Native knowledge holders alike consider salmon to be an ecological keystone species as well as a prime indicator of ocean, estuary, river, and watershed health or "integrity," i.e., adequate ecological function with all watershed components intact. Since salmon are central to Indigenous cultures of Pacific North America, they can also be described as a cultural or ecocultural keystone species.

The Salmon Homecoming Ceremony, now being revived by some tribes and bands after a hiatus in some cases of 150 years or more, celebrates the return of salmon to their birthing rivers and streams, at the same time it highlights the social harmony between humans and salmon. Salmon were thought by some cultural groups to be humans who lived in houses under the sea, who would return as salmon. Representing Salmon Nation, they were accorded the respect and honor deserving of royalty, part of an ancient Indigenous story that Lichatowich has recorded in his book, *Salmon Without Rivers: A History of the Pacific Salmon Crisis* (Lichatowich, 1999: 36). A salmon feast was held and the remaining salmon bones and skin would be placed on western red cedar sprigs (a cultural keystone tree species) and taken to the bottom of the river by young Native men. Remembering the "Original Compact" between animals and humans, the salmon would see the remains and, knowing they were being treated with the requisite respect, reconstituted themselves and returned the next season and for as long as humans treated them as befitting visiting royal salmon ambassadors. Following the ceremony and after the community had taken what it needed, a newly constructed weir spanning the river and temporarily blocking salmon passage (usually for 10 days) would be opened daily, allowing salmon to again swim upstream to spawn, feeding neighboring upstream communities. All of the animals, birds, and creepy-crawlers, as well as the forest itself, benefited from these nutrients – mostly from the ocean where the salmon had been for several years (in their decomposing bodies following spawning and spread by the birds, animals, and insects to a distance of up to one kilometer on either side of streams) – and depended on this prodigious feast for survival and regeneration. In the case of some bear, bird, and insect species, salmon nutrients were distributed a distance of several kilometers and affected entire watersheds. The people then had shown their appreciation to the salmon dignitaries. The salmon would return again, and ocean and forest and humans and salmon were ritually and materially united – with benefits spread out over the entire watershed.

Indigenous peoples of Pacific North America are Salmon People and want to *continue* being Salmon People. Because of salmon they were an affluent people of great social and cultural richness with a sophisticated political and legal system that was linked to similarly sophisticated river/land-care and harvest technologies. A stable food supply was ensured by the deliberate spread of salmon, increasing their abundance, diversity, and distribution, while enhancing the complexity of salmon habitats through a diversity of cultural practices. Ocean conditions, then as now, were constantly changing. Given the uncertainty of the ocean, Native peoples focused on caring for salmon freshwater habitats: estuaries, rivers, and streams. Failures were not common but they were not unknown and were never forgotten, providing a compelling reason for conservation and honoring of the Original Compact. The most recent example that I know is the 2012 sockeye salmon run that missed its normal southern route when the fish were pushed north by El Niño-driven warmer waters, missing western Washington and Oregon completely and ending up in northern British Columbia and Arctic rivers, including the Fraser River in British Columbia where I was able to observe the largest sockeye run in living memory. But Puget Sound tribes got very little. Similar events would happen periodically in the past – even occurring over several years running according to oral accounts.

Historic salmon river-care practices are not well known. Lacking today's sophisticated statistics and algorithms of science, Indigenous peoples did not crunch numbers, but they knew well how salmon populations were faring, what interventions were called for, and when and how frequently they were needed. What were some of these historical practices? Nigel Haggan, Irish-Canadian fisheries professor at the University of British Columbia's Fisheries Centre, has done pioneering research in the history of Indigenous marine and aquatic cultural salmon-care practices, assisted by his close familial and professional association with the Nuu-chal-nulth First Nations of Vancouver Island. Some of his findings are included here. For example, following large storms, Natives cleaned gravel-spawning beds, and when necessary, they removed log jams. Sandspits blocking late summer/early autumn Chinook salmon runs were also opened.

The oral tradition in southwestern Oregon and northwestern California reports cases where early white settlers did not allow Indians to unblock sandspits that build up at the mouths of rivers or estuaries, blocking salmon's entrance to rivers when sufficient rains arrived. The result was that very soon an entire late-summer/early-autumn Chinook salmon run was extinct (Lake, personal communication, 2010). This story illustrates the dependence of some species on human care. Trees were felled to divert stream flows into side channels, creating storm-safe back eddies and side channels for overwintering Coho salmon and flushing sediments from spawning beds. Salmon spawn were transplanted in damp moss to streams with few or no salmon (Sproat, 1968). Clam and oyster beds were constructed in the coastal intertidal zones in Washington state and British Columbia. Herring nurseries, consisting of hemlock boughs stuck in estuary and river-mouth bottoms where herring laid their eggs, were regularly maintained (and still are in some places on the British Columbia and Alaskan coasts). Sophisticated fish and lobster traps were constructed that could screen unwanted fish while allowing desired species into the trap, eliminating by-catch waste. Intertidal stonefish traps were also constructed; remnants of these can still be observed from the air. Drying racks and smoking/storage methods enabled the people to have their fish dinners and smoked and cured salmon "candy" desserts throughout the year (Gunther, 1926: 424–26; Haggan, 2013; Williams, 2006). Salmon were flumed or carried around landslides or ice blockages (Campbell and Butler, 2010: 17; Sproat, 1968). This practice occurred most recently in 1913 following a huge slide in the Fraser River at Hell's Gate Canyon – with Coastal Salish Indians saving sockeye salmon runs (Lichatowich, 1999: 173–75).

Watershed terrestrial systems were also well tended. Prescribed burning was the primary land-care tool, especially in southern parts of the salmon region and in the interior mountains everywhere. Deliberately set low-intensity fires were frequently set – every one to ten years or more depending on vegetation type, cultural use or objective, and season. The fires created and maintained a constantly changing patchy landscape mosaic of burns with vegetation in varying stages of development. The most recent vegetation-free burns (called "black lines" by prescribed fire professionals today) also prevented fires from getting away and burning more than was intended. These burns had a number of objectives, including keeping forest fuels low enough to prevent major conflagrations. Burns were beneficial to salmon and other freshwater aquatic species and habitats because they reduced water loss via evapo-transpiration from brush and small trees. Larger mature and old-growth trees help create higher humidity and, in some cases, rain and fog-drip through the condensation of atmospheric moisture on leaves and needles. Appropriate burning increased groundwater quantity and quality as water slowly filtered underground to emerge cold enough to benefit salmon and other aquatic species in stream headwaters. In this way, fire can be a tool for water conservation (Bonnickson et al., 1997: 439–70; Lewis, 1973; Martinez, 1993: 23–28).

These and other land-care practices were sustainably maintained by a land tenure system that divided responsibilities for the care of fisheries and other life-forms – terrestrial freshwater aquatic and marine, e.g., good fishing places, farmed herring, clam and oyster beds, and intertidal fish traps – into units of local responsibility. There were harvesting rights by individuals, families, and clans nested within a larger collective band or tribal regulatory structure through which experienced knowledge specialists and other leaders had the last word on harvest practices. These practices were based on several key variables including appropriate year, season, harvestable amounts, kinds of species, places off limits, amount of time allowed for harvesting in a particular place, fallowing schedules, kinds and scheduling of land or river-care practices, limits during both normal times and times of regional or seasonal shortages, and observance of dozens of special tabooss. Indigenous regulatory authority and responsible use of the commons avoided Garrett Hardin's (1968) well-known and quite misunderstood "tragedy of the commons." This kind of local responsibility with oversight during hard times and the experience of knowledge specialists generally was the key to Indigenous environmental sustainability, and sets the Indigenous ethical-economic model apart from the dominant modern capitalist model and its irresponsible winner-take-all "free market" – the true tragedy of the commons that was once mistakenly blamed on regulated collective harvesting practices.

One could argue that industrial fishery researchers also have access to their own "knowledge specialists": Western science specialists and local fishers who are well-acquainted with their particular fishing locales can offer informed opinions on the number of harvestable fish, spawning and rearing places, ratio of juvenile to mature fish, prey-predator relationships, habitat quality, diseases, and so on. Theoretically at least, fishers and industry managers discourage overharvesting, as do government fishing regulations enforced by fines and jail sentences. In spite of this knowledge, regulations, and government policing and punishment, fish populations have been declining for a long time and, now, commercially important fish species such as cod and salmon, once so numerous that the idea of their endangerment was unthinkable, are on the edge of extinction.

The industrial ethos of maximizing profits and the fishing methods that facilitated profit making at any cost, fisher greed or desperation, and an ideology or belief system that encouraged free-wheeling fishing are critical factors in fish endangerment. The main factors leading to the debacle that fish and fisheries are in now are: industrial managers sitting on political fisheries oversight committees; extremely lax fishery regulations (until recently due to public-political pressure); and the scientific belief in mechanistic fixes such as hatcheries (all exacerbated by global warming). Simply put, the industrial fisheries' managers have the political clout to influence government oversight agencies and state legislatures to write regulations that benefited their bottom lines. Ethics, in the end, has not played a significant role in the harvesting of fish.

A key aspect of the kincentric model is the personal and familiar relationship between the people and salmon, a relationship that has been severely weakened by industrial fisheries. Indigenous fishers know well the penalties for overharvesting or failing to practice good salmon-care such as restoring and maintaining quality aquatic habitats. They have seen it happen before many times.

Fisheries historian Lichatowich puts his finger directly on the real problem when he tells us that "the industrial economy set the co-evolutionary clock back to zero, throwing aside all that had been learned since humans harvested their first salmon. ..." Lichatowich's remarks underscore the great length of time that humans have understood kincentricity and how quickly this understanding of respectful behavior toward other life forms has been lost (Lichatowich, 1999: 44). Indigenous subsistence fishing is informed by "a sustainable relationship between the natural economy of the region's ecosystems and the gift economy of the Indians ... This change [industrialization] weakens the negative feedback loops between fish and fishers, making it virtually impossible for a sustainable relationship to co-evolve between the fish and industrial economy" (Lichatowich, 1999: 44).

In other words, if Indians had overharvested fish long enough, they would have starved. No such negative feedback is possible in a horizontally integrated industrial fishery with several other commercial options available besides fishing. The big fisheries companies profited while the small fishers barely made a living or were forced out (the fate of most fishers today) as each tried to maximize his or her catch – the tragedy of the commons that the Indigenous ethical-economic model had prevented due to its relationship-based kincentric gift economy. The same impossible endeavor to achieve "maximum sustainable yields" has been the primary reason for the destruction of the Northern Hemisphere's temperate old-growth forests. "Maximum" and "sustainable" do not belong together. Indigenous peoples know that the natural world has its own evolved ways and rates of change, and that humans are obliged to work within these parameters or fail. Put another way, *Natural Law is non-negotiable.*

Lichatowich argues that the ultimate cause of the spectacular decline of salmon is the clash of two very different economies: The natural and the industrial. He sums up the difference this way: "The gift economy of the Indians evolved a sustained balance with natural economy. Eventually the industrial economy will have to evolve a balanced relationship with the natural economy of the Pacific Northwest." The different objectives, operating principles, and perspectives lead in opposite directions and to opposing outcomes: "The industrial economy encourages individualism, extraction, economies of scale, and simplification of natural systems, whereas the health of the natural economy depends on interdependence, renewal, dispersal of production and diversity" (Lichatowich, 1999: 47). We see the results of the near-total commodification of nature in the present imminent-extinction of wild salmon, even though their mortality rates are half that of hatchery salmon (Lichatowich, 1999: 47). The few remaining rivers and streams that still offer adequate habitats to reproduce and rear young salmon *naturally* are not enough to save wild salmon despite genetic diversity borne of their adaptation to place. Yet most salmon biologists continue to support hatcheries.

I return to Whitehead's idea of "misplaced concreteness" to explain this willful ignorance when the empirical evidence fails to support the use of hatcheries to reproduce salmon that are able to survive ocean conditions for two to five years without high mortality. As scientists well know, hatchery salmon are becoming increasingly vulnerable to extreme climate events. The continuing loss of quality riverine or estuarine habitats and water quality are likely to worsen as climate destabilization continues to test the ability of poorly adapted salmon to survive. Only a long-entrenched ideology seems capable of trumping empirical evidence for otherwise intelligent scientists. In *Adventures of Ideas,* Alfred North Whitehead writes, "When the routine is perfect, understanding can be eliminated ... A system will be the product of intelligence. But when the adequate routine is established, intelligence vanishes, and system is maintained by a coordination of conditioned reflexes" (Whitehead in Deloria et al., 1999: 101–02).

A *"scientific"* way of thinking becomes "*a coordination of conditioned reflexes*" given enough time. Hunkpapa Lakota thinker and author Vine Deloria, Jr. adds to Whitehead's remarks: "We are living in a strange kind of dark ages where we have immense capability to bring together information but when we gather this data, we pigeonhole it in the old familiar framework of interpretation, sometimes even torturing the data to make it fit. Discordant facts and experiments are simply thrown away when they do not fit the prevailing paradigm" (Deloria et al., 1999: 101). This is how much of Western science works. Historian of science Thomas Kuhn makes the same argument as Deloria in his 1962 seminal study, *The Structure of Scientific Revolutions* (although, ironically, Deloria uses this Kuhnian argument to show how poorly science performs). Kuhn (1962) tells us about paradigm "anomalies" that eventually become so numerous that they refuse to fit present theory, so a scientific "revolution" occurs and a new theory emerges over a generation or two that is able to make sense of and finally incorporate the anomalies.

Students are taught that science, through the slow and linear process of a gradual accumulation of knowledge, becomes ever closer to "the truth" and that sooner or later all mysteries will be explained by science. In fact Western science progresses through fits and starts and the eventual overturning of former closely held and cherished beliefs. So let's examine some scientific beliefs: the belief in hatcheries, the belief that technological progress (including green technology) will save us from climate change; the belief that capitalism is potentially sustainable, that it is the solution and not the problem and will be able to feed the world without damaging the environment; the belief that Indigenous peoples are too primitive and technologically inept to have influenced the environment for the better; the belief (for conservationists) that nature works best without human interference and, therefore, Indigenous peoples should be removed from conservation reserves and parks; and so on. This is *opposite* of the other popular industrialists' perspective that nature doesn't work well *unless* manipulated by science and technology.

Having examined the failure of the Western neoliberal economic model to provide a pathway to sustainability, I now turn to the Indigenous ethical–economic model in order to show the ways Indigenous stewards go beyond mere ecological *classification* to *modeling* what Reichel-Domatoff (1976) hypothesized as *"trophic webs and energy flows"* inherent in Indigenous peoples' cosmologies (International Indigenous Commission [IIC], 1991: 2).[1] However, even more relevant, the Indigenous model is based on the ways in which Native peoples integrated their kincentric ethic of reciprocity into land-care praxis and the restraints that control resource harvesting.

Traditional Land-Care Practices Defined: Models, Objectives, and Controls

What follows is based on the International Indigenous Commission (IIC) (1991) report, *Indigenous Peoples' Traditional Knowledge and Management Practices,* circulated at the 1992 Rio Earth Summit and presented to the United Nations Conference on Environment and Development. The report was provided to the UN and later to the World Parks Congress (WPC) to show that Indigenous environmental caregiving is as important to the conservation of nature in protected areas as universal human rights. IIC, however, stressed secure *land tenure rights* that legally allowed Indigenous stewards to continue to exercise their conservation responsibilities. Both rights and secure stewardship are important to conservation, but the global protected-areas conservation movement,

---

[1] For example, the work that non-Indigenous ethno-scientists have done documenting *Indigenous* taxonomies and identifying Indigenous cultural flora or fauna that could be useful to the world, is often associated with "bioprospecting" for pharmaceutical plants. Rarely are Indigenous communities compensated for what amounts to blatant burglary.

represented by the World Parks Congress, was more interested in the rights issue than in the Indigenous land-care expertise that IIC believed was critically important to the future of conservation. Human rights, critical to social justice, are based on our inherent or reserved rights as human beings with every right to be secure in our places (Poole, 2012). *Period*. But this kind of universal right says nothing specifically about the value of Indigenous land management. While the IIC report refers to "management," most Indigenous people prefer not to use the term because it implies domination or control; some prefer *land-care* or *care-giving* (as I do), or other terms that convey keeping the earth in balance; or, in the way expressed by one Cree elder, "*match* [the land] *to their thinking*" (IIC, 1991: 3). The IIC also rejected the Western idea of "pristine" nature – an arrow aimed right at the heart of a protected area and conservation movement that believed it was protecting an autogenic or self-organizing nature that worked best *without* people – code for: worked best without Indigenous stewards.

Another Indigenous group, The Indigenous Agendas for Conservation (IAC), is composed of an international network of 100 Indigenous communities. As of 2011, ninety-six are still active. During the period of 1970–1990, IAC documented 100 community-driven stewardship/conservation projects throughout North America. Peter Poole, a longtime British-Canadian Indigenous cultural and land tenure rights activist and aerial cartographer, has reported on both IIC's and IAC's work, documenting numerous global tribal conservation/stewardship community land-care practices and projects. In the 1991 IIC UN report, traditional land care is divided into three dimensions: models, objectives, and controls. We have already encountered *controls* in the traditional harvest regulatory structure discussion. Ultimately, it comes down to personal responsibility, rewarded, as IIC informs us, with "high status" in Native communities. IIC notes that, in general, control of resources is inherent in what the Western world calls a "conservation ethic." Many Western anthropologists and other academics assumed that the highly rational subsistence hunting-gathering practices are wasteful or mindlessly destructive, and certainly by no means close to an ethic. But resource use for Indigenous peoples is a matter of making "*social choices*" about the "*rate of resource use*" within the limits of sustainability *in order to increase the availability of useful resources* (IIC, 1991: 1; Poole, 2012). This was usually done by prescribed fire to enhance ecological productivity as well as the creation of a biodiversity surplus.

Indigenous land-care praxis attempts not to overuse resources, unlike Western "utilitarian" conservation ethics that, while attempting not to overuse resources, stop short of the Indigenous ethical-economic model, which not only conserves resources but also increases their availability and diversity through appropriate land-care practices. This fact belies another Western myth: the lack of technology is one reason Indigenous peoples could not greatly affect their environments (even as some accuse Indigenous peoples of destroying their environment). Technology was never an issue because social choices were made about resource use based on sustainability, not technology (IIC, 1991: 1), although generally Indigenous peoples will use introduced technology that can make life easier, e.g., guns, skidoos, and matches.

For IIC, these *models* accurately reflect an understanding of ecosystems: "how the component species of ecosystems interact, and how they are affected by human activities." The report tells us that since the universe "is continually running down (entropy) it requires periodic renewal by its human occupants." Nature "is dynamic, finite, and fragile"; this perception influences the conservative way that Indigenous peoples take care of their resources (IIC, 1991: 2). Canadian Blackfoot (Blood Band) elder and philosopher Leroy Little Bear sees nature in "continual flux" (Little Bear, 2000: x). His comment corresponds roughly to a relatively new and influential paradigm in ecological theory: Nature is dynamic, stochastic, chaotic, complex, unpredictable, and random.

IIC sees *objectives* as reflecting the human aspect of ecology. "Objectives" is where ethics meets economics in the Indigenous ethical-economic model. The report points out a critical difference between the Indigenous model and Western market-oriented economies: "the maintenance of large resources of unexploited capacity and sharing of output" (IIC, 1991: 3).

To summarize, the essence of the Indigenous model is the *conservative* nature of traditional land care: Maintaining surplus biodiversity with limits always in mind and with people and resources always in balance. I have found five essential categories of IIC "objectives" that are the principle expressions of the Indigenous ethical-economic model integrating the conventionally separated categories of social and ecological. The first is the Indigenous concept of *ownership*: ownership of resources (berry patches, good fishing places, oak groves, basket plant stands) includes the responsibility to take care of the resources one uses; assuming conservation responsibilities for one's own turf; and sharing in time of need. Second: "Minimum necessary yield" or leaving a biodiversity surplus trumps "maximum sustained yield." We have already learned that so-called maximum sustained yield (clear-cutting of forests) is an illusion that has profited a few and harmed others, as well as the environment. Third: people are obliged in the creation of biodiversity to promote ecological stability and diverse production in a constantly changing environment (IIC, 1991: 8). This enhancement goes beyond the Western utilitarian ethic by intentionally promoting increased production, but in ways that are ecologically appropriate, even if humans are not the primary beneficiary (e.g., prescribed fire positively affects many more species than only the cultural targets). This enlarged scope of ecological enhancement promotes diversity that has a long-term stabilizing effect on ecosystems (IIC, 1991: 5). Intentional Indigenous burning was (and still is, where allowed) the most important land-care tool for creating biodiversity. Fourth: Obey Natural Law, e.g., do not force plants or animals to grow, for instance, by using genetically modified organisms (GMOs), because doing so leads to loss of long-term ecological stability and productivity as well as species extinctions. Fifth: Use incentives for wealth redistribution; examples include Potlatch ceremonies, sharing in hard times, kinship obligations, community-enforced shame for the greedy, harvest taboos, and spiritual retribution.

These five categories are part of "kincentric ecology" and constitute the Indigenous redefinition of sustainability. Kincentric ecology encompasses the principles embedded in biodiversity surplus, including the creation of diverse economies and habitats via prescribed fire. It is conservative and not risk averse, planning for the *worst* yearly outcomes, not for an average year as in Western economics. This approach understands that continuous economic growth is a destabilizing force. Additionally, sharing and wealth redistribution is essential to real sustainability. This approach is based on the careful observance of Natural Law, such as creating diversity to make and maintain stability or not pushing plant or animal growth to unnatural destabilization levels, such as those seen in genetic engineering (IIC, 1991: 7).[2]

Continuing with the concept of positive human involvement in ecosystems, I now outline the importance of *ecocultural restoration* (its analogue term *biocultural* is used more frequently, especially internationally).[3] By *ecocultural restoration*, I mean "the process of recovering as

[2] For a detailed explanation of how Kincentric ecology can be applied to current political ecological thinking, see Altieri and Toledo, (2011: 587–612). The authors discuss how Indigenous agroecological paradigms driven by the Indigenous economic/ethical model are challenging neoliberal modernization policies in Latin America.
[3] A term that Jeffrey Thomas of the Puyallup tribe in western Washington state and I began using around the same time in 1993.

much as is recoverable of the key historic precontact or preindustrial eco-system structure, composition, processes, and function, along with tra-ditional, time-tested, ecologically appropriate and sustainable Indigenous cultural practices that helped shape ecosystems, while simultaneously building in resilience to future rapid climate disruptions and other envi-ronmental changes in order to maintain ecological integrity in a way that ensures the survival of both Indigenous ecosystems and culture" (Higgs and Martinez, 1996). This definition is novel in that it explicitly recog-nizes that much, though certainly not all, of what is called "nature" has included a strong positive cultural component until the advent of Western industrial society. Because Western science has rarely acknowledged the positive contributions of Indigenous cultures to nature, the Western envi-ronmental movement has advocated the removal of Indigenous peoples from their homelands. This strategy has had severe unanticipated reper-cussions for natural systems and Indigenous peoples alike because of a universally accepted fact in the fields of ecology and wildlife biology: the removal of *any* keystone or apex species leads to the unraveling of intact food webs and eventually to ecological collapse. Until Western science and conservation/environmental communities understand that Indigenous peoples and/or a modern equivalent (where Indigenous mod-els are lacking) belong in so-called pristine ecosystems, we may have lost our last good opportunity for sustainability.

The issues before us, before the world, are serious. The global situ-ation for Indigenous peoples is worsening, the enclosure of the global commons is extending to the last open spaces, and the last traditional peoples who carry the living ecocultural heritage of all humanity, a her-itage that extends back tens of thousands of years, are disappearing. Traditional Ecological Knowledge, or TEK, indeed all traditional knowl-edge, is not safe or helpful buried in the libraries and archives of aca-demia unless it continues as *living* knowledge rooted in the homelands of Indigenous peoples, continuing to adapt and change as environmental conditions change. When lands are lost, the peoples dispersed, traditional knowledge and hard-won environmental know-how *and* Western sci-ence lose. Ecological understanding by science is diminished. Accurate knowledge of what restoration should be restoring and what conserva-tion should be conserving is lost. An understanding of sustainability from an Indigenous perspective is lost, a meaning that is neither economics-without-environment nor nature-without-humans but both, requiring appropriate human interventions in nature that are based on a sustaining model of kincentric reciprocity. This model restrains economic activities when they infringe on our relationship to the natural world, of which we are a contributing and caring part.

To our future generations!

WORKS CITED

Alcorn, Janice B. "Indigenous Peoples and Conservation." *Conservation Biology*, 7 (2), 1993, 424–26.

Altieri, Miguel A., and Victor Manuel Toledo. "The Agroecological Revolution in Latin America: Rescuing Nature, Ensuring Food Sovereignty and empowering Peasants." *The Journal of Peasant Studies*, 38 (3), 2011, 587–612.

Bonnicksen, Thomas, Katherine Anderson, Henry Lewis, Charles Kay, and R. Knudson. "Native American Influences on the Development of Forest Systems in Ecological Stewardship." *Humans as Agents of Ecological Change*. Oxford, UK: Elsevier Science, 1997, 439–470.

Campbell, Sara K. and Virginia L. Butler. "Archaeological Evidence for Resilience of Pacific Northwest Salmon Populations and the Sociological System Over the last ~7,500 years." *Ecology and Society*, 15 (1), 2010, 17.

De Bary, Theodore and Richard Lufrano. *Sources of Chinese Tradition: From 1600 Through the Twentieth Century*, Volume 2. New York: Columbia University Press, 2000.

Deloria, Vine, Jr., Kristen Foehner, and Sam Scinta. *Spirit & Reason: The Vine Deloria, Jr. Reader*. Golden, CO: Fulcrum Publishing, 1999.

Dobyns, Henry. *Their Number Became Thinned*. Knoxville: University of Tennessee Press, 1983.

Dowie, Mark. *Conservation Refugees: The Hundred Year Conflict Between Global Conservation and Native Peoples*. Cambridge, MA: MIT Press, 2011.

First Peoples Worldwide. Field Report, 2011. [online] URL: www.firstpeoples.org

Foster, John Bellamy. "The New Imperialism of Globalized Monopoly Finance-Capital." *Monthly Review*, 67 (3), 2015. [online] URL: https://monthlyreview.org/2015/07/01/the-new-imperialism-of-globalized-monopoly-finance-capital/.

Foster, John Bellamy, Brett Clark, and Richard York. *The Ecological Rift: Capitalisms War on the Earth*. New York: Monthly Review Press, 2010.

Foster, John Bellamy and Michael Yates. "Thomas Piketty and the Crisis of Neoclassical Economics." *Monthly Review*, 66 (6), 2014, 1–24.

Gaonkar, Dilip Parameshwar. *Alternative Modernities*. Durham, NC: Duke University Press, 2001.

Georgescu-Roegen, Nicholas. *The Entropy Law & Economic Process*. Cambridge, MA: Harvard University Press, 1971.

Gunther, E. "An Analysis of the First Salmon Ceremony." *American Anthropologist*, 28 (605), 1926, 617.

Hardin, Garrett. "The Tragedy of the Commons." *Science*, 162 (3859), 1968. 1243–48.

Higgs, Eric and Dennis Martinez. *Minutes of the Board of Directors of the Society for Ecological Restoration: Revision of Definition of Escological*

Restoration by Science and Policy Working Group Co-chaired by Eric Higgs and Dennis Martinez. Rutgers University, New Jersey, 1996. [online] URL: www.ser.org

International Indigenous Commission (IIC). *Indigenous Peoples' Traditional Knowledge & Management Practices.* Report circulated at 1992 Rio Earth Summit and presented to the United Nations Conference on Environment and Development, 1991, 1–8.

International Labor Organization (ILO) Convention 169, article 14. *Refugees: The Hundred Year Conflict Between Global Conservation and Native Peoples,* edited by Mark Dowie. Cambridge, MA: MIT Press, 2011.

Krugman, Paul. "Why We're in a New Gilded Age." *New York Review of Books,* May 8, 2014, www.nybooks.com/articles/2014/05/08/thomas-piketty-new-gilded-age/.

Kuhn, Thomas. *The Structure of Scientific Revolutions.* Chicago: University of Chicago Press, 1962.

Lewis, Henry. *Patterns of Indian Burning in California.* Menlo Park, CA: Ballena Books, 1973.

Lichatowich, James. *Salmon Without Rivers: A History of the Pacific Salmon Crisis.* Washington, DC: Island Press, 1999.

Lichatowich, James and Seth Zuckerman. "Muddled Waters, Muddled Thinkers." *Salmon Nation: People and Fish at the Edge,* edited by Edward C. Wolf. Portland, OR: Ecotrust, 2003, 17–31.

Little Bear, Leroy. "Foreword." *Native Science: Natural Laws of Interdependence, edited* by Gregory Cajete. Santa Fe: Clear Light Publishing, 2000, ix–xiii.

Magdoff, Harry. "Remarks on Capitalism and the Environment it Produces." *Monthly Review,* 67 (4), 2015, 9.

Malthus, Thomas R. *An Essay on the Principle of Population.* Cambridge, UK: Cambridge University Press, 1992.

Mann, Charles C. *1491: New Revelations of the Americas Before Columbus.* New York: Alfred Knopf, 2005.

1493: Uncovering the New World Columbus Discovered. New York: Alfred Knopf, 2011.

Martinez, Dennis. "Karuk Tribal Module for the Main Stem River Watershed Analysis: Karuk Ancestral Lands and People as Reference Ecosystem for Eco-cultural Restoration." *Collaborative Ecosystem Management,* Issue 41, US Klamath National Forest, 1995.

"Managing a Precarious Balance: Wilderness versus Sustainable Forestry." *Winds of Change,* 8 (3), 1993, 23–28.

"The Missing Delegate at Cancun: Indigenous Peoples." *National Geographic News Watch,* December 8, 2010, online publication.

Marx, Karl. In John Bellamy Foster, "Marxism and Ecology: Common Fonts of a Great Transition." *Great Transition Initiative,* October 2015. [online] URL: www.greattransition.org/publication/marxism-and-ecology.

Merchant, Carolyn. *The Death of Nature: Women, Ecology, and the Scientific Revolution.* San Francisco: Harper & Row, 1983.

Pearce, David. *Blueprint 3: Measuring Sustainable Development.* London: Earthscan, 1993.

Pearce, Fred. *The Land Grabbers: The New Fight Over Who Owns the Earth.* Boston, MA: Beacon Press, 2012.

Piketty, Thomas. *Capital in the Twenty-First Century.* Cambridge, MA: Harvard University Press, 2014.

Reichel-Domatoff, Gerardo. "Cosmology as Ecological Analysis: A View from the Rainforest." *Man*, 11 (3), 1976, 307–18.

Saito, Kohei. "Marx on Ecology: New Insights from his Notebooks." *Monthly Review*, 67 (9), 2015, 26.

Salmon, Enrique. "Kincentric Ecology: Indigenous Perceptions of the Human-Nature Relationship." *Ecological Applications*, 10 (5), 2000, 1327–32.

Shephard, Paul and Florence R. Shephard. *Coming Home to the Pleistocene.* Washington, DC: Island Press, 1998.

Sproat, Gilbert Malcolm. *The Nootka: Scenes and Studies of Savage Life.* London: Smith, Elder, 1968.

Tarnas, Richard. *The Passion for the Western Mind: Understanding the Ideas That Have Shaped Our World.* New York: Random House, 1991.

Toledo, Victor. "Indigenous Peoples & Biodiversity." *Encyclopedia of Biodiversity*, edited by Simon A. Levin. Amsterdam: Elsevier Academic Press, 2001, 451–463.

Whitehead, Alfred North. *Adventures of Ideas.* New York: Macmillan, 1933.

Williams, Judith. *Clam Gardens: Aboriginal Mariculture on Canada's West Coast.* Vancouver, BC: New Star Books, 2006.

Worldwide Fund for Nature (WWFN). "Global 200 Projects." Reported in Steven Sanderson's keynote address to Conservation Biology's annual convention, October 7, 2008.

10

Indigenous Food Sovereignty in Canada

Priscilla Settee

Some years ago, for an Indigenous women and wellness national conference, I put together a poster called "the Garden: a metaphor for health." The poster was based on my interest in community gardening as an excellent pastime for good physical and mental health, as well as a beneficial source of tasty and healthy foods and a way to meet and work with people interested in the same issues. Coming from hunting and gathering and agricultural peoples, I have always had an interest in food as an inspirational focal point around community well-being, Indigenous sovereignty, land protection, community development, exercise, and health. All these issues inevitably have women at the center. This essay will define and discuss food sovereignty and describe some of the work Indigenous peoples are involved in regarding "food sovereignty." It outlines some causes of the loss of food sovereignty, some history of Indigenous food traditions and contributions, the impact of Western "development" and the energy sector on food sovereignty, health consequences caused by a lack of good food, and solutions to the challenges. The issue will be placed within a broader context of community wellness and health and Indigenous sovereignty.

During the 1970s, I worked for Saskatchewan Indian Agriculture Program as a field worker. My job was to assist communities growing gardens and to identify agricultural challenges. My work was not named food sovereignty but in many aspects that's what it was. I was there for two years and was interested in seeing how communities could restore balance and healing through the regeneration of community gardens from the ground up. As a second-generation urban First Nations person, I was intrigued by the self-sufficiency and knowledge of northern and land-based communities. Working in northern Saskatchewan in the mid 1970s, I witnessed an environmental transformation of communities that went from self-sufficiency to being negatively impacted by development in the form of forest clear-cuts and mining. Virtually the only reliable and nutritious community foods were those that were traditionally hunted and gathered, which were increasingly threatened. Local stores offered foods imported from the south at inflated prices. Junk foods, brightly packaged and high in calories and carbohydrates, were readily available. These foods have had devastating impacts on the health of my people in a relatively short period of time.

Working in southern Saskatchewan, I saw that industrial agriculture, while it helped feed the nation, did not acknowledge what impact it was having on small family farms and Canada's food system. I was trying to do a larger and perhaps socio-political analysis of how Western culture's food production was actually creating poverty, hunger, and injustice both locally and globally. The evidence was everywhere, particularly in northern communities. At the time I was deeply inspired (and still am) by the work of Susan George, who is president of Transnational Institute, an Amsterdam-based organization whose work focuses on global social justice, underdevelopment, and debt. Shortly thereafter I was "released from my duties" for showing the film *How the Other Half Dies*, a documentary that says food famines are avoidable, but food is increasingly under the control of the corporate sector, not ordinary farmers. The film was apparently too radical for the organization (which has since folded).

I was interested in food security/sovereignty in those early days because my own community experienced tremendous disruptions resulting from an upstream dam built in the 1940s. The dam, which has led to the near economic collapse of the community (Settee, 2013), is only one example of the development policy and practices of various governments in Saskatchewan's north. The impact of the dam on the tiny First Nations and Métis community of Cumberland House, which depended on the area's natural resources, was catastrophic yet, ironically, the northerners' (primarily Indigenous) power rates were much higher than southerners. Any disruption to the natural environment can have devastating impacts on local and Indigenous peoples in a hunting and gathering society, and Cumberland House was no exception. The dam altered water levels in the Saskatchewan River, which made the area uninhabitable for many animals. The dam wiped out many local gardens and dried up natural wetlands, forcing much of the wild bird, duck, and moose populations to disappear from the area. Because of the dam, within a few years the community went from a thriving subsistence economy to one that was no longer able to adequately provide for its members.

Today, Indigenous people of Cumberland House and elsewhere are faced with epidemic rates of diabetes and other preventable diseases brought on by a number of socioeconomic/development and food-related factors. The film *My Big Fat Diet* describes how Indigenous peoples are suffering particularly from high rates of diabetes, obesity, and related diseases. The film tells the inspiring story of an Alert Bay community in Northern British Columbia that identified food-related illnesses and began focusing on food challenges under the leadership of Dr. Jay Wortmann, a Métis physician from northern Alberta. Alert Bay's traditional seafood diet included shellfish, cod, and salmon but, because of a loss of traditional food sources, a diabetes crisis arose that was three to five times higher than the national average. In response, people gave up sugar and starch for one year and saw a dramatic change in their weight, wherein they collectively shed thousands of pounds. Similarly in *Harvesting Hope*, a film based on stories from northern Manitoba, the University of Manitoba research team headed by Dr. Shirley Thompson describes the epidemic of diabetes that plagues the region with graphic stories of loss of limbs and lives. The film also describes community-based responses, such as school gardens, and raises awareness of larger food-sovereignty issues.

Many of us can tell personal stories of relatives losing eyesight and limbs or, worse, suffering an early death as a result of diabetes, loss of traditional foods, sedentary lifestyles, and the availability of "junk" foods. The loss of traditional and usually outdoor work and means of production contributes to the diabetes epidemic. Even though some young people have taken jobs at fly-in mining sites, this response to new employment opportunities has not helped and may have contributed to epidemic youth suicides that plague our communities. It is a simple equation that when land is taken, the local economy suffers along with the sense of Native identity, and a people's physical and spiritual health deteriorates.

Fast forward to 2013: accelerated resource extraction has spelled further disaster for Indigenous peoples, including clear-cuts, toxic sludge pools in Alberta's tar sands, nuclear dumpsites in northern Saskatchewan, expropriation of traditional hunting and gathering lands for the Primrose Bombing range (and other land grabs), and mercury poisoning from pulp-mill effluent of the Anishinabe people of Grassy Narrows, among other environmental devastation. Saskatchewan is particularly vulnerable because, in addition to clear-cuts and dams, the area is a major uranium-mining province. While no studies have been done in Saskatchewan, other Indigenous regions mined for uranium produce troubling statistics. For example, in the American Southwest, uranium mining has produced cancers and greatly damaged food-producing lands. In terms of both short- and long-term environmental impacts, uranium mining is by far the most environmentally problematic of any mining activity because the ore's radioactivity presents an intangible that cannot be chemically mitigated. Even after mining activities ceased on the Navajo Nation, the legacy of environmental harm continued, such as the 1979 disaster at Church Rock, the largest accidental release of radioactive material in US history. At the New Mexico site, a tailing dam burst, sending eleven hundred tons of radioactive mill wastes and ninety million gallons of contaminated liquid into the Rio Puerco River, pouring into Arizona. The Navajo still cannot use this water (see Ali, 2003).

These and other examples represent a direct threat to traditional food sovereignty and related water security of Indigenous peoples. Food sovereignty, as defined by the Nyelani Declaration, means having access to healthy, culturally appropriate, delicious, and nutritious foods. The Nyelani Declaration is named after a legendary West African woman who worked hard and innovatively to feed and care for her people from Mali. Food sovereignty requires that the producer benefit from his/her work. Another definition says:

Food sovereignty is the right of peoples to healthy and culturally appropriate food produced through ecologically sound and sustainable methods, and their right to define their own food and agriculture systems. It puts those who produce, distribute and consume food at the heart of food systems and policies rather than the demands of markets and corporations. It defends the interests and inclusion of the next generation. It offers a strategy to resist and dismantle the current corporate trade and food regime, and directions for food, farming, pastoral and fisheries systems determined by local producers. Food sovereignty prioritises local and national economies and markets and empowers peasant and family farmer-driven agriculture, artisanal – fishing, pastoralist-led grazing, and food production, distribution and consumption based on environmental, social and economic sustainability. (Via Campesina, 2015)

But it is something more. Considering the many environmental catastrophes on Indigenous lands, food sovereignty is linked to the energy sector, i.e., mining of oil, gas, and water. A critical relationship exists between the energy sector, how mainstream food is produced, and

Indigenous land and food sovereignty. Our mainstream food system – industrial agriculture, intensive livestock production, including factory farms – has a troubling and problematic reliance on the fossil fuel industry (Ervin et al., 2003). Food production has been taken out of the hands of the community and is controlled, with devastating consequences, by the corporate energy sector.

Indigenous Knowledge Contributions to Global Food Security

Another food security issue related to intellectual property rights is the recognition of Indigenous peoples' contributions to world food supplies. Despite the fact that Indigenous nations developed and perfected many of the world's great foods, such as beans, corn, squash, potatoes, berries, and herbs, we receive no acknowledgement or compensation (Weatherford, 1988). For Indigenous peoples, lands and foods are at the center of what it is to be Indigenous. In some instances nomadic cultures required access to vast territories and ensured access to traditional foods. Tribal values of giving, sharing, and trading are at the heart of land care and food sovereignty. Indigenous peoples hold lands, foods, medicines, and animals as sacred and freely gifted. Without them, Indigenous values of reciprocity and relationship diminish and a loss of Indigenous humanity results.

It was Indigenous foodways that kept the first Europeans alive – whether a cure for scurvy for Jacques Cartier and the early explorers or the sharing of pemmican, a highly nutritious preserved food made of dried meat and berries that allowed explorers to cross the continent with healthy sustenance. Without this food, European settlement would have developed at a far slower pace, if at all. Many Indigenous foods from the Americas, such as corn, potatoes, and tomatoes, were introduced into Europe, which in turn led to better nourishment for Europeans in general and ironically to "national cuisines" – for example, Italians with tomatoes and Irish with potatoes. For Indigenous peoples, the land, food, and identity were seen as parts of a whole system. The land and food exist to feed the whole community as an extension of the family unit.

Jack Weatherford, a non-Indigenous scholar, writes about Indigenous knowledge of food and medicinal contributions. Prior to writing his 1998 book *Indian Givers*, Weatherford spent considerable time in South America and other parts of the world learning about Indigenous knowledge. He states, "Without the experimental and trial and error methods of early Indian farmers, modern science would have lacked the resources with which to start. The limited agricultural background of the Old World would have been far too meager and would have required centuries more of research before science reached its present level" (Weatherford, 1988: 82).

According to Weatherford, Indigenous peoples in South America were the first to develop the "planting" method (as opposed to the Old World "broadcasting" method) of seeding the land. Corn was adapted to grow with a protective husk that saved the seeds from both drought and insects. Prior to their adaptation away from wheat-based foods to potato diets, many Old World people died from famine because wheat was wiped out more easily than underground potato crops. Weatherford states that without potatoes many populations (including the Irish and Russians) would not have survived. Indigenous peoples of South America were the first to freeze-dry potatoes for storage, to use after the growing season had come and gone.

In the tiny jungle community of Genaro Herrera, South American Indians are teaching scientists how to cultivate a wide variety of yams, potatoes, and tubers. These Western-trained scientists have no understanding, knowledge, or language for many of the plants. Weatherford states, "[T]he American crops required new ways of farming that appeared bizarre to Old World farmers and violated all past agricultural principles of good farming. The scientists working at Ganaro Herrera strive to unravel the complex technology of native agriculture and food processing as much as they strive to understand more about the biology of the plants themselves" (Weatherford, 1988: 82).

Weatherford also describes the general superiority of Indian medical knowledge and pharmacology. It is common knowledge that Indigenous peoples saved the lives of many men who came with Jacques Cartier during the early voyages. Today the Incas still prevent goiter with seaweed (high iodine content), and kelp is harvested by large commercial ships from California to Peru for a variety of pharmaceuticals, foods, and toiletries (Weatherford, 1988). Other Indigenous medicines include petroleum jelly, oil of wintergreen, aspirin, quinine, and muscle relaxants from curare. The Andean region has been identified by Western science as one of the eight centers of origin of cultivated plants, and the variety of cultivated plant species is legion. Indigenous peoples grow some 1,500 varieties of quinoa, 330 of kaniwa, 228 of tarwi, 3,500 of potatoes, and 610 of oca, another tuber (Apffel-Marglin, 1998).

In many respects, Indigenous relationships to food differ from mainstream relationships which, for the most part, view food only in a utilitarian way, for individual caloric input and as part of the market economy. Natural laws, embodied in our languages and traditions that embrace the sacredness of all life, are part of what it is to be Indigenous. Plants, animals, and Mother Earth are not resources; they are the source of life itself and are at the center of our ceremonies. Traditional harvesting and management strategies and practices were adapted over millennia. As representatives of nations that represent collectivities, Indigenous peoples have opposed privatization of their lands and food systems that are intended for profit only.

Biotechnology Threats to Food Sovereignty and Indigenous Mobilization

Research, policies, and practice have also created troubling issues for "Indigenous Food Sovereignists." Specifically, genetically modified organisms (GMOs), in addition to corporate foods and patents on life, have raised questionable and ethical issues for communities; patents, a form of exclusive property rights, strike at the heart of cultural sovereignty of Indigenous peoples. Many international Indigenous groups, including La Via Campesina, have called for a halt on genetically modified organisms. Indigenous Mexican farmers insist on rejecting GMOs after witnessing two decades of negative impacts on traditional foods: "Commercial liberation of GMO maize presents immense dangers to human health, biodiversity, culture and to our national sovereignty." Indigenous tribes of Mexico state that despite protections such as the precautionary principle and calls to protect biodiversity from academics and scientists, organizations, various government ministries, and their agro partners have pushed through on genetically modifying our foods.

The food crisis in our Indigenous lands has caused the mobilization of many communities and a return to the traditional knowledge of our ancestors. Stories tell of a developing awareness that is growing within Indigenous communities, and that people are creating multiple strategies for Indigenous Food Sovereignty plans of action. *Eating the Landscape* is an inspiring research book on "Indigenous Food, Identity and Resilience" by Native Studies scholar Enrique Salmon. He states that our peoples, in his case, the Raramuri, are related to our environment, which includes food, through kinship (Salmon, 2012: 21). In the majority of Indigenous nations, kinship and relationships are the foundation of what it means to be Indigenous (see Settee, 2013). This growing awareness has led the development of community-based organizations and initiatives that address the global crises – north, south, east, and west.

The Peoples Food Policy is a Canadian organization that has an Indigenous peoples sector addressing Indigenous Food Sovereignty. In May 2011, the Indigenous sector helped produce *People's Food Policy for Canada*. This document, the outcome of two years of kitchen table meetings, is a thirty-five-page report that outlines the challenges relating to food sovereignty. Indigenous contributions describe local, national, and global concerns and were written under the guidance of a group of Indigenous community-based activists, scholars, and storytellers involved in food sovereignty issues. Representing fishing, hunting, gathering, and gardening peoples, our group brought an understanding of the impact of colonialism on our region's foods and food production. Indigenous food systems include land, soil, water, air, and culturally important plants, fungi, and animal species that have sustained Indigenous peoples over thousands of years. In many communities of origin, biological diversity lends itself well to an abundance of traditional foods, and Indigenous peoples throughout Canada, as well as other regions of the world, have developed distinct cultures based on traditional harvesting strategies and practices in their respective traditional territories. These practices are in contrast to the highly mechanistic, linear food production, distribution, and consumption model applied in the industrialized food system.

As a result of the harmony in our traditional food systems, Indigenous peoples exemplify food sovereignty. The rapidly expanding Indigenous food sovereignty movement intends to restore and enhance access to traditional Indigenous foods in the forests, fields, and waterways. Contemporary food sovereignty is directly linked to the historic claims to hunting, fishing, and gathering grounds in their respective traditional territories. This network of Indigenous food growers, community activists, and academics has inspired the development of public awareness workshops, community engagement, and an Indigenous Food Sovereignty course through the Department of Native Studies, University of Saskatchewan. The course and awareness workshops have created opportunities to build linkages with the community, so participants can learn what is being done to build allies and food sovereignty. As academics we are inspired by the enthusiasm of our students who long for knowledge and who, through the course, eagerly embark on innovative work within the community that focuses on food security and food sovereignty.

Within the Canadian context, colonial relationships with settler nations have ravaged Indigenous nations and their relationship with land. Legal categories such as Treaty, non-Treaty, Métis, nonstatus, status, reserve, and urban-based separate us. These separations further exacerbate larger food issues as legal definitions and impacts have restricted the movements of land-based peoples, while determining who can hunt and gather foods for family sustenance. Métis and nonstatus Indians and Treaty/ Status Indians have restricted access to land due to Canadian policies of exclusion. Like other First Peoples throughout the world, Indigenous peoples of Canada are often paupers in their own lands, with destroyed local economies and disrupted ways of life. Often international aid and trade is available only if tribal nations accept food that is nonculturally appropriate, overly processed, and genetically modified; meanwhile trade agreements through structural adjustment programs are designed to undermine Indigenous sovereignty and local autonomy. State laws often abrogate Indigenous food sovereignty by giving license to transnational corporations over our land. Shrinking and contaminated lands and rapacious resource extraction based on colonial models have forced many land-based peoples into cities. In urban areas deprived of traditional foods we experience food deserts, extreme hunger, and the onset and entrenchment of preventable diseases leading to early death (Lemstra et al., 2006: 3).

In many urban centers, the vast majority of First Nations – Inuit and Métis – are marginalized, with minimal resources to provide the necessities of life. Shelter, warmth, and food are priorities due to limited financial resources. Food insecurity, which is a reality for Indigenous people in the best of times because of land degradation and laws limiting harvesting, fishing, and hunting, can become even more desperate following relocation to the urban centers. In "Health Disparity by Neighbourhood Income," authors Lemstra, et al. (2006) describe Saskatoon's six lowest-income neighborhoods and health disparities. "Although disparity in health outcomes by socioeconomic status is well known, the magnitude of the disparity in health outcomes found in Saskatoon is shocking for a city in the western world. For example, the infant mortality rate in Saskatoon's low income neighbourhoods was 448 percent higher than the rest of the city, which is worse than developing nations" (Lemstra et al., 2006).

Deep discrimination is at the heart of Canadian nationalism and prevents similarly affected peoples from working together to address our common dilemmas and food challenges. Our collective experiences will help formulate and strengthen the larger food sovereignty movement. Many of our First Nations contributions are foundational and without these traditional ecological knowledges many settlers would have perished. The current socioeconomic and political system of neoliberalism has meant disaster for Indigenous Nations and others where traditional lands and a way of life are being commodified and destroyed. Colonialism and neoliberalism have resulted in a loss of language, cultural identity, and biodiversity, as well as a food system that focuses on monocultures, capital-intensive food production, an excessive use of pesticides and herbicides, and a profound loss of respect for soils and waters.

While Indigenous peoples have participated in processes such as the Convention on Biological Diversity and Species at Risk discussions, our voice is seldom considered. Mostly our presence is taken as consent for many issues that nation states put forth. We are not given a formal vote on any issues. In addition, governments pay lip service to species at risk initiatives while their development practices and lack of environmental protections show the real intent. We emphasize the value of traditional knowledge that is foundational to maintaining cultural and biological diversity, and we decry the notions of monocultures or patents on life forms.

We in the food sovereignty movement believe that traditional knowledges, as well as addressing the social determinants of health, should be at the heart of government food policies and practices. Indigenous peoples in different areas have sustained themselves on the wildlife and plants that their areas have produced. Various forms of agriculture have been practiced by Indigenous peoples in order to sustain the soil, seeds, plants, and water. This knowledge has been used by Indigenous peoples and in many cases shared with their non-Native brothers and sisters. The uses of plants and animals as medicines and foods were common among Indigenous peoples. This unique knowledge belonging to Indigenous peoples has also assisted the Canadian people to live on the land and to prosper.

We have deep concerns for industrialized forms of agriculture that national and international "food security" embraces. Industrial agriculture undermines small farmers, is heavily reliant on agrochemicals, is fraught with health concerns, and strikes at the core of food sovereignty. Industrial agriculture's sole purpose is to support market economies of scale. We join our Indigenous relatives throughout the world when we voice our concerns about genetic modified organisms, species destruction, and other desecrations of life. These issues threaten our foods, community fabric, and ultimately our ability to survive.

As the United Nations Declaration on the Rights of Indigenous Peoples states, Indigenous peoples, under the concept of free, prior informed consent, have a right to approve or disapprove any incursions on their land, especially as it affects food sovereignty. This decision includes oil exploration, forest clear-cuts, dams, mining, road development, bombing test sites, and other colonial practices that strike at the heart of food's sacred nature and reduces Indigenous capacity to gather culturally appropriate foods. Despite the fact that our human rights are identified under Section 35(1) of the Canadian Constitution, in our own lands we have been charged and jailed for practicing traditions and challenging life-destroying forces. A northern Saskatchewan Dene community has an outstanding charge for taking animals out of season. Tragically, rapacious corporate behaviors require more access to Indigenous homelands and legally supersede Indigenous rights to hunting, fishing, and gathering.

Not unrelated to land sovereignty is the recent issue of "land grabs," the theft of large tracts of land often belonging to Indigenous and local small farmers/land holders. While some may argue that land grabs have taken place since settler societies first entered Indigenous homelands, the level of land grabs has increased recently, due in part to the neoliberal philosophy of open borders promoted by various free trade agreements. These pacts are largely imposed on the backs of poor nations by the more powerful and northern countries known as the G-8. The policies have benefitted foreign and Western interests while creating a borderless world dominated by the interests of wealthy individuals and powerful corporations, undermining Indigenous and local sovereignty on lands, traditional foods, and local autonomy. More recently land grabbers are the elite from countries where the land is taken.

The unique global colonial experience of Indigenous peoples requires that Indigenous peoples' history and culture are valued and recognized. We represent a stronger voice when unity is based on listening, mutual respect, and proactive strategies. Our survival and the survival of the natural world require that we work toward mutual understanding to strengthen our voices. Finally our voices must be heard in the important work of policy development, food sovereignty as a framework for reconciling past social and environmental injustices, and relationship between Indigenous peoples and Canadian society.

Returning to traditions, while questioning the politics of petroleum-dependent food systems, helps to counteract the breakdown of the family unit and lessen the extreme poverty and hunger that plagues so many Indigenous communities. As Winona LaDuke, Anishinaabekwe activist, environmentalist, economist, and writer has stated, "[T]he recovery of the people is tied to the recovery of food, since food itself is medicine: not only for the body, but for the soul, for the spiritual connection to history, ancestors, and the land" (LaDuke, 2005: 210).

The trends occurring among Indigenous peoples in Canada and globally represent the beginnings of a new Indigenous food sovereignty movement. By establishing projects under their own leadership, Indigenous peoples are continuing to determine what should be grown, cooked, taught, and shared. In time, these decisions will pave the way for greater food security based on traditional knowledge and armed with information about new developments in food sovereignty. The larger Indigenous land struggles and food sovereignty issues are not mutually exclusive, even when the struggle remains centered in an urban setting. Food sovereignty, which is never static, links traditional Indigenous knowledge with contemporary urban realities that in turn contribute to new forms of knowledge and action. In this time of dynamic change, the traditional Indigenous way of looking at the land may help Canadian society and other societies and nations to understand the practices needed to protect the earth.

Conclusion

Since the report of the People's Food Policy in Saskatchewan, several developments have occurred that will potentially contribute to Indigenous food sovereignty. They include the growth of community garden projects in urban Saskatoon, which now number seven; and the expansion of the "Good Food Box," which feeds inner city school children and provides healthy food boxes to the Saskatchewan Urban Native Teacher Education Program (SUNTEP) at the University of Saskatchewan. Another development is the Good Food Junction, a full-size grocery store in a previous food desert in inner city Saskatoon. Additionally, there is the expansion of a northern organic vegetable producing initiative on the Flying Dust Cree First Nations in northern Saskatchewan. While these are important developments, they are only part of the solution. The struggle for Indigenous Food Sovereignty involves addressing, firstly, the problem of unequal power relations in which Indigenous peoples are denied access to overdue land claims. Secondly, the rapacious nature of dangerous corporate developments on traditional Indigenous lands results in poverty that ensures our people are kept in a state of governmental subservience and disempowerment. The final issue is the lack of transparency in scientific research, which curbs, curtails, and possibly results in devastating consequences for the intellectual property and traditional knowledges of Indigenous peoples. Until this bigger picture of the loss of autonomy is corrected, Indigenous food sovereignty will continue to be a major concern for many Indigenous peoples but will move forward in small but powerful, community-based initiatives such as community gardens, local economy grocery stores, and farm-to-school programs.

WORKS CITED

Ali, Saleem H. *Mining, the Environment, and Indigenous Development Conflicts.* Tucson: University of Arizona Press, 2003.

Apffel-Marglin, Frederique. *The Spirit of Regeneration: Andean Culture Confronting Western Notions of Development.* London: Zed Books, 1998.

Ervin, Alexander M., Cathy Holtslander, Darrin Quanlman, and Rick Sawa. *Beyond Factory Farming: Corporate Hog Barns and the Threat to Public Health, the Environment, and Rural Communities.* Saskatchewan: Canadian Centre for Policy Alternatives, 2003.

Food Secure Canada. *Resetting the Table: People's Food Policy for Canada.* Food Secure Canada, Creative Commons 2011.

LaDuke, Winona. *Recovering the Sacred: The Power of Naming and Claiming.* Cambridge, MA: South End Press, 2005.

Lemstra, M., C. Neudorf, and J. Opondo. "Health Disparity by Neighbourhood Income." *Canadian Journal of Public Health*, 97 (6), 2006, 435-39.

Salmon, Enrique. *Eating the Landscape: American Indian Stories of Food, Identity, and Resilience.* Tucson: University of Arizona Press, 2012.

Settee, Priscilla. *Pimatisiwin: The Good Life, Global Indigenous Knowledge Systems.* Vernon, BC: JCharlton, 2013.

Weatherford, Jack. *Indian Givers: How the Indians of the Americas Transformed the World.* New York: Ballentine Books, 1988.

Wilson, Shawn. *Research Is Ceremony: Indigenous Research Methods.* Winnipeg: Fernwood, 2008.

Wittman, Hannah, Annette A. Desmarais, and Nettie Wiebe, Eds. *Food Sovereignty: Reconnecting Food, Nature and Community.* Halifax, Nova Scotia: Fernwood, 2010.

11

The Radiant Life with Animals

Linda Hogan

"The Eyes of the Animals"

Looking into the eyes of the elephant
I am looking also into the eyes of the great land tortoise
with its life more than a hundred years
and I see the sand, the salt water from those eyes, the mouth,
claws, flippers, hoof, trunk, all on the way to any water,
across a changed world
where nothing is familiar.
And looking into the eyes of the mountain gorilla infant
holding green bamboo with her black hands
and fingernails so perfect,
the eyes look back at me
so unwillingly gentle and alive,
so unable to say, take from me this fur
as the turtle would not say, take from me the great shell
or the elephant its tusk or hoof.
It would say I am light, kind.
I am the same as you.
I see the red eyes of the tree frog,
climbing with yellow webbed feet
hanging on, calling out for rain.
Dear life, let's you and I talk
about the orangutan surrounded by shining fur
all amber jewel, golden eyes
copper arms stretched thin,
open and reaching, holding the emerald plant
and the shining light of morning.
A diamond cutter could not make anything so great
so needed
so needy

so desired and desirable
as this red ruby of a child. So,
dear life, protect this world.
Life, look into the eye of the whale. There are no words
a man can speak so great as theirs.

And then there are the eyes of the wolf.
A god was named for them.
And when you see any of these you know
all they want is to live
to survive, to care for their playful young
just as we do
knowing god is not who or what
or anything but all this, Life,
even the circle of fern is unfolding,
and the eyes of the universe
look back at you
with the true knowledge of what you are,
saying, human, woman, man, child,
this world, even your self
you must learn to love.

Linda Hogan

One thing to remember is to talk to the animals. If you do, they will talk back to you. But if you don't talk to the animals, they won't talk back to you, then you won't understand, and when you don't understand you will fear, and when you fear you will destroy the animals, and if you destroy the animals, you will destroy yourself.

Cree speaker (attributed to Chief Dan George)

The whole of nature touches and intertwines in one great embrace. The wind that brushes against my skin, the sun that kisses my face, the air that I breathe, the fish swimming in the water, the far-off star, and the gaze in which I hold it are all in contact.

Ernesto Cardenal from *Abide in Love*

The Radiant Life with Animals

One of my grandmothers was an eagle, a golden eagle. From the beginning she and I knew one another in a particular and mysterious manner of kinship. In all her injured shining, she was the "killer bird" the veterinary school didn't want to handle, and so they sent her to the rehabilitation center where I worked.

Sigrid, the woman who created the facility, took the eagle out from the cardboard box that had housed the bird, speaking gently the entire time.

Reaching in, holding onto the bird's legs, she lifted the eagle out of the closed-in darkness.

"Some killer bird," she said, smoothing the feathers down around the eagle's face and eyes, comforting the beautiful golden with her kind words. She cleaned the dirty beak with her own ungloved and vulnerable fingers. The membrane closed over the eagle's eyes in relief.

One wing we pulled open to a wide and magnificent spread of feathers. The other wing drooped, clearly broken, probably from an automobile.

When the eagle was moved out of intensive care, she was placed into the flight cage with the many other eagles. But this one never flew. Instead she leapt up and claimed a tree stump for her perch. She remained with us a long while and I helped look after her, taking food, checking the claws for problems.

The wing was too broken for flight, but we always hoped for healing. We believed in impossibilities. Perhaps that was part of the magic of a world that revolved around birds, magic that sometimes made a broken life whole. We called it *a wing and a prayer*. If nothing else, we wished for the absence of pain and the life of the bird for education purposes.

As the eagle stood on that trunk of tree, I brought food to her, cleaned the ground around her, and picked up the undigested pellets she spit up, which contained fascinating bones, claws, and the fur of animal remains. The birds need a diet of a total animal, all parts.

As with all the great birds, I knew their possibilities, the claws, the sharp beaks, but I never felt afraid or endangered. Some days as I bent down below her to clean the ground, she held the healthy wing out over me with care, so kindly, so wide and perfectly feathered that even as I felt the comfort, the broken wing seemed even more heartbreaking. One day I called her *Grandmother*. The name remained. Soon she was called Grandmother by everyone else. And like a grandmother, there were times she tried to straighten my hair to be sleek enough for flight, the way she would have done with her young.

But she required something of me in return. Grandmother, like all the animals I have known, maybe even more, required that when I enter, I be present with fullness, with all my heart and being. I learned to stop outside the door before entering the enormous flight cage or any of the others, stopped long enough to place myself in a quiet balance.

In my life with many different animals, I found that each species I have met prefers those who are at an internal peace, a wholeness, a person who does not dwell too strongly in the chattering mind.

After many years of work with different species, I have considered this state of human being and its place inside and without us. Perhaps, from the animal soul, it is the human mind that is the hard-edged and dangerous part of us. It can be as devious as it can be beautiful and creative. The human mind can plan threats as well as artistic works, cruelty in place of gentleness. It can hate as deeply as it can love. In contemplating human thought, we haven't designated what the mind might wholly contain, just as we can't say where the human spirit truly dwells. But animals recognize the soul of the human and know when we are fully present, our intent, even our caring. They see us.

A mutual respect between humans and animals appeared in the words and hearts of our Native ancestors, so often quoted. In earlier days we had an agreement, something of a treaty with the animals. It was binding. We would care for them. They would care for us. This was true in a small way with Grandmother, but it is also the ethical context of our cultural life and being.

When we look to the earlier days of our many Indigenous cultures, we find that care for each part of the world around us has been the most basic similarity and connection between the peoples of all continents. It is the singular cornerstone of cultural memory, and it is the strongest remaining cultural knowledge that is essential to who and what we are as people. Our ancestors respected not only animals, but all the other forms of life with which we shared this world, from the soils that nourished seeds, the trees that sustained us, to the grains and grasses that fed us and our animal relatives in our co-inhabited and tightly interwoven ecosystems. This cultural and spiritual ecology was central to our lives. An infringement on one part affected the rest. Thousands of centuries of observation made clear that survival depended on this knowledge then, just as it does now.

We expressed gratitude for the lives that sustained ours. When the life of an animal was taken, it was honored for its gift to the people. Plants were thanked before being removed and again while being used as medicine or food. Traditionalists still know that limits were set down for us in the first times, limits that tribal people knew as necessary to survival and to future sustenance. The act of cooperation and caretaking is known as natural law, which was in existence in the Indigenous past and needs, even now, to take precedence over laws created by humans.

I have long considered the reality and ways people formed according to their cultural understandings and perceptions. Europeans had ways of seeing and knowing the world that were very unlike ours. Our numerous cultural ways of working with and caring for the world around us was deeply embedded in our histories, languages, and the complex cultural developments that took place long before the arrival of Europeans on other continents. Indigenous peoples had a long-standing knowledge about their environments, the animal ways, the relationship between life forms. It was important that we had developed agricultures that didn't deplete the land, but in spite of the witness of the richness of the new worlds, the Native people were less than human to the early invaders. We were considered to be pagans for the knowledge and respect we had of other lives. In those days, that was often the cause of death.

The knowledge and practices long in place were abruptly changed with the invasions that occurred from the European continent. Europe was a place whose warring peoples saw the world in anthropocentric terms. Theirs was a world that existed for human needs and desires. It was a group of nations with continuous war, with monarchies and crises. Their sense of animals, most no longer present, except the domestic, was reflected in their bestiaries. Complete with griffins, gargoyles, sea monsters, and strangely depicted animals from other continents, the bestiaries revealed little true knowledge of the animal world. Some of the drawings, even into the eighteenth century, showed mechanistic animals appearing like items, even machines, instead of the living creations they actually were.

Beginning with the violence of European invasions, Indigenous histories changed. These were times that began the breaking of our own natural laws and our agreements with animals. Along with the broken histories, many Indigenous peoples lost the awareness of our human place and our need for cooperation as part of the planetary kinship. For those who survived the first invasions, the world changed in the greatest of ways. Out of new needs and changed economies, often in forced compliance with an alien view of life, our own knowledge began to disappear. Much of the time, human survival was at stake.

I can't speak for entire continents, or all tribal people, but on our North American continent, the Southeastern experience may represent many others. First, the horrors of a violent first contact remained in the stories and memories of the people for many centuries. Our tribal nations, those who survived, first offered many gifts to welcome the visitors, but later the people relied on the fur and skin trade in exchange for weapons and ammunition to protect loved ones. Desperate for rifles to protect ourselves, we overkilled deer, bear, and other animals to trade the fur and skins of our animal sisters and brothers for weapons to save ourselves from the warfare that was fought or fueled by Europeans. Enormous shipments of animal skins were sent to Europe. Weapons were also needed to protect us from being captured, sold into the slave trade, and sent to the West Indies, primarily Barbados, to labor and early death. New threats constantly rose, even as we were set to fight against one another.

This period was also one of the first breakdowns of our time-held traditions, including the loss of enormous knowledge of ecosystems and medicines. With entire nations of people vanishing under siege, we had little time and possibility to continue passing on our knowledge and intelligence about the world. All the while, we witnessed with grief how the newcomers from Europe made drastic changes to the environment, first from the animal losses and, later, from great deforestation. Cities grew around sawmills. Then, our intelligent planting methods were forced into an agriculture guaranteed to fail, as it already had done in deforested Europe.

Living with sudden war, the loss of animals, and wave after wave of disease, our ancestors suffered the great stresses expected with such abrupt change, loss, and trauma. It isn't surprising that so many nations were unable to maintain knowledge systems that had sustained the people for millennia.

Gary Nabhan (2003), in his book *Singing the Turtles to Sea*, writes that knowledge is embedded inside the culture, language, and history of a people and that we can't know a people without knowing their environment or ecosystem. They are linked to one another. In restoring our relationships with the world still here, we are many. We are reconsidering the places we inhabited and the species that remain. This has been especially important for those of us whose tribes were removed from their homelands long ago. We need to learn again the great intelligence of animals and trees and the understory that sustained the forest waters, even the need for predator and prey relationship in forest health, especially in a time when we are experiencing great losses of predators to trappers and hunters.

In the past, as our understanding and knowledge of the world was broken, the wholeness of our human lives was likewise broken. But now we are in need of restoring our agreements with our Earth and animal relatives. In recent years, many have been reaching back in time to study what practices kept the environments sustainable, and to put back together our traditional ways of physical and spiritual being in the world.

We are still in the process of decolonizing ourselves and examining how Western educations and histories have damaged Native knowledge systems and ecologies. Looking to ways that existed before the invasions is a great and difficult work. It requires much interdisciplinary research, contemplation, and also understanding a way to heal the spiritual and psychological disordering that came from the new ways we had to take on in order to survive. These ways of enforced education and religion made for a world that was less sustainable in a time when we seek to take care of what comes after us.

Some traditional keepers of knowledge retained a portion of our once fullness. Some have consciously worked to restore themselves and their cultures. Some are born with the knowledge of our ancestors, a rare gift that comes from the past. Few Indigenous peoples escaped the processes that dominated every continent. For those who did, they are now facing what most of us experienced centuries ago. But we've learned from one another. Recently, tribes in the rainforest set up blockades to stop timber industries from destroying the precious forest environments that provide water and support for people and animals that live in those forests. In addition to initial deforestation, those losses change climates in the forests that remain. The one still standing may not survive because of the changed water table and atmosphere needed for its support. Forests are also interconnected organisms to be studied.

While traditional Indigenous knowledge systems are being rekindled among Native peoples, our partially restored knowledge hasn't yet taken us across the boundary from where we stand, longing for change, to the true transformation that will make the planet more sustainable. The question is, How do we use Traditional Ecological Knowledge to take us over the border from this vastly changed world into another, more sustainable, way of living?

I remember Oren Lyons, Iroquois faith-keeper, saying at the UN Geneva Convention in 1978 that he saw no seat for the eagle. How important his statement was at the time. The people needed to hear this. Even more, he spoke us back into our human place as only part and parcel of the creation. Humans exist somewhere between the mountain and the ant, he said, there and only there. His words helped to set back into motion our own early traditions with the rest of life. The earlier history of all our continents was alive with this knowledge, and our humility among all the other creations was a way of living and knowing. All creature life, even trees and soil, has the same breath that flows with great mystery through each of us. Losing sight of this importance of animals, their fine embodiment of the sacred being called life, has taken some people time and effort to restore.

We do not hear from the animals themselves. They have been vanishing at an alarming pace, and they've had no voice in their own struggle and desire to live. Some of the disappeared are species not even known by us, but with each one missing, we lose something of great, unknown value, and it doesn't return. It leaves an empty place in the world that will never be filled. This is why I am moved to speak for animals and plants in my life and work.

Hannah Arendt believed it was the poet/historian who set a world into motion. I hope she was right and that there are words strong enough to begin this motion, a wave that travels out to great distances to move others into new ways of perceiving the world about them, that they may be moved to take on the task of caring for the fates of other lives on Earth.

Knowing this, serving the needs of animals, thinking of how to touch the lives of others, I also think of those many years caring for owls, hawks, and eagles. It was good work. I carried long hoses to clean guano, fill water for birds, clean walls, and then drain the heavy hoses outside in the heat of summer or in the ice of winter when the birds roughed out their feathers to hold in their bodily warmth. I helped in small ways, even feeding finely chopped mice to infant falcons. There was never time for all the work that needed doing.

My own affinity for animals and for plants is shared by many others, and has been throughout our histories. I continue trying to learn the many complex connections between humans and the other lives traditional people once had as a given.

Years after working with birds, my life expanded in many ways, but the same requirements of human balance and ways of being with animal life remained. First I met and swam with dolphins in Florida. At one research center, some of the dolphins were used for human-focused therapies and diagnostics. I traveled with a friend, and we also had a brief, heartbreaking visit with the Navy dolphins who were going to be returned to their pod in the wild after they had been taken away and then attached to humans. They were starved for human affection and did everything, including leaving the water, to be cared for by us. Withholding affection and attention felt cruel, even if it may have been necessary for their return to the wild sea. The dolphins were going back to their known pods. They had been failures in military planning, unwilling to carry bombs or obey any intentions having to do with warfare.

Later, observing the unique spinner dolphins in Hawaii, a years-long life with whales began. Maybe it began one day, out in a kayak with my friend, Brenda, when we came into close contact with a humpback whale.

As odd as it seemed, before we saw it, we heard the song coming from beneath us. It rose up, a peculiar and mysterious sounding, strangely felt in our bodies. We were accustomed to the feel of dolphin sonar clicking through our swimming bodies, taking our measure for their lifetime of memory, but this was something different. As it occurred to us that a whale song had pervaded each person's full being, we looked at one another, both of us with tears in our eyes. The whale surfaced then, extremely close, holding us in her gaze, eyes enormous, intelligent, and beautiful. She remained close, in our presence, without leaving. The three of us stayed together for a while. But since most whales only passed by this location in their daily journey, we thought something was amiss. Feeling we were out of our place, we went to shore and watched the whale, still surfacing and diving, and we were thrilled with the sound and sight of each great spume of exhalation.

The whale remained. Then, after what seemed a few hours, we saw not just the single great spume of a single breath, but suddenly, nearby, a much smaller one spouted. We were overjoyed. A birth had taken place. The whale had been in mammal labor. In all its shining newness, the newly born infant surfaced, then gently curved back into the great ocean. For a while they remained, rising and diving. Then the mother, with her new life, continued on with their passage. We had witnessed something of a miracle. In a book I can't recall, one person had written about the love between a mother whale and her infant, saying the mother sent milk out in a stream to the open mouth of her offspring.

As if by some strange fate, our life with whales was just beginning. Not long after, two Native women elders from a tribal community called on us to interview them and hear their story about the political business behind their council's plans to return to killing whales. The women wanted their own stories published. One was the keeper, by inheritance, of the ancient whaling implements her nation once used to kill whales in earlier days. Her home had been overturned in a break-in to search for these weapons. In earlier days, the whale kill had been very dangerous work and men didn't always survive their quest for whale meat and fat. Because of the danger involved in the killing of so great an animal, swordfish were considered great friends because whales were sometimes killed by swordfish and washed ashore, gratefully eliminating the necessity of a human kill that may have also resulted in human deaths.

Now today's weapons have removed the past dangers. The implements had been searched only for show, it seems. The two women seriously wanted to protect the gray whales in their region, a species only recently having made a comeback. Gray whales have long been extinct in the Atlantic, where they were once plentiful until the object of whalers. But most important to the women was the political and business machinery at work behind the scenes. The "hunt" had been described to the world at large as a return to tradition and the eating once again of traditional food. However, it was not a call to tradition. It was a money making venture for a few businessmen in their tribal nation who had already arranged to sell the whales at a high price to Japan for their popular whale sushi.

While it is easy to judge these men harshly, the same violations have been taking place since early contact in a society based on our present economy. After the numerous American wars against us, many ethical concerns we once had toward animals and the environment no longer held. I think of this as the result of an imposed process of thought and perceiving the world in ways that came from the violent process of colonization and loss of tribal values. For many, our Indigenous reverence for life has changed drastically. With Christianity and a singular, invisible god who counts for more than all the sacred lives around us, the animals we honored, and the environment loved and nurtured, no longer matters to many.

Despite the efforts of the women, their interviews, and their truth telling, a whale was killed.

There is no humane manner in which to kill a whale. Numerous weapons were used, including war weapons. The coast guard protected the men who killed the whale. But the whale's suffering was obvious, and its bleeding from multiple wounds was witnessed widely on television. When it sank beneath the water, the coast guard helped bring it back to the surface for the unprepared men. After it was hauled to shore, some reporters had no choice but to busy themselves, helping to prepare the meat with experienced whalers, flensers who came to assist from the far north. Many of the local hunters had gone inside to watch a televised ball game. To make the situation worse, the whale was a local, considered a "friendly" who had trusted humans. It lived in the same vicinity most of the time, loved and watched with affection by many.

A public outrage followed. Unfortunately, so did a renewed racism. This event set off a series of reactions. The men who killed the whale publicly said they'd been on drugs that day, as if offering an excuse. Instead, it made the situation worse.

As I said, this was the beginning of a journey for us. After the interviews with the women, after the terrible death of a whale, and the following

actions by and against the International Whaling Commission, and many
other unforeseen consequences, we decided to follow a group, or pod, of
gray whales from their birthing lagoons to as close as we could travel into
the Bering Sea. The journey lasted for years.

The gray whale is a species tied to land, needing shallow water and
sunlight to charge and photosynthesize the plankton and foods they eat.
The year the whale was killed, the others left their feeding grounds and
migration routes close to land. Now they vanished from sight. Soon they
were reported by tuna fishing boats far out at sea, and they were thin
from lack of food.

Some of the biologists who reported on the whales, not considering all
of the variables, such as their food needs in shallow, sun-worked waters,
concluded that perhaps their population was becoming too great for their
food supply. We were surprised by that conclusion. Perhaps it was the
logic of only one discipline in an educational system with only singular
parcels of knowledge at work. They didn't take into account the possibility of the whales' renewed fear of humans, their communication skills
and memory of the past, and especially not the necessary foods absent at
that distance from shore.

At Tofino, British Columbia, the traditionalist who knew the behavior
of whales over generations and in context, exhibited a breadth and depth
of knowledge from his own tribal sources. As he took us out to look for
the whales, he told us they were now afraid of humans. Only one had
remained nearby during the migration season when numerous whales
had always before passed by until that year. That one whale had always
remained there in place with the people, another friendly.

The whales we met who had been so open toward us in their birthing
lagoons, whales who brought their infants on their backs to show us their
new great beauty and wonderful life, the whales who playfully pushed
or lifted our skiffs, were now afraid as they left those protected lagoons.
They seemed to know what had happened to the one who was shot and
suffered. Using a great intelligence we are only beginning to understand,
whales, like prairie dogs and other animals and birds, communicate with
one another in known, recognized, and researched languages.

Part of the crisis of our continent's historical past is the white men who
were celebrated for their abilities to hunt and kill, and even to overkill,
without regard for what had once been ethical to our own ways. Buffalo
Bill, for reasons difficult to understand, was one of the men who became
a celebrated killer and then a showman using dignified and well-known
tribal leaders, some of whom had been imprisoned; almost all of them

had loved their people and had been forced to hide or war against the American military. However, Bill Cody is primarily known for his great slaughter and waste of bison until only a small number of the animals, once thundering across the plains and prairies, remained.

Whaler and naturalist, Charles Melville Scammon (2007), one of the many men who nearly made the gray whales as extinct in the Pacific as they were in the Atlantic, also carefully revealed their biology in his drawings. His was an attention and respect for whales that strangely accompanied his work at decimating the creature he wrote about, sketched, and appeared to respect. He wrote with care about the love of the mothers for their infants, and yet he wounded the young to attract the mothers to the calls of their infants, so they could both be more easily killed. Such a bewilderment of the mind and such violence we could now consider a form of mental illness. Yet these men received accolades, as do trophy hunters in some circles, proud of their kill, as are those who import or keep "exotic" animals illegally, often for canned hunts. More tigers exist now in Texas in artificial settings than in their own wild environments. In other countries, poaching for the "exotic," or for parts of endangered species, is rampant and increasing as quickly as habitat destruction. Overkill continues, hidden from most of us. But for the animals who witness the killings by poachers, they remember and they also exhibit more aggression and other symptoms of traumatic stress for what they have seen.

Maybe the past centuries have taken us too great a distance from remembering the lives we shared with the living Earth, but tribal nations still maintain their songs and stories about the animals. Many animals were creators and originators. Some sang the land into being. Others, in our origin stories, created the land for human beings, saw our needs and tended them, brought us fire, or taught us to weave. Some gave their lives and were honored for their sacrifice by humans. Our creation stories are rich with the lives of animals. For us it was crayfish. For others, it may have been turtle who brought land from the bottom of water, as Gary Nabhan relates in his work on the Seri. The same is true in many Northeastern nations.

Peoples throughout the world have accepted the intelligent presence of animals not just as helpers in the beginning, but as teachers, mediators, helpers, and providers through our lives. They have served us in all capacities of our existence, including our knowledge of which plants were medicinal.

Knowledge about other species sustained us for millennia, even before the large, complex societies, cities, and ceremonial centers that once existed here. At least two cities in the Southeast, from CE 700 to 1000, were the size of London and Paris at the time. These, the Mississippians, were just one of many people extremely informed about animals and plants. For them, as for the Maya, and the visitors to Chaco Canyon, the sky also was a key part of their world.

Even centuries after the invasion, people continued to wear tattoos of the sun, moon, and constellations on their bodies. It seems that this was a way to bring their Earth bodies into concert with what was above. Some of these were depicted by early European artists, and mentioned later by William Bartram, the botanist, as late as the 1700s. The Skidee Pawnee had created a leather star bundle with the sky constellations depicted as swimming ducks and a herd of antelope. Astronomy was a practical knowledge, in predicting runs of fish in the river, the migration of animals, and times to harvest or pick fruits and nuts. The sky was a guiding force for knowledge of animal routines throughout the year.

The Greeks also lived beneath a sky filled with animals, the constellations most of us are now taught, with a bear, ram, scorpion, and other lives. On this continent, thousands of earthworks remain, shaped as animals. Many of them are present in the shape of bears, eagles, serpents, turtles, and other amphibious animals, all created with great labor, lasting many years, and with what can only be described as love and honor. If they have not already been bulldozed, these earthworks remain intact because of the architectural intelligence that went into their creation.

I have found it most interesting that nearly all tribal nations on both sides of the Mississippi, including the Pueblo regions and farther west into California, observed a constellation of the great serpent, similar to the earthwork of the well-known Serpent Mound in Ohio. The Rainbow Serpent is also significant to Australia, and the shape is easily seen by any sky watcher who ignores the stories of the Greek sky we have been taught. And in our own Chickasaw tribal story of the Milky Way lives the sacred white dog we followed in an early migration. While it once led the living, the dog now helps lead the dead through the sky maze and into the world of souls.

Looking back to the time of the first journeys of Europeans to other continents may be a key to the continuing violence against animal life, including the whale death. Those early journeys to other locations resulted in great animal and plant loss. In Europe, with its history of constant warfare and monarchies, the disregard for life was clear in their practice of sadistic human and animal cruelty as entertainment. As they brought back lives from other continents, crowds watched them fight to the death. Bears against lions. Man against man. Bloodshed and suffering were a common pleasure to observe. We need only to consider the instruments of torture created there. A disease of the mind existed on the conquering continent at the time and it was contagious.

The significance of this contagion is of utmost importance in my mind when I consider our relationship with the animal world, but so is a consideration of our sustainable future and how we can practice sustainability without significantly changed attitudes about animals and other life forms on our Earth. We have to examine every aspect of our relationship with the animals, how they are treated, and the habitats in which they thrive. We have to examine our own selves as part of this.

For those whose own first struggles in the past were to stop the large numbers of killing, their views toward the earth and animals were not only animistic, but childlike. Even later, prominent psychologist Eric Fromm believed that only children went through a phase where all the world was seen as alive. In our own language, the word for animal is *Nan Okcha*, which means *All Alive*. As adults, this view of the world was apparently taught out of people, yet it constitutes the dominant knowledge of Indigenous cultures. While this presented problems to the newcomers at the time, now large numbers of people in the world are looking toward this Earth intelligence of our historically suppressed ways of living.

The grand narrative of our continent and others, a narrative created by historians and other scholars, hasn't changed over the centuries because of what we once knew, or still know, in our traditional knowledge systems. It is not because tribal scholars aren't at work changing the earlier histories that still influence those in the present. We have to consider who determines the histories, who decided and regulated what was recorded in the past. We need to consider, also, what our own people learn in schools and universities, what that grand narrative has taught everyone without regard for their histories, and with very little room for argument.

Now, considering the most recent information, it may be hard for us to comprehend how anyone came to believe that other animals do not have feelings of fear, stress, and most especially, pain. Gay Bradshaw's (2010) work on elephants in her book, *Elephants on the Edge*, addresses post-traumatic-stress disorder in these large and intelligent, very sensitive animals. The effects on them are the same as those of humans in warfare.

For those who did not grasp this earlier, there had to have been a distancing from their own observations and what they had been taught to believe. It is a continuation of the mental distancing and chaos of mind that allowed killers not to feel about what they had done, the slaughter of bison, Indian horses, even the massacres of people. The distancing still applies to war zones where, in addition to humans, we rarely, if ever, consider the animals and vast environmental damages that accompany the human death counts. Entire worlds of humans, animals, and habitat are at stake – a constant in the ongoing wars where so little is said of so vast a destruction.

The bridge between differing views of this world sometimes seems impassible. I recall seeing Werner Herzog's (1984) film, *Where the Green Ants Dream*, based on an actual court case that even included some of the original activists – Australian aboriginal people who tried, unsuccessfully, to explain to Western miners why they couldn't mine in the sacred place of the Green Ant Dreaming. The place, they said, was pertinent to creation, a sacred site laid down by the first ones at the very beginning of time, which exists also in the present, a world still associated with life from the creation. No one was able to cross or bring together the vastly different systems of thought. This place of the Green Ant was laid down when the great river of beings passed across and through the earth in its beginning, and the people are yet charged with its care.

A culture that endured for over 60,000 years deserves to have its world and knowledge tended, but Western miners were not able to comprehend this most significant aspect of place and meaning to people who had a continuous knowledge of land, waters, and animals, as well as their own continued protection of the place and its diversity.

From this complex example, we see the great respect for life, for creation, for the underlying nature and habits of lives shared with other lives, but especially the ancient past thrown up against the Western view with its lack of comprehension.

Western science has only recently documented the ways different species collaborate with and rely on one another. Prairie dogs, with their complex language, contribute not only to the aquifer; they also strengthen the protein in the grasses for grazing animals, including cattle in pastures. We know how necessary each species is to the well-being of the earth network of connections, and prairie dogs are a keystone species, providing shelter for some animals, food for many. The old Navajo have said that prairie dogs call down the rains. Once dismissed as folklore, we now know how significant this information is. Water calls itself just as trees bring down rain. Aquifers are increased by these "pest" animals who work the earth and in their work sustain water tables.

The compartmentalized mind has been educated in a way that rarely sees the world in its wholeness and the numerous interconnections that exist in the world around us. Our need for new ways of education begins with the treasures of our ecosystems, their dependence on all the lives in an environment, in all their simple complexity. We might even pass this knowledge on to children from an early age. But even so, we still have to address how many of the factors affecting our lands and all that live on them fall, truly fall, under our economies.

Economic factors have resulted in an even greater loss of compassion than we want to imagine. We need to know about the inhumane treatment in factory farms, and the other long lists we read each day that violate the life force for financial gain. This ethical breach in our relationship with animals destroys the possibilities of sustainability. These factors are a true breach of traditional Indigenous understandings of the relationships in the world. The sometimes sadistic cruelty that exists toward animals in factories or slaughterhouses does not transfer to thoughts of food on the table, nor do the abundant chemicals used. The frequent transport of what is merely called "livestock" contributes a large part to climate change.

Throughout the world, wildlife is removed or fenced out of ranch lands. Rivers have been diverted and dams have been built, destroying important habitat to furnish energy to developments and growing cities. We haven't learned from centuries of the terrible consequences of our poor human decisions. Recently, the Shasta dam was enlarged, resulting in the loss of twenty-six square miles of land and water sources belonging to California Wintu and other tribal peoples.

The list is lengthy and we never want to hear it: the trade in international wildlife for Asian medicines; driftnets that pull in miles of living animals from the oceans, including those already endangered; and deplorable medical research methods. Add to this list the trees orangutans and others need for their lives are now being felled for palm oil, previously cut for lumber.

Some years ago, I remember seeing a film presented in a lecture by Birute Galdekas, one of the original women Leaky sent to work with primates, women chosen for their compassion. Galdekas went to live with the orangutans, moved into their world, physically and eventually socially. A most memorable vision that remains with me from her talk and visuals is a scene of a young orangutan watching the great trees fall, the look in that beautiful animal's eyes as its world was being destroyed. The women all became advocates for habitat protection in order to save the animals they cared for so powerfully.

While researching the ecosystem in Florida's Everglades for work on the Florida panther, I learned that the few remaining animals were sick beyond healing because of contaminants in the environment. Because of compromised immune systems, the animals had a form of feline leukemia, primarily caused from agricultural run-off, industrial waste, and decomposing plants, which give off methyl mercury, a toxic poison. Numerous other human-created poisons exist in that one endangered location. Some are hormone disruptors. For the males, the hormone-altering chemicals have resulted in undescended testicles. The same estrogen imitators now affect all the animals in the Everglades, as well as the humans. As for the cats, they are left unable to reproduce, and while signs near Miami ponds say the fish are not safe for human consumption, the poor still fish there for food.

After the Florida panther became endangered and unable to reproduce, a federal agency decided to place a Texas cougar in the area to help with the fertility of at least one female, to begin an increase in their numbers. Some argued whether the panther is the same species as a mountain lion. The cougar placed in its new environment did not survive. It did not know how or what to hunt or how to move through an ecosystem as unique as the glades. It was a new and strange world, a dangerous world.

As Cristina Eisenberg (2011) points out in her study on wolves, the loss of any species has a cascade effect, altering and resulting in the loss of others, eventually changing an entire ecosystem. Those who lived within their own worlds for millennia knew what could happen and understood how to keep a system in its balance.

Our lack of information and knowledge, and our ignorance about the primary relationship of the natural world, extends to our human lives as well. What affects the animals also affects us, from the toxic environment, antibiotics and fattening agents, to the lack of care given to other life forms. Nor do we hear of the men who are paid to dive for lobsters eaten at famous fish food chains across the United States, men disabled by their work in deep water. Yet the demand for animal and marine food is great. Unfortunately, many developing countries are modeling their own growth after our economies. A Cree expression says,

> Only when the last tree has died
> and the last river has been poisoned
> and the last fish has been caught
> will we realize
> we cannot eat money.

Our knowledge isn't expansive enough to take us to the sustainable world we so desire in this sacred place, where we once knew the means to keep this planet healthy. We have let our world down.

Aside from the economically based factors that affect entire ecosystems, we need to continue an examination of our own thought systems. The question now is, as asked earlier, How do we cross the borders to a different way of life? Aside from new forms of energy, desperately needed, we also need a new kind of education, as I mentioned, beginning with our young people.

When we speak of other life forms or of other humans, perhaps our learning is not another way of "knowing," as is often said when we speak of Indigenous knowledge, but as with the animals I have met intimately, another way of "being." This is what the animals still teach many of us in our continuing histories with them, each with its own grace and intelligence aside from ours, and each with its own integrity and reason for being on Earth in one interwoven terrestrial intelligence.

When we consider sustainability, our interests are now global and not just our own continent, our own wildlife, or our own relationship to them. Entire environments are to be considered, because the planet is so small. We are all one interconnected world. Everything travels: radioactivity, toxins – even those traveling through the oceans – disease, even dust crosses oceans. Think of the topsoil of Oklahoma flying east with the winds all the way into the Atlantic Ocean in the 1930s dustbowl. The narrative accepted historically is not the story held and known in our original traditional knowledge systems. Humans did not have dominion. The religion that granted such a gift was not our own, which came under attack for being animistic in its vision.

Insight into animals and their ways of being are a part of that traditional knowledge, and we know each species is a creation, different but not less than our human selves.

It is important for us to know the animal lives and their ways lost because those forgotten attitudes and knowledges about animals and plants are the key to a sustainable future. To consider the past is just as important as thinking ahead seven generations into the future. Even when poor decisions were made, the past still is a map and a guide for the future. It is a true path for our behaviors and choices, our actions that we now want.

Our presence with the other lives on the planet calls for the development of a certain kind of heart as well as intelligence, one that has partly, but only partly, been taught out of us.

When Lakota Alex White Plume directed the Forest Service in his region, he brought back a herd of bison. The weight of the bison and the power of their feet on the land brought water back to the surface of dry earth, waters old people said hadn't been seen in many years, streams and creeks they had only heard about. The water made the grasses once present begin to grow. When the grasses returned, so did certain insects. These insects attracted birds thought to have vanished long ago. The land began to resemble what it had been in the past.

Years later, when a herd of wild horses was also released near those same lands, the bison stood at the crest of a hill and watched these other missing animals, also shot in large numbers, once again run free. Who knows what memories they may have had in mind, those with a shared history? We don't know what this continent would have become without the numerous creature losses to which it has been subjected, but it is significant enough for us to know that water missing from the earth would like to return to the surface, that given the return of one form of life, others will follow, will return, and that there is a regeneration waiting to take place.

Considering the many losses, including that of the gray whale some years ago, we may put this loss side by side with our human compassion. In a location farther north, a killer whale was understood to be the spirit of a great spiritual leader who had died, and the whale was held in great esteem, adamantly protected and not allowed to be disturbed by tourists or researchers. Constant watchers remained in the water, protecting the whale.

Elsewhere, whale eaters saved the lives of three gray whales who remained too long among rich food, migrated too late, and became frozen into sudden, early ice. Great care went into the twenty-four-hour labor of the Indigenous people and their friends who worked without relief to free the whales from the ice that formed around them.

The empathy and love that went into freeing the three whales frames any discussion of the relationship between Native peoples and Earth's creatures. The animals and the people are connected. Those in the Northwest say, *Without the salmon, we are no longer a people.* The Gwichin say, *Without caribou, we will cease to exist.* The people realize that we can't, for reasons of survival and cultural integrity, afford to lose any species.

The Gwichin of interior Alaska, the Caribou People, have suffered calamitous effects from climate change. The warming of ice and permafrost has caused the loss of thousands of migratory birds and waterfowl. Melting permafrost has left tree roots vulnerable and trees have fallen over. The released mercury and methane gas of decaying vegetation in waters nearly dry have poisoned the atmosphere, and the once great herds of caribou upon which people's lives have depended no longer pass through their aboriginal lands in large numbers.

In 2009, at The Parliament of World Religions, Norma Kassi showed slides of what had happened to the Gwichin land in interior Alaska, and the audience wept. She said her father had seen it coming and had spoken of a day when only two birds would come back to the remaining water. While there had been thousands of migratory birds and waterfowl, his words came to pass. That year only two wild geese had arrived. The caribou, once passing through in great numbers, were dwindling.

The survival of the animals is of primary importance to us all, and cultural survival is a significant part of it. The animals, the land, and all its inhabitants are part of our Native cultural histories, and they are a necessity to our lives.

Culture is the deciding factor in our way of seeing and knowing the world, and yet our values extend now to people other than those who are indigenous to the continent. Many of us know that the borders between us are slender ones, skin and fur, skin and feather, skin and fish scale. While there is little division in reality, a great division exists in the mind where we have lived too long without one another and not returned strongly enough, searchingly enough, to Indigenous understandings of the world and the intelligence of Traditional Ecological Knowledge.

In our time, we have mistakenly delisted numerous animals from the endangered species list. Yet the animals are leaving us at a high rate. Some are forced into new locations by climate change, fire, habitat destruction, and other human-caused forces. Some exist now only in zoos or elsewhere, protected, even breeding, with the human hope – as unlikely as it is – that one day their habitat will be restored. Even then, will they know how to live in it? As with humans, perhaps they will be as lost in their old lands new to them that they will not recall or remember their food sources – if those remain – that they will not have a genetic memory, enough to survive.

Also, considering habitat, the fish in waters near the enormous area of destruction called the Alberta Tar Sands are cancerous. They are deformed. They bleed from their scales. The Native people of the region have always lived off the fish and the forest lives, and what can they survive on now that is in any way intact? With the entire top of the earth cut open, the health of the human habitat has been destroyed. This area is one of such great devastation that it can be seen from space. We need the precious lands, waters, and animal life to survive for our health, as well as theirs. When we talk about subsistence, what we mean is survival into the future for all of us.

While the cultural relationship goes back to our long ago beginnings, now it is a necessity to take back the ability to birth our own vision and speak back our knowledge, to see our lands remain in healthy existence and to restore a world we still care for so strongly. Many thousands of years of knowledge, agriculture, astronomy, animal and plant connections all brought back together might offer us a renewed, ancient, if difficult beginning.

Now, too, a multifaceted way of knowing and perceiving our world is a necessity. Many of us are piecing together what knowledge we can, and learning, through re-searching, our true histories through a variety of disciplines combined together. To continue our research, we need to consider how we maintained animal lives, plant life, and the habitat that supported all, although many historians will belie this changed narrative, the new story. It is a large job, one requiring a remapping of the mind, a new fitting together of old pieces that were taken apart. It is a new cartography of thought. It is necessary for our wholeness and our future, one in which we may keep our unique ecosystems and knowledge from collapse, as our ancestors had once done.

While at the Amerind Museum in 2013 for a seminar, I noticed a ceramic pot in the process of restoration. It was partially recreated, the shards fitted together as in a puzzle, yet already the jar had life, and a unique shine was given off by it. It seemed already whole, the pot with its beauty of given-off light.

As for us, it is our same challenge to bring back that light of the past and remember ourselves.

As in this ceramic construction, in recreating a whole, we also reassembled our traditional ecosystem knowledge, not just for ourselves, but for all people because we are not the only ones searching for an ancient way of being and living. We needed to find the pieces that had been broken in order to repair ourselves, and revive our search for empathy with one another, animals, and plants.

Searching for the new story is also a search for a language of healing. The renewed knowledge and histories, truly ancient as they are, are a language like a river. It flows through the country of our spirit, our heart, and moves toward great oceans of new being. Its power opens us to the world and takes to the old riverbeds as well as creating new pathways and tributaries to be learned, known, and followed.

It seems that words have always been the glue that held together the broken vessel of our cultures. They are the carriage of sustainability, when we possess the right ones to speak. Our lives are recreated in language used for re-cognition, return, re-storying, and re-searching all that has already been searched, storied, and turned over.

While our tribal nations do not have the same shared histories or myths, nor do they share the same stories of how the world was created, we do share with one another that the story lives in the land, with all its relations, and we can illuminate the sacred world, our unity with all other lives. In this way, the word has power to keep meaning alive for us, to hold our cultures strong in our hearts, not only through stories, shared experience, and remembrances, but through our songs, songs for plants, songs for animals, and so many of these remain. So do the numerous dances. And, of course, the songs came from the animals to us at some time in the beginning, as most of our stories go.

What the animals told us, and how we sing the plants upward from the earth, even the songs of ceremony are still present. New forms, new writings, and new incantations are present for us. After all, our lives are an ongoing process. And, as I said earlier, we are searching for a new way, a new story, in addition to seeking what our ancestors spoke into the current of our present lives.

Sometimes I think of the stories I have heard from others and how they have remained alive within me. I remember Joe Little Coyote, in a Native science gathering, telling how the wolves retained songs for the Northern Cheyenne who were being chased around the country by the cavalry. The people, he said, were re-learning their songs from the wolves. Elder Howard Luke, Otter Clan and Alaska Native traditional hunter, says, "You have to be careful what you say about the animals. They can hear you."

Other times I remember a poem in which Ernesto Cardenal (1995), a poet, priest, and activist in Nicaragua, writes that animals loved the revolution; even the armadillo was happy with it, because what was right for the people was right for all lives no longer being destroyed. For him, language was a certain road to change, but he lived in a world where poetry was dangerous work; it was the poets and singers who lost their lives to regime changes because of the power of words.

Thinking of the pottery being put together at the museum, I realize that putting the past together in the present is a work of changing the existing dominant narrative and returning it to the cherished knowledge that allowed us to survive over centuries. Our work is knowing that creation is an unfinished thing, that it's a daily ongoing process and we are participants in it, co-creators. As such, our labors and words will continue to unfold and open our way back to what has been taken apart.

The shining pot, the smoothing of it so that the fracture lines are no longer visible, this work is an amazing task. As for our own human vessel, our traditional ecosystem knowledge can be placed within this realm with a language that brings together pieces of who we were, what we are now, and the possibilities for a future becoming whole. The collective ethics of our ancestors, however painful they were at different times, truly still begins with love – compassion not only for human beings, but for all lives. Consider singing to the plants as they grow. That song came from the depth of the hearts of our people. This dimension of the human is an acknowledgment that all is powerfully alive – exquisite forms of all the radiant living beings, from seedling to bison to ceremonies for food killed. We may, we just may, continue to find a way into the wholeness of our beloved and Earth-created ancestors, the animals who kept us alive from the first creation.

WORKS CITED

Bradshaw, Gay. *Elephants on the Edge: What Elephants Teach Us About Humanity*. New Haven, CT: Yale University Press, 2010.
Cardenal, Ernesto. *Abide in Love*. Maryknoll, NY: Orbis Books, 1995.
Eisenberg, Cristina. *The Wolf's Tooth: Keystone Predators, Trophic Cascades, and Biodiversity*. Washington, DC: Island Press, 2011.
Herzog, Werner, Dir. *Where the Green Ants Dream*. Project Film production, 1984. Film.
Nabhan, Gary Paul. *Singing the Turtles to Sea: The Comcaac (Seri) Art and Science of Reptiles*. Berkeley: University of California Press, 2003.
Scammon, Charles Melville. *Marine Mammals of the Northwestern Coast of North America*. Berkeley, CA: Heyday Books, 2007.

PART IV

GLOBAL AND LEGAL IMPLICATIONS OF INDIGENOUS SUSTAINABILITY

12

Home: Resistance, Resilience, and Innovation in Māori Economies of Well-Being

Rachel Wolfgramm, Chellie Spiller, Carla Houkamau, and Manuka Henare

Introduction

Sustainable societies flourish over generations and are wise enough not to undermine either their physical or social systems of support. As such, sustainability requires understanding relationships between natural and social ecologies (Berkes, 1999; Berkes et al., 2003; Meadows et al., 1992: 209). However, there are many different cultural dimensions to sustainability that have yet to be explored.

To address these cultural elements, this chapter examines resistance, resilience, and innovation in Māori economies of well-being. With specificity we ask, in the twenty-first century, how are embedded and evolving realities of Home manifested in Māori economies of well-being? What is the role of Traditional Ecological Knowledge (TEK) in these transformations? We engage the notion of Home as a touchstone as it is inextricably associated with enacting and asserting sovereignty (*tino rangatiratanga*) over environs and destinies.

We also note that Māori are the *tangata whenua* (people of the land) or Indigenous peoples of Aotearoa New Zealand. In its recent history, it is a nation founded on a partnership between Māori and the British Crown. Because encounters with Indigenous peoples were not unusual in the expansion of the British Empire, in 1840, a treaty, later named the Treaty of Waitangi (*Te Tiriti o Waitangi*), was signed by 540 Māori chiefs and representatives of the British Crown including Governor Hobson (Kawharu, 1977, 1989; Orange, 2004; Walker, 1990). While intertribal warfare existed pre- and post-European settlement, warfare between Māori and the New Zealand government after the treaty was signed was brutal. In the period 1845–1872, known as the New Zealand Wars, 18,000 British troops fought against 4,000 Māori warriors at the peak of hostilities.

Thus, the issue of sovereign rule by Māori over their own affairs, a matter termed *tino rangatiratanga,* continues to be at the heart of on-going negotiations between Māori, the Crown, and its representative governments in New Zealand. Although warfare in defense of Home has shifted from battlefields to boardrooms, Māori continue to contest the dispossession of lands, rights, and autonomous sovereignty.

However, Māori grievances are now addressed through a tribunal named the Waitangi Tribunal that was established in 1975 by the Treaty of Waitangi Act. Specifically, the Tribunal is a permanent commission of inquiry charged with making recommendations on claims brought by Māori relating to actions or omissions of the Crown that breach the promises made in the Treaty of Waitangi. Māori grievances are researched and settlements awarded. Settlements include formal apologies, the return of stolen lands, returned place names, and financial reimbursement. Currently, one in seven people (598,605 or 14.9 percent of the population in New Zealand) belong to a Māori ethnic group (Statistics New Zealand, 2013) and there are hundreds of tribes, tribal affiliates, and Māori organizations within all sectors of New Zealand society. In addition, there is Māori representation in New Zealand's broad political spectrum including a distinct political party.

The chapter begins by detailing issues pertinent to this discussion of embedded and evolving realities of Home. This is followed by a section that draws on TEK to elucidate how Māori economies of well-being are embedded in holistic relational systems. Four frames of reference are then used to provide explanatory emphasis in our discussion: Home as Identity, Home as Kainga and community, Home as Waka Aoturoa (a journey of social transformation), and Home as Navigating Futures to advance economies of well-being. The conclusion provides a summary of the contributions this chapter offers.

Context

We locate our discussion of resistance, resilience, and innovation in Māori economies of well-being for a number of reasons. First, a current estimate of the collective Māori asset base is NZ$42.6 billion (Te Puni Kokiri Ministry of Māori Development, 2013). Second, as noted earlier, Māori economies have developed in the face of sustained socio-political, cultural, and environmental trauma, which indicates a high level of resilience. Third, a major proportion of Māori development is occurring in industries such as forestry, fishing, farming, energy, and tourism, which impact the sustainability of immediate environs of Home from *whanau* (extended family), *hapu* (sub-tribe) and *iwi* (tribal) perspectives. Therefore, seeking innovative solutions grounded in Traditional Ecological Knowledge and environmental integrity, referred to as *kaitiakitanga* (guardianship), is often foremost in the minds and hearts of Māori when considering development plans.

The fourth point we make is that Indigenous peoples are not unique in these concerns. In fact, in order to satisfy human needs and limitless desires, exploitation of planet Earth, the Home of the global human family, has accelerated over the last two hundred years in a period of condensed industrialism with both positive and negative consequences (Gladwin et al., 1995; Hamilton, 2003; Hawken, 1993; Jackson, 2005; Max-Neef, 1995). Simply put, a global meta question is, How do we continue to undertake economic activity on Earth in the face of diminishing resources, a population estimated to climb to 9 billion by the year 2050, accelerating water and food security issues, and unmitigated negative externalities? These issues, coupled with mismanagement of current resources, much needed investments in aging infrastructure in cities worldwide, climate change adaptation, and hyper consumption, are now reaching critical levels (Jackson, 2005). Therefore, developing a deeper understanding of embedded and evolving realities of Home and seeking wise and innovative solutions to current challenges has broader sustainability implications (Wolfgramm et al., 2013).

The fifth point we make is that the word *economy* (c.1530) derives from the Latin term *oeconomia* and from Greek *oikonomos*: "manager, steward," and *oikos* "house." These Greek terms are related to the Latin *vicus* (district), *vicinus* (near), dwelling, village, and villa and to *nomos*, "managing," from Latin *nemein*. Therefore, the word *economy* derives from the concept of both Home as a physical place and the notion of managing Home.

Finally, as a science, economics is concerned with social behaviors and institutions involved in optimizing resources to produce and distribute goods and services. Products and outputs are then consumed by all. Therefore, the dynamics of social institutions and behaviors related to Home are of ongoing interest in wider analyses of economies of well-being and sustainability.

Home Through a *Kuwaha* (Gateway)

Drawing on Traditional Ecological Knowledge defined by LaDuke (1994) as the culturally and spiritually based way in which Indigenous peoples relate to their ecosystems, we now invite the reader to enter our discussion through a *kuwaha,* or gateway, in which we illustrate how Māori economies of well-being are embedded in *holistic relational systems.* Natural, social, and spiritual worlds are interrelated and the well-being of the individual is central to the well-being of the collective.

In this world, Home conjures up words that hold distinct meanings, such as *turangawaewae* (a place to stand), *whakapapa* (genealogical recital; layering of relationships), *whenua* (lands), *taua* (warfare), *maunga* (mountains), *awa* (rivers), *moana* (oceans), *tupuna* (ancestors), *urupa* (burial grounds), and *whanau* (family). As such, the notion of Home may evoke conflicting feelings of *aroha* (love), *manaakitanga* (kindness and caring), joy, sadness, melancholy, happiness, belonging, fear, comfort, remorse, and expectancy to name a few.

Home in this world incorporates *tikanga,* the intellectual and spiritual ideas *and* practices that relate to Māori ways of being and doing (Smith, 1999; Henry and Pene, 2001; Mead, 2003). *Tikanga* emerges from a Māori worldview and influences cultural and spiritual traditions, social kinship systems, and rituals. To explain further, Henare (2015) offers a matrix of interwoven ethics that underpin a Māori approach to ecological economics and the good life: "*He Korunga o Ngā Tikanga, a Philosophy of Vitalism and Reciprocity.*"

He Korunga o Ngā Tikanga, a Philosophy of Vitalism and Reciprocity	*Matrix of Māori Ecological Economics and the Good Life*
Te ao marama	Ethic of wholeness with the cosmos
Te ao hurihuri	Ethic of change and tradition
Tapu	Ethic of being, potentiality, sacred
Mauri	Ethic of life essence, creation
Hau	Ethic of reciprocity
Mana	Ethic of authority, common good
Tika	Ethic of finding the right way, justice
Whānaungatanga	Ethic of belonging, dignity of humanity
Wairuatanga	Ethic of spirituality
Kotahitanga	Ethic of solidarity
Tiaki (Kaitiakitanga)	Ethic of guardianship, *relational and reciprocal*

| *Hohou rongo* | Ethic of peace, reconciliation, restoration |
| *Manaaki* | Ethic of love, honor and care |

Source: Henare, 2015

Hence, economies as relational systems are both embedded in and emerge out of worldviews. For Indigenous peoples, worldviews and cosmovisions are both abstract and concrete as sophisticated *lived in* belief systems (Deloria, 2005; Nelson, 2008). For example, living in the natural world and observing its intelligence over centuries led Māori to accord nature with divinity, such that a Māori pantheon includes many gods representing the natural world. Examples include Papatuanuku, Mother Earth; Ranginui, Sky Father; Tangaroa, god of the oceans; Tawhirimatea, god of winds; Haumiatiketike, god of wild foods (Barlow, 1991).

This approach resonates with Cajete's writings, which emphasize the force and scope of eco- and Native philosophies. When combined, he suggests a worldview emerges that includes a spiritual orientation, a perpetual state of dynamic and multidimensional harmony in the universe, human knowledge related to the creation of the world, and the emergence of human cosmology. For Cajete (2000), Native Science highlights relationships with all natural phenomena, dreams as gateways to creative possibilities when used wisely and practically, and artefacts as symbolic containers of energies and thought. In this context, elders and specialist knowledge holders play a role as keepers of essential knowledge and wisdom to guide collective and individual development.

In terms of sustainability, Māori also needed to be conservationists, because long periods of isolation meant they could not rely on external help. Survival was linked to community and subsistence living that relied on available resources. Adaptation included ensuring the conservation of natural resources, as with many societies, Māori learned lessons from the over-exploitation of natural resources. Over time, social norms, structures, rituals, and institutional practices were developed to adapt (Wolfgramm and Henry, 2006). An example includes the practice of *rahui*, a form of restricting access to, or use of, an area or resource. It is still practiced to protect species and to replenish diminishing stocks.

Having explained the foundations of relational systems based on Māori traditional ecological knowledge, we now weave together four frames of reference to highlight the dynamics of Māori economies of well-being: Home as Identity, Home as Kainga and community; Home as *waka ao turoa*, a journey of social transformation; and Home as navigating futures to advance economies of well-being.

Home as Identity

Reflecting on the first frame of reference, Home as identity, Houkamau (2006, 2010) argues that Western psychological perspectives of identity view "it" as a person's answer to the questions "Who am I?" (self-definitions) and "What does it mean to be 'me' as a member of society?" (self-descriptions and evaluations). Following on, Western theories of identity formation cohere around the premise that people derive self-definitions through affiliation and interactions with others. Traditional Māori conceptions of identity also emphasize the centrality of relationships as evident in the *whakatauki* (proverb) – *He aha te mea nui o te ao? He tangata! He tangata! He tangata!* "What is the most important thing in the world? It is people! It is people. It is people."

Māori, therefore, place significant emphasis on *whakapapa* (genealogies) and sub-tribal and tribal connections (*hapū* and *iwi*). In this context, traditional Māori notions of identity formation tend not to be separated from places of geographical origin. Emphasis is given to the role of ancestral communally shared tribal lands in cementing *hapū* and *iwi* relationships and shaping Māori identity. In fact, identity for Māori may almost be described as coterminous with "Home" and "Land." In testimony, Walker observed that significant tribal geographical characteristics (lands, sacred places, lakes, and rivers) are all indicative of one's Home and therefore are all an intrinsic part of identifying as Māori.

The arrival of *pākeha* (European settlers) and subsequent colonization meant circumstances for Māori changed rapidly and irrevocably. From the turn of the twentieth century Māori lost most of their Home lands and thus lost contact with their Home – their *hapū* and their *iwi*. A recent history of assimilation into European culture alongside urbanization has meant that the traditional sources of Māori identity have been eroded, undermined, and in many cases removed. At the same time identity remains a central focus for Māori people, as well as a central theme of contemporary and political activity and academic scholarship.

For some time, Māori academics have argued that the history of colonization experienced by Māori predisposes modern Māori to a form of psychological distress (Dewes, 1975; Durie, 1985; Sachdev, 1989, 1990a, 1990b), which has been termed "cultural depression" by Lawson Te-Aho (1993, 1998a, 1998b). Referring to the psychological impact of colonization on Māori (particularly urban migration and acculturation into Pākehā society), Sachdev (1990b: 102) observed that the disconcerting increase in Māori psychiatric admissions in recent decades "… may reflect the impact of psycho-cultural stress on the community" (cited in Hirini, 1998: 206). In her description of this phenomenon Lawson Te-Aho writes:

> Loss of cultural identity as Maori is the result of colonisation. First, the removal of land rendered Maori unable to maintain cultural traditions which, for centuries, had been based around identificaiton with the land as a source of spiritual and physical identity for Maori *whanau, hapu* and *iwi*. Second, the active process of assimilation rendered Maori values, traditions, beliefs and world views irrelevant to the values and beliefs of the dominant culture. It created an imposed inferiority through the denigration of Maori identity. (Lawson-Te Aho, 1998b: 15)

Houkamau (2006) says the implicit assumption that because Māori are deculturated and are now unable to live according to their "essential being as Māori" is both compelling and influential from a sociological perspective. However, it fails to consider that the evolution of identity and culture is a transformative and ongoing process.

In fact, she argues the view that identity is somehow defective for urban and deculturated Māori does not hold true for many contemporary Māori who have found new ways of expressing their Māori identities – through relationships and by creating new "Homes" in new spaces and places. This is particularly so because Māori are a diverse social group, many of whom function adaptively in New Zealand society and abroad, yet differ in their perceptions of the relevance of culture and geographical location for them personally (Sibley and Houkamau, 2013).

With respect, Houkamau says it is time to unpack our assumptions about Māori identity. We need to understand how Māori identity is a personalized social construction that reflects individual contexts and the diverse sociocultural realities in which Māori now live. In highlighting the evolving realities of Home, she argues that the greatest potential for Māori now sits with valuing our uniqueness and ability to adapt to new geographical locations and new sets of relationships while maintaining a clear sense of self-acceptance as Māori.

Home as Kainga and Community

Considering the second frame of reference, Home as *kainga* and community, economic historian Henare introduces critical aspects of *kainga* and notes its continued dynamic function within larger social groupings. *Kainga* is a term that encompasses notions of Home as residence, village, encampment, region, or homeland (Henare, 2003). A related term, *papakainga*, denotes a Home base, a true Home as *papa* refers to a house-site or the earthen floor of a traditional home that connects directly with *Papatuanuku* (Mother Earth). The collective care of the *papakainga* is grounded in a sense of community within the wider tribal *rohe* (districts). The term *wakainga* refers to Home recalled from a distant place, and the phrase *kainga tautohe* (quarreled-over homeland) refers to areas where different *hapu* or other groups claim conflicting rights of use or access. Historically, economic activity in *kainga* included proactive and adaptive management of physical environs for small and large scale production in agriculture, horticulture, sea, river, and forestry resources and continues to do so.

According to Henare, the human dimension of the *kainga* is historically the *whānau*, who were the agents of change in settlement patterns and developments. By the nineteenth to early twentieth century, notions of *iwi* had neither usurped the significance of the *kainga* and the *whānau* or their primary economic functions in society.

In terms of evolving realities of Home, as the system of social organization adapted to meet the conditions of given times, so too did the meanings attached to *kainga* transform. In eliciting historical understandings of Home, Henare argues that the pre-eminent space and place of Māori people in history is the *kainga*, whether they were part of fortified villages known as *pā*, or in the many unfortified villages scattered throughout the country. Hence, Home is embedded in notions of *kainga* and community, evolving over time to meet the economic needs of *whanau, hapu,* and *iwi* Māori.

Home as *Waka Ao Turoa*: A Journey of Social Transformation

In this section, Wolfgramm engages the term *waka ao turoa* to explore Home as a journey of social transformation. *Waka ao turoa* is in part inspired by the shared Polynesian *waka* traditions linked to exploration, trade, and settlement across the vast Pacific Ocean (Hiroa, 1954; Howe, 2003; Irwin, 1992). For Māori, as an ancient concept, *waka* implies an eternal dynamic interaction of light and movement, *wa* referring to time and motion, *ka* to light and fire (Fraser Puroku Tawhai, in Wolfgramm, 2007). *Waka* can also mean the tail end of a constellation, the medium of an *atua* (divine diety), a flock of birds, a physical vessel used by tribes for various purposes and also a tribe (Williams, 1975: 478). *Ao turoa* can mean several things. *Te ao turoa* can literally mean "long-standing world" (Williams, 1975: 12) and in a metaphysical sense can imply the enduring nature of the world, a world that stands within pluralities. *Te ao turoa* also relates to stewardship of the environment including *whenua* (land), *ngahere* (forests), *moana* (oceans), and *awa* (rivers).

Waka is also an important part of one's identity construct, as being able to identify with *waka* links directly to a sense of Home as a journey and a place, both of which are central to socio-economic activity. How so? *Waka* as vehicles of transportation are significant to tribes whose ancestors formed the crew of one of the many canoes that landed on the shores of Aotearoa New Zealand. After Māori settled Aotearoa, in the defense of new Homes, *waka* were developed for political, economic, and military operations. *Waka taua* are imposing, and elaborately carved. The primary role of *waka taua* was to transport warriors to and from battle. Often large *kaupapa* (fleets) were utilized. Battle confrontations were dangerous, and when they did occur, opposing *waka taua* would often be driven against each other, the objective being to destabilize or capsize the enemy's *waka* in order to attack warriors when vulnerable. Hand-to-hand combat with various weapons of war such as *patu*, *mere*, and *taiaha* would ensue in water and on land (Ballara, 2003). Warfare in the defense of Home for *iwi* Māori is historically significant and revealed in archaeological findings, particularly in the proliferation of *Pa* (fortified villages) sites.

In providing for Home, a *waka tiwai* is a vessel used for fishing, food gathering, transportation, and races. It is propelled by poles and paddles, and a *waka tete* is a seagoing vessel used for deep-sea fishing trips, coastal journeys, trading, and deep river work (Nelson, 1999). Māori also invested in large ships in the early part of the nineteenth century to engage more effectively in local and international enterprises (Petrie, 2007).

In terms of social organization, for Māori, *te waka* also refers to a group of people with a common territory and common links to members of a voyaging canoe and is used to identify groups larger than *iwi* or *hapū*. Identification with *waka* is simpler for some tribal groups but more complex for others (Ballara, 1998). For example, depending on the circumstances or context of *hui* (meeting, gathering), Māori may choose to identify with (*whakapapa*, layering of relationships) to particular social groups by naming several *iwi* and *hapū* and *waka* affiliations when introducing themselves.

However, in giving voice to Home as a journey of social transformation, resistance, and resilience, many aspects of Home altered irrevocably for Māori when legislative changes were imposed by the British Crown and its representative government in New Zealand. For example, acquisition, control, and expropriation of land were key factors in consolidating Crown sovereignty and according to Durie (1998), significant expropriation was heavily engaged in between 1840 and 1852, with millions of acres of land being acquired or taken from Māori. In addition, Walker considers the Native Land Act of 1862 to be one of the most damaging legislative contributions to the expropriation of Māori land. Although Māori have since made gains in terms of the settlement of treaty claims, the legacy of Crown control through represented institutions and enforced political and legal change is still evident. This is most notable in the enduring and uneven distribution of recognition, access, opportunity, rights, resources, economic, political, and social opportunity for Māori.

However, *whanau* (extended family) is still considered the most enduring form of social arrangement in Māori society. Within *whanau*, individual well-being is critical to maintaining and advancing the well-being of the collective. However, the term *whanau* may emcompass both *whakapapa* (kin-based) and *kaupapa* (purpose driven) *whanau* (Metge, 1995). Home now has a sphere of engagement that may include church, sports, leisure, community, social events, and so forth.

Building upon the *whanau* or extended family, *Hapū* have always been strategically important to Māori for socio-political and economic advancement, and they continue to weave relationships between *whānau*, *iwi*, communities, and national and regional government agencies. However, *iwi* (tribal institutions) are now primary vehicles for Māori development with some now surpassing the billion-dollar mark.

Marae (meeting places) are culturally designed institutions that are authentic expressions of Māori social innovation and are often a key center point of Home. However, legislatively constructed *iwi, rūnanga*, a wide variety of Māori trust boards, representative government agencies, Māori/government co-management, and administrative boards have also emerged in recent decades and are reshaping notions of Home. Such entities operate within a dual frame of reference: *tikanga* and legal identity. Within a *tikanga* context, regulation according to tribal customs remains important in terms of managing Home in a holistic relational sense, while the legal context requires compliance to legislation. In addition, co-management systems that include government agencies and Māori tribes working cooperatively are often included in tribal settlements. Responses to such models couched in a partnership discourse are mixed, with some viewing them as an important opportunity to co-develop resources and sustainable wealth, while others view these models as ongoing forms of de facto sovereignty.

Corporate *iwi* enterprises, tribal federal alliances, Māori owned and operated businesses, Māori organizations located in mainstream bureaucracies, *hapū* partnerships, cooperatives, and new strategic global alliances are evidence of Māori engagement in social transformation designed to enhance and advance individual and collective aspirations while retaining unique relationships with lands, lakes, rivers, oceans, and forests.

In terms of resistance, resilience, and innovation, this journey of social transformation illustrates how Māori, as proactive agents, continue to use new organizations as *waka* (vehicles) to deliver economies of well-being that benefit all. In a post-treaty settlement era, the ongoing demand for autonomous institutions will continue to elicit new forms of social organization that once again reshape evolving realities of Home.

Home as Navigating Futures

Reflecting on Home as navigating futures to enhance economies of well-being, Spiller draws insight from life energies captured in the term *mauri ora*. *Mauri* is a binding force, and energy that unites diverse elements in the universe (Marsden, 2003: 47, 60) ascribing intrinsic worth to all (Morgan, 2008). *Mauri ora*, meaning well-being, is, from a Māori perspective, intentionally realizing and manifesting the full potential in relationships as *ora* denotes "well" and "in health" (Williams, 1975). When *mauri* and *ora* come together, it is with the intention to bring about well-being (Spiller et al., 2010).

Mauri as a life-force is oriented toward healing and sustaining life (Marsden, 2003; Tipu Ake ki te Ora, 2011); thus, in a Māori worldview, wisdom is linked to consciously creating well-being. Spiller argues that organizations must therefore act consciously to create economies of well-being. Such creation involves stewardship whereupon care and conservation are at the heart of values systems, which call upon humans to be *kaitiaki*, stewards of the *mauri*, the life force, in each other and in nature. She notes this resonates with the original meaning of the old English "welth," meaning "to be well" (Zohar and Marshall, 2004: 2). Well-being, then, is the goal of wisdom, not wisdom for wisdom's sake – but how wisdom serves others.

In reinforcing the point that Home is about navigating futures, Spiller asks, How does the concept of Home enable us to chart new trajectories in business? She suggests that Māori businesses continue to think inter-generationally, an important concept for understanding traditional ecological integrity. While mindful of "now," their outlook is aligned with what Shirres (1986: 18) calls an "eternal present" that embraces ancestors and events of the past. The eternal present is situated in an understanding of a greater reality where "the universe is not static but is a stream of processes and events" (Marsden, 2003: 21) and is very much a "matter of present experience, a living and lived-in reality" (Metge, 1995: 45).

Spiller suggests the navigational orientation system of Māori businesses can be likened to that of Oceanic traditional navigators, described as the "local reference" system and wayfinding (Spiller et al., 2015). In this system, directions relate to local prominent features, and voyagers rarely lose connection with their point of departure. As wayfinders, they remain simultaneously aware of both their destination and Home base. The self is not perceived in terms of "self-centered-ness" (Gatty in Lewis, 1972: 169) but inhabits a woven universe of "related-ness" with communities and ecologies. Thus, a sense of belonging is central to a Māori relational view of the world, which holds that all people are called into being through relationships where "I belong therefore I am" (local referencing system) (Spiller et al., 2010). This sense is unlike much Western philosophy, which is a response to Descartes' proposition, "I think therefore I am," promoting a philosophy that asserts primacy of the individual (self-centered referencing system). So how can we cultivate a sense of Home and belonging in business? Spiller believes one way to keep strengthening the relational dimensions in every aspect of business, to enable flourishing economies of well-being, is to ensure the business is grounded spiritually, culturally, socially, and environmentally.

Conclusion

The primary aim of this chapter was to contribute a cultural perspective to sustainability. To do this, the authors focused on giving voice to the story of resistance, resilience, and innovation in Māori economies of well-being. The notion of Home was used as a touchstone as it is inextricably associated with enacting and asserting sovereignty (*tino rangatiratanga*) over environs and destinies.

The two questions raised at the outset were: How are embedded and evolving realities of Home manifested in Māori economies of well-being? What is the role of Traditional Ecological Knowledge in these transformations?

To answer these questions, we highlighted that Home from a Māori perspective is embedded in holistic relational systems where the natural, social, and spiritual worlds are interrelated, and the well-being of the individual is central to the well-being of the collective. Home and economies in this world emerge from traditional knowledge that combines cultural and spiritual traditions with social kinship systems and practices known as *tikanga*.

In extending the discussion, four frames of reference were used: Home as Identity; Home as Kainga and community; Home as Waka Ao Turoa, a journey of social transformation; and Home as Navigating Futures. The chapter highlighted that Home as identity is subject to transformative influences that change relationships and lead to creating new "Homes" in new spaces and places for Māori. Home as *kainga* and community has evolved over time to meet the economic needs of *whanau, hapu,* and *iwi* Māori and continues to be manifest in the dispersed social geographies Māori now inhabit. Home as *waka ao turoa,* a journey of social transformation, highlighted the evolution of social organizations that continue to shape and reshape our concepts of Home. Finally, Home as navigating futures highlighted the need to unite life energies based on concepts of *mauri ora* (well-being) and *kaitiakitanga* (stewardship and guardianship) in ways that assist businesses and organizations to intentionally create economies of well-being.

In sum, this chapter has contributed a cultural dimension to sustainability by highlighting the ongoing relevance of TEK in the study of economies of well-being. We conclude with a *whakatauiki* (proverb) that guided the thoughts offered in this chapter.

"Matariki ahunga nui, Matariki tapuapua, Matariki hunga nui, Matariki kanohi iti."

Matariki ahunga nui is a season of bounteous harvests and plentiful food supplies; *Matariki tapuapua,* when the abundance of sacred waters flow from above providing spiritual and physical refreshment; *Matariki hunga nui,* when many followers congregate together to work cohesively and collaboratively in social arrangements engaged in "seeding, planting, sowing, harvesting and replenishing the sources"; *Matariki kanohi iti,* with the little faces of Matariki guiding the way, providing insight and vision *i te ara hou,* on the pathway to new beginnings.

WORKS CITED

Ballara, Angela. *Iwi: The Dynamics of Māori Tribal Organisation from c.1769 to c.1945.* Wellington, NZ: Victoria University Press, 1998.
——— *Taua: Musket Wars, Land Wars or Tikanga?: Warfare in Māori Society in the Early 19th Century.* Auckland: Penguin, 2003.
Barlow, Cleve. *Tikanga Whakaaro: Key Concepts in Māori Culture.* Auckland: Oxford University Press, 1991.

Berkes, Fikret. *Sacred Ecology.* New York: Routledge, 1999.

Berkes, Fikret, Johan Colding, and Carl Folke. *Navigating Social-Ecological Systems: Building Resilience for Complexity and Change.* Cambridge, UK: Cambridge University Press, 2003.

Cajete, Gregory. *Native Science: Natural Laws of Interdependence.* Santa Fe: Clear Light, 2000.

Deloria, Vine, Jr. "Indigenous Peoples." *The Blackwell Companion to Religious Ethics,* edited by William Schweiker. Malden, MA: Blackwell, 2005, 552–59.

Dewes, Te Kapunga. "The Case for Oral Arts." *Te Ao Hurihuri: The World Moves On,* edited by Michael King. Wellington, NZ: Hicks and Smith, 1975, 55–85.

Durie, Mason. "A Māori Perspective of Health." *Journal of Social Science and Medicine,* 20 (5), 1985, 483–86.

Te Mana, Te Kawanatanga: The Politics of Māori Self-Determination. Aukland: Oxford University Press, 1998.

Gladwin, Thomas N., James J. Kennelly, and Tara-Shelomith Krause. "Shifting Paradigms for Sustainable Development: Implications for Management Theory and Research." *Academy of Management Review,* 20 (4), 1995, 874–907.

Hamilton, Clive. *Growth Fetish.* Crow's Nest, New South Wales: Allen & Unwin, 2003.

Hawken, Paul. *The Ecology of Commerce: A Declaration of Sustainability.* New York: HarperCollins, 1993.

Henare, Manuka A. "The Changing Images of Nineteenth Century Māori Society." Unpublished PhD thesis. Wellington: Victoria University, 2003.

"Lasting Peace and the Good Life: Economic Development and the 'Te Atanoho' Principle of Te Tiriti o Waitangi." *'Always Speaking': The Treaty of Waitangi and Public Policy,* edited by V. M. H. Tawhai and K. Gray-Sharp. Wellington, NZ: Huia, 2011, 261–75.

"Tapu, Mana, Mauri, Hau, Wairua. A Maori Philosophy of Vitalism and Cosmos." *Indigenous Spiritualties at Work, Transforming the Spirit of Enterprise,* edited by Chellie Spiller and Rachel Wolfgramm. Charlotte, NC. Information Age Publishing, 2015, 77–98.

Henry, Ella and Hakiwai Pene. "Kaupapa Māori Research: Locating Indigenous Ontology, Epistemology and Methodology in the Academy." *Journal of Organization Studies,* 8 (2), 2001, 234–42.

Hirini, Paul. "Te Kaimatai Hinengaro Māori: The Māori Psychologist." *Proceedings of Te Oru Rangahau: Māori Research and Development Conference,* edited by Te Pumanawa Hauora. School of Māori Studies, Massey University, July 1998, 204–11.

Hiroa, Te Rangi. *Vikings of the Sunrise.* Wellington, NZ: Whitcombe and Tombs, 1954.

Houkamau, Carla. *Identity and Socio-historical Context: Transformations and Change Among Māori Women.* Unpublished PhD thesis. Auckland: University of Auckland, 2006.

"Māori Identity Construction and Reconstruction: The Role of Sociohistorical Contexts in Shaping Māori Identity." *Social Identities: Journal for the Study of Race, Nation and Culture,* 16 (2), 2010, 179–96.

Howe, K. R. *The Quest for Origins: Who First Discovered and Settled New Zealand and the Pacific Islands.* Auckland: Penguin, 2003.

Irwin, Geoffrey. *Prehistory Navigation and Colonisation of the Pacific.* Cambridge, UK: Cambridge University Press, 1992.

Jackson, Tim. *Motivating Sustainable Consumption: A Review of Evidence on Consumer Behaviour and Behavioural Change: A Report to the Sustainable Development Research Network.* Surrey: Centre for Environmental Strategy, University of Surrey, 2005.

Prosperity Without Growth: Economics for a Finite Planet. London: Earthscan, 2009.

Kawharu, Ian Hugh. *Māori Land Tenure: Studies of a Changing Institution.* Oxford, UK: Oxford University Press, 1977.

Waitangi: Māori & Pakeha Perspectives of the Treaty of Waitangi. Auckland: Oxford University Press, 1989.

LaDuke, Winona. "Traditional Ecological Knowledge and Environmental Futures." *Colorado Journal of International Law and Policy,* 127, 1994, 127–48.

Lawson-Te Aho, Keri. "The Socially Constructed Nature of Psychology and the Abnormalisation of Māori." *New Zealand Psychological Society Bulletin,* 76, 1993, 25–30.

Kia Piki te Ora o te Taitamariki: Strengthening Youth Wellbeing. New Zealand Youth Suicide Prevention Strategy. Wellington, UK: Ministry of Māori Development, 1998a.

A Review of Evidence: A Background Document to Support Kia Piki te Ora o te Taitamariki: Strengthening Youth Wellbeing. New Zealand Youth Suicide Prevention Strategy. Wellington, UK: Ministry of Māori Development, 1998b.

Lewis, David. *We the Navigators.* Honolulu: University of Hawaii Press, 1972.

Marsden, Māori. *The Woven Universe: Selected Readings of Rev. Māori Marsden,* edited by Te Ahukaramu Charles Royal. Otaki, NZ: The Estate of Rev. Māori Marsden, 2003.

Max-Neef, Manfred. "Economic Growth and Quality of Life: A Threshold Hypothesis." *Ecological Economics,* 15, 1995, 115–18.

Mead, Hirini Moko. *Tikanga Māori: Living by Māori Values.* Wellington: Huia Publishers, 2003.

Meadows, Donella, Dennis Meadows, and Jorgen Randers. *Beyond the Limits: Confronting Global Collapse, Envisioning a Sustainable Future.* Post Mills, VT: Chelsea Green, 1992.

Metge, Joan. *New Growth from Old: The Whanau in the Modern World.* Wellingto, NZ: Victoria University Press, 1995.

Morgan, T. K. *The Value of a Hapū Perspective to Municipal Water Management Practice: Mauri and its Potential Contribution to Sustainability Decision-making in Aotearoa New Zealand.* Unpublished PhD thesis. Aukland: University of Auckland, 2008.

Nelson, Anne. *Nga Waka: Maori Canoes.* Wellington, NZ: IPL Press, 1999.

Nelson, Melissa K. "Lighting the Sun of Our Future: How These Teachings Can Provide Illumination." *Original Instructions: Indigenous Teachings for a Sustainable Future,* edited by Melissa K. Nelson. Rochester, VT: Bear & Company, 2008, 1–19.

Orange, Claudia. *Illustrated History of the Treaty of Waitangi.* Wellington, NZ: Bridget Williams Books, 2004.

Petrie, Hazel. *Chiefs of Industry: Maori Tribal Enterprise in Early Colonial New Zealand.* Auckland: Aukland University Press, 2007.

Sachdev, Perminder Sachdev. "Psychiatric Illness in the New Zealand Māori." *Australian and New Zealand Journal of Psychiatry*, 23 (4), December 1989, 529–41.

"Behavioural Factors Affecting Physical Health of New Zealand Māori." *Social Science and Medicine*, 30 (4), 1990a, 431–40.

"Mental Health and Illness of the New Zealand Māori." *Transcultural Psychiatric Research Review*, 27 (2), 1990b, 85–111.

Shirres, Michael P. *An Introduction to Karakia.* Unpublished PhD thesis. Auckland: University of Auckland, 1986.

Sibley, Chris G. and Carla A. Houkamau. "The Multi-dimensional Model of Māori Identity: Item Response Theory Analysis of Scale Properties." *Cultural Diversity and Ethnic Minority Psychology*, 19, 2013, 97–110.

Smith, Linda Tuhiwai. *Decolonizing Methodologies: Research and Indigenous Peoples.* London: Zed Books, 1999.

Spiller, Chellie, Barclay-Kerr Hoturoa, and John Panoho. *Wayfinding Leadership: Groundbreaking Wisdom for Developing Leaders.* Wellington, NZ: Huia Publishing, 2015.

Spiller, Chellie, Ljiljana Erakovic, Manuka Henare, and Edwina Pio. "Relational Well-being and Wealth: Māori Businesses and an Ethic of Care." *Journal of Business Ethics*, 98 (1), 2010, 153–69.

Statistics New Zealand. [online] URL www.stats.govt.nz/census/2013-census/profile-and-summary-reports/quickstats-about-maori-english.aspx

Tipu Ake ki te Ora. Retrieved May 11, 2011, from www.tipuake.org.nz

Te Puni Kokiri. Ministry of Māori Development: The Māori Economy Report 2013. [online] URL: www.tpk.govt.nz/en/a-matou-mohiotanga/business-and-economics/maori-economy-report-2013.

Walker, Ranginui. *Ka Whawhai Tonu Matou: Struggle Without End.* Auckland: Penguin, 1990.

White, C. "Anthropological Analysis of Social Structure, Organisation and Values." *Sustainable Māori Development in Tai Tokerau, Ngapuhi Region.* James Henare Māori Research Centre, University of Auckland, 1998.

Williams, H. A. *Dictionary of the Māori Language.* Wellington, NZ: A. R. Shearer, Government Printer, 1975.

Wolfgramm, Rachel. *Continuity and Vitality of Worldview(s) in Organisation Culture: Towards a Māori Perspective.* Unpublished PhD thesis. Auckland: University of Auckland, 2007.

Wolfgramm, Rachel, Sian Flynn-Coleman, and Denise Conroy. "Dynamic Interactions of Agency in Leadership (DIAL): An Integrative Framework for Analysing Agency in Sustainability Leadership." *Journal of Business Ethics*, 126 (4), 2013, 649–62.

Wolfgramm, Rachel M. and Ella Henry. "Ancient Wisdom In a Knowledge Economy Before and Beyond Sustainability: Valuing an Indigenous Perspective." *International Indigenous Business Conference*, Sandia Casino Resort, Albuquerque, July 2006.

Zohar, D. and I. N. Marshall. *Spiritual Capital: Wealth We Can Live By.* San Francisco: Berrett-Koehler, 2004.

13

Indigenous Peoples and "Cultural Sustainability": The Role of Law and Traditional Knowledge

Rebecca Tsosie

Introduction

The protection of tribal cultural heritage is closely linked to the cultural survival of Native peoples. Because of this, American Indian and Alaska Native peoples within the United States have successfully lobbied for federal statutory protection for certain categories of tangible cultural resources. The Native American Graves Protection and Repatriation Act of 1990 (NAGPRA), for example, protects the rights of federally recognized tribal governments, as well as Native Hawaiians, to ancestral human remains and funerary objects, sacred objects, and objects of cultural patrimony. In addition, Congress has protected the tribes' commercial interests in producing authentic Native art (such as baskets, rugs, and jewelry) for sale through the Indian Arts and Crafts Act (IACA). This statute precludes non-Indians from selling these types of products as "Indian-made," thereby conferring a trademark in the identity of "Indian" to federally recognized Indian tribes and their members.

There is, of course, a great deal of cultural knowledge that is embedded within tangible cultural resources, as well as Indigenous art forms. However, this "traditional knowledge" is currently not recognized as a cultural resource that merits legal protection. Rather, the intangible essence of an object is generally not part of the calculus of ownership for purposes of Western property law. This was demonstrated in the June 2013 public sale of Hopi ceremonial objects by a Paris auction house to the highest bidders, which went forward against the protests of the Hopi Tribe. The "purchasers" obtained the legal right of possession without the cultural obligation to honor the duties of care required by Hopi tradition. Within many Indigenous societies, sacred objects, such as medicine bundles, require elaborate feeding and care by their stewards. Within those traditions, the bundles are alive; they have an essence, an identity, and they exert power in the material world. Consequently, there are songs and prayers that go with the object. In such cases, Native cultural practitioners would consider it ridiculous, and probably dangerous, to compartmentalize the object separately from its qualities, and the duties and obligations that are required. Why should non-Indigenous possessors have any "right" to do what the Indigenous cultural practitioner could not do?

The answer to that question relates to the predominant Euro-American view of property rights and the powers of a sovereign, such as the United States or state governments, to regulate the use and transfer of property, domestically and internationally. With respect to tribal property rights, another set of norms, embedded in federal Indian law, becomes pertinent. United States federal Indian law describes tribal governments as "domestic, dependent nations," under federal protection. Tribal property interests in land or natural resources are protected under federal law because of the federal government's "trust" duty to the tribe. Tribal trust lands and water resources are not alienable without federal consent. However, if the tribal property interest does not fall into a protected category of intellectual property (and most tribal intangible resources, including songs, ceremonies, and traditional knowledge would not), then the interest receives no legal protection, unless Congress explicitly enacts legislation authorizing such protection (as it did with NAGPRA and the IACA). Congress is perceived to have the authority to legislate on behalf of the Indian nations in the exercise of its "plenary power" under the Indian Commerce Clause.

Traditional knowledge is a valuable resource, as evidenced by international discussions on sustainability policy. Unfortunately, tribal governments are not directly represented in those discussions, which often leads to confusion about the nature of their rights. A panel of experts from the United Nations (2007) recently expressed concern that the latest draft of the UN Sustainable Development goals had deleted all references to "Indigenous peoples," substituting instead the phrase "Indigenous and local communities." The shift might seem harmless to the uninformed reader. However, as the UN experts noted, the effect of the change was to undermine the successes that Indigenous peoples have made in claiming their rightful identity as "peoples" with the right to self-determination. Self-determination entails autonomy over land and resources, including cultural resources. Indigenous peoples consider their traditional knowledge to be a "cultural resource," and one that is vital to their continued ability to thrive and maintain an intergenerational presence on their lands. Sovereign governments can own resources, as can individuals and corporations. On the other hand, ethnic and cultural groups do not own collective resources. Individual members may speak the language or practice the customs, but no entity is perceived to "own" the culture. So, identity is very much a key component of the debate over ownership of traditional knowledge.

In comparison, the nation-states increasingly see Traditional Ecological Knowledge (TEK) as a resource that can benefit global society, particularly in an era of climate change. For example, the United Nations University Institute for the Advanced Study of Sustainability maintains a Traditional Knowledge Initiative, which seeks to study Indigenous sustainability practices and knowledge systems as a way to understand how to use resources efficiently, improve waste management, and adapt to climate change. Such initiatives are valuable, but run the risk of exploiting Indigenous peoples to the extent that they proceed without adequate attention to the right of self-determination.

In this chapter, I will address the question of whether and how Indigenous traditional knowledge should be protected under international law, domestic federal law, and tribal law. I am arguing for a concept of "cultural sustainability," and it is my position that traditional knowledge is part of the "cultural heritage" of Indigenous nations and that they have the full authority to control and regulate this knowledge in the exercise of their traditional governance authority. I will further take the position that the United States has an affirmative duty to safeguard tribal rights to traditional knowledge, and the international human rights framework ought to be invoked in service of the duty of all nation-states to collaborate in order to protect the interests of Indigenous nations in safeguarding traditional knowledge.

Traditional Knowledge: Understanding the Foundational Issues

The traditional knowledge possessed by Indigenous peoples represents a holistic system of cultural knowledge when considered from the perspective of the group. However, when outsiders explore the utility of the knowledge, they typically divide Indigenous knowledge into categories that align with the dominant society's intellectual property system.

Consequently, the nation-states generally place "traditional cultural expression" (TCE) into a category similar to that governed by copyright law (art, literature, songs, stories), while sustainability practices and health innovations are linked to patent law, which governs science and technology. In both cases, Indigenous knowledge generally fails to meet the operative standards for protection under Western law. Indigenous cultural expression is generally quite old and songs and stories are transmitted intergenerationally, while intellectual property law generally protects "new" forms of creative expression. Moreover, the group possesses the knowledge, and so it is difficult to assign "ownership" because there is no "artist" or "creator" for purposes of copyright protection, and no "novel and unique invention" for purposes of patent law. In addition, Indigenous knowledge may be linked to material objects, such as the knowledge that traditional healers often possess about medicinal plants. However, the resource (e.g., the plant) is considered separately from the knowledge about its useful qualities. Because this knowledge is not accompanied by a technological innovation, the plant, as a product of nature, will not be eligible for patent protection. The knowledge that accompanies the plant may also be unprotected, unless there are equitable arguments in favor of "benefit-sharing" to avoid exploitation of the traditional knowledge holders.

Thus, there are several foundational issues that commonly occur in any discussion of traditional knowledge, including the nature of traditional knowledge, the ability to develop meaningful categories for legal protection, whether the holders of the knowledge should be considered "owners" or "beneficiaries," and the scope of protection (which involves the question of what actions would be at least morally wrongful, constituting, for example, "biopiracy").

What Is the Scope of Traditional Knowledge and What Actions Are at Least Morally Wrongful?

Traditional knowledge is a broad category, inclusive of ritual knowledge, historical knowledge, social knowledge, medicinal knowledge, and scientific knowledge, among other categories. Angela Riley notes that Indigenous peoples' Traditional Knowledge (TK) includes "ancient medicines, farming techniques, literature, music, ceremonies, folklore, and art" (Riley, 2007: 373). In the sustainability literature, most attention is focused on the traditional knowledge that Indigenous and local communities have about their environments (inclusive of human/natural environment). In all cases, this knowledge has been gained through successive generations of habitation within traditional territories and thus constitutes a valuable and irreplaceable body of knowledge. However, it is a continuing challenge to define the identity of the knowledge holders in a way that allows them to claim legally protectable rights. If the knowledge holders are from a "traditional or local community," this is less important, because the discussion will focus on principles of "equitable benefit-sharing" between the knowledge holder and the external entity on the basis of a transaction. If the knowledge holders are "Indigenous peoples," however, the issue is very important. International human rights law struggles with the effort to define "Indigenous peoples," and there is no definition at all in the Declaration on the Rights of Indigenous Peoples, which is the most recent human rights document dealing with Indigenous rights.

Who Is "Indigenous"?

Although there is no uniform definition to describe "Indigenous peoples," I will use the term in its most basic sense, to describe "the original inhabitants of traditional lands," who maintain their traditional values, culture, and way of life. The term may comprise the First Nations of given lands, such as those in Canada, New Zealand, Australia, and the United States, that were colonized by Great Britain and then placed under the political sovereignty of the European nations that settled the lands and reorganized as new "multicultural" nation-states. In these "settler societies" the demarcation between Indigenous peoples and the peoples who settled the lands is quite clear, historically, politically, and culturally. However, in its larger sense, the term may describe "local communities" that share ethnic and cultural traits with the dominant society, and yet are distinctive because they maintain traditional, land-based economies and socio-cultural modes of organization. In Africa and Asia, for example, the historic shifting of populations and territories is notable and the demarcation depends mainly upon the type of lifeway practiced by the group. Traditional tribal societies operate according to customary law, while the dominant society is likely to have a modern, multicultural social and political structure, and an integrated "global" economy.

Although the Declaration on the Rights of Indigenous Peoples does not define the term "Indigenous peoples," it does recognize that Indigenous peoples have the right of self-governance in their domestic affairs, and should be treated with respect and dignity by the national governments in their collective capacity. Thus, individual members of the Indigenous group are entitled to claim the rights of national citizens on an equal basis to others, but they also have rights that derive from their membership in the collective. The collective (as a "people") is entitled to self-determination, including rights to self-governance and rights to control property and resources. The Declaration contains 46 Articles that delineate the rights of Indigenous peoples to protect their lands and national environments, safeguard their cultural heritage (including language, religion, and cultural resources), and maintain their own institutions of self-governance. The Declaration also counsels national governments to involve Indigenous peoples in policy making decisions, and to obtain their "free, prior and informed consent" before taking actions that would jeopardize their fundamental rights. In that sense, the Declaration imposes procedural and substantive norms to ensure the equitable treatment of Indigenous peoples.

For purposes of this chapter, I will argue that the United States already possesses a framework that recognizes tribal governments as sovereigns capable of holding and managing property and resources. Thus, the definitional issues are more constrained under US domestic law, and largely concern those groups who claim Indigenous status but lack formal recognition by the US government. The status of non-recognized groups is compelling, but it is not an obstacle for the vast majority of Indigenous peoples in the United States, who already have status as recognized tribal governments.

The Categories of Traditional Knowledge

The World Intellectual Property Organization (WIPO) is in the process of crafting a treaty on Traditional Knowledge. The Treaty is useful in its draft form because it seeks to identify the relevant categories of traditional knowledge and prescribe standards for equitable treatment. In the most recent draft, "Traditional Knowledge" is defined to include "the know-how, skills, innovations, practices, teachings and learnings" (Anaya, 2017) of Indigenous peoples, local communities, and states that are "dynamic and evolving, and that are passed on from generation to generation," and may exist in "codified, oral or other forms." Of this broad category, the document provides that protection would only extend to particular forms of knowledge that are internal to the community, associated with its cultural and social identity, and maintained by the group through each generation. If the knowledge is available outside the group or has fallen into the "public domain," it would not be eligible for protection.

The document specifies that this knowledge may be associated with fields "such as agriculture, environmental, healthcare and indigenous and traditional medical knowledge, biodiversity, traditional lifestyles and natural resources and genetic resources, and know-how of traditional architecture and construction technologies." However, the document maintains a special section defining "Traditional knowledge associated with genetic resources," which means "substantive knowledge of the properties and uses of genetic resources and their derivatives held by indigenous peoples and local communities and which directly leads to a claimed invention."

This set of definitions is important because it illustrates the difficulty of trying to fit categories of Indigenous knowledge into a form that approximates that of the Western intellectual property law system. The categories of Indigenous knowledge often seem broad to cultural outsiders. Therefore, the document attempts to disassociate that which is protectable – because its use has been kept out of the public domain and is essential to the cultural survival of the group – from the vast stores of knowledge that are shared more broadly. In addition, the document defines the relevant knowledge holders as "beneficiaries" and suggests that nation-states may claim beneficiary status for themselves if they pass appropriate legislation. The idea that Indigenous knowledge can be "nationalized" by the encompassing nation-state is problematic, but fits with the notion that "society at large" is a potential beneficiary of some traditional knowledge.

The category of knowledge associated with genetic resources is an interesting hybrid because it disassociates the knowledge from the material object (e.g., a plant), and also from the broad category of traditional knowledge, by developing a description that links this knowledge to the development of an invention. In that respect, the document moves toward the language of patent law.

For purposes of sustainability policy, it is perhaps more useful to speak of the category of "traditional ecological knowledge." Indigenous peoples are unique because they have a longstanding and intergenerational presence upon their traditional territories, and this "ethics of place" is deeply embedded within their cultures and social organization. For most Indigenous peoples, sustainability is the result of conscious and intentional strategies designed to secure a balance between human beings and the natural world and to preserve that balance for the benefit of future generations. Indigenous sustainability is represented by generations of practices, governance structures, and complex knowledge systems. These sustainability practices, structures, and systems have enabled Indigenous peoples to survive and adapt over many generations, despite the massive shifts in their social and environmental worlds caused by European settlement of Indigenous lands. Resilience, stability, and balance are fundamental values within the constellation of Indigenous sustainability practices. Today, Indigenous nations continue to invoke those values, as they develop and reinvigorate their own survival mechanisms to meet contemporary challenges.

Traditional Ecological Knowledge

As a subcategory of TK, Traditional Ecological Knowledge comprises the "culturally and spiritually based way in which indigenous peoples relate to their ecosystems" (LaDuke, 1994: 127). Importantly, Traditional Ecological Knowledge reflects Indigenous systems of environmental ethics as well as the group's scientific knowledge about environmental use that has resulted from generations of interaction. For example, the Traditional Ecological Knowledge of the Dene people of Canada "consists of a spiritually based moral code or ethic that governs the interaction between the human, natural and spiritual worlds" (Tsosie, 1996: 225) and it "encompasses a number of general principles and specific rules that regulate human behavior toward nature" (Tsosie, 1996: 273).

There are striking parallels among many Indigenous groups. For example, most Indigenous peoples who retain their traditional ecological knowledge have land-based subsistence economies, rather than industrial or market economies. Most Indigenous peoples perceive their traditional structures to be separate and distinct from the colonial systems that were imposed upon them. Many Indigenous peoples believe that the core aspects of their identity as distinctive peoples of a specific territory are defined in relation to this traditional knowledge. A central feature of many Indigenous world views is found in the "spiritual" relationship that Indigenous peoples maintain with their environment. Spiritual rights are unique to Indigenous peoples in the human rights literature and importantly linked to their lifeways, which often consider lands and other natural resources to be sacred to the people. Spiritual rights are often conflated with religion, but this is not an adequate account. There may be functional integration of the economic and religious orders of the Indigenous society (for example, Pueblo Nations have this type of functional integration), and yet it would be incorrect to conflate spiritual values with religious values. Rather, Indigenous spirituality reflects central norms of identity, kinship, and relationship that anchor the moral ordering of the society within an overall environmental ethic.

Although Indigenous peoples possess distinctive cultures, a notable commonality exists among Indigenous environmental ethics. Indigenous peoples share a perception of the earth as an animate being (Tsosie, 1996: 276–79). Most consider human beings to be in a kinship relationship with other living beings, and they consider their traditional lands to be essential to the identity of the people. Most groups maintain a guiding ethic of reciprocity and balance that extends to relationships among humans, including the future generations, as well as relationships to other living beings.

Because the overall category of "traditional ecological knowledge" may seem quite broad, outsiders may believe that appropriation is permissible. For Western cultures, "ideas" are considered "free as the air that we breathe" and appropriation is the norm, unless an exceptional circumstance (e.g., a patent) forbids nonconsensual transfer. This norm enables the exploitation of Indigenous peoples and is therefore unjust as applied to them. We must do a more particularized analysis of the intercultural norms at stake and assume that nonconsensual transfers are likely to constitute "biopiracy," a wrongful act. In all cases, Indigenous peoples must be consulted and asked to give free, prior, and informed consent before outsiders use their knowledge.

What Constitutes "Ownership" of Traditional Knowledge, and Who Are the "Owners"?

The issue of ownership is also complex. Under Western property law, ownership is an attribute of individuals and of certain collectives, such as nations and corporations, which maintain collective standing to own particular resources on behalf of their constituent members. For example, nations may own "public property," such as national parks, on behalf of the citizens of the nation. No single citizen could own the property for the benefit of the public. The nation is uniquely situated to maintain this form of public ownership.

Corporations have a legal identity similar to that of individuals, although they are accountable to their shareholders as the relevant constituent owners. Thus, the corporate entity owns the resources as would an individual, though profits are distributed among group members. The ownership of Indigenous nations is more similar to that of national governments, although there may be important cultural differences. For example, Indigenous nations commonly place specific stewardship responsibilities with subgroups, such as clans, moieties, and religious societies, even though the collective (tribe) actually owns the property. In such cases, the specific custodians exercise the duties of care and control for the benefit of the larger Indigenous nation. This is the argument, for example, that pertains to cultural patrimony under NAGPRA, which is defined as property that is central to the identity of the group and cannot be alienated from the group by any particular individual member, without first securing the consent of the group.

For these reasons, the concept of ownership is best defined according to the customary law of the Indigenous nation. It is very difficult for cultural outsiders to understand the identity of Indigenous groups as "peoples," "tribes," or "nations" because each of those words constitutes a term of art under international law and, in some cases, under domestic law. The Western definition may or may not map onto the term used by the Indigenous peoples themselves, particularly where the traditional mode of social organization is by local band, rather than overarching "nation." This is apparent from treaty law, where certain historic treaties (e.g., the Treaty of Ruby Valley with the Western Shoshone people) were signed with the overarching collective of culturally related bands, while particular subgroups (e.g., the Fallon Paiute-Shoshone Tribe) constitute the current federally recognized tribal governments.

In addition, the understanding of duties and obligations with respect to resources is likely to be highly contextualized according to the culture of the group and the nature of the resource. For example, the specific duties may be those of stewardship, rather than ownership, if we look to the role of those entrusted with managing the resource. The Blackfeet Nation in Montana, for instance, possesses a cultural norm that requires circulation of medicine bundles throughout the nation to ensure the well-being of the collective. Yet those norms do not authorize transfer outside the group to non-members.

One significant problem concerns the fact that traditional knowledge may be shared among culturally related groups that today maintain different political identities. So, for example, to the extent that an Indigenous people (like the Lakota) are now divided into several distinctive tribal governments (Pine Ridge, Rosebud, Yankton), one government has the political authority to consent to transfer traditional knowledge, even though the transfer may violate the understanding of the group's cultural authority among other governments. This has been a point of contention in many of the land claims cases, such as that of the Western Shoshone, where different factions of the historic people dispute the justice of receiving a monetary settlement in lieu of the land in a takings claim.

What Rights Accrue from the Fact of Ownership?

If we invoke a Western European lens, the legal fact of "ownership" entails a full bundle of rights, including the right to use, the right to control, the right to exclude, and the right to share. However, we must be careful not to invoke Blackstone's conception of "absolute" ownership (the "despotic" rights of land ownership) if this is not consistent with the cultural view of the Indigenous nation. So, again, I would maintain that these rights are to be described according to the worldview of the Indigenous group and then negotiated with the nation-state to afford adequate protection to the resource.

My central argument is that solutions cannot be found in our current legal structure nor can they come from the predominant moral framework of Western liberal theorists. Rather, protection of Indigenous traditional knowledge must be informed by intercultural norms. Because of this, it is entirely likely that the protection of Indigenous traditional knowledge will require us to structure a "sui generis" system of legal protection. In this respect, federal Indian law in the United States offers a beginning template for such a structure.

The Basic Structure for Legal Protection of Indigenous Rights in the United States

American Indian and Alaska Native governments are separate sovereigns that preexisted the formation of the United States, and many of the tribal governments entered treaties with Great Britain, France, and Mexico prior to their treaties with the United States. Tribal governments retain inherent sovereign authority to regulate their lands, resources, and members, and they may also regulate nonmembers who enter tribal territory or engage in consensual relationships with the tribe or its members, provided that there is no acknowledged legal barrier to this exercise of jurisdiction. Thus, tribal law is of paramount importance to the issue of how to protect Indigenous traditional knowledge. Tribal law may be unwritten, customary law, or it may be formalized into a written code. Many tribal governments are drafting legislation to protect tribal cultural heritage, including traditional knowledge, genetic resources, and intangible cultural heritage, such as songs and ceremonies.

Under federal Indian law, tribal governments are held to have all the sovereign powers that they possessed at contact, except those that were ceded by treaty or taken away by Congress in the exercise of its plenary power. Starting in 1978, the Supreme Court held that tribes were also "implicitly divested" of powers to adjudicate non-Indians where this would be "inconsistent" with their "dependent status." In particular, the Supreme Court reasoned, the exercise of criminal jurisdiction over non-Indians and could jeopardize the liberty interests of non-Indian citizens (see *Oliphant v. Suquamish Indian Tribe*, 1978). However, with limited exceptions, tribes still retain full powers of inherent sovereignty to regulate their lands, resources, and members.

The federal government has a duty to protect the sovereign authority of tribal governments, except where this would impair federal interests, protected by the Supremacy Clause. As a result, statutes of nationwide application, such as the federal pollution control statutes, may apply to reservation lands, as well as state and federal lands. In these cases, complex doctrines articulate the jurisdictional parameters of federal, state, and tribal authority, and Congress often must enact amendments to specify how the jurisdictional rules will be operationalized within Indian Country.

Congress has never enacted legislation removing the rights of federally recognized tribal governments to their cultural resources. To the contrary, NAGPRA requires the repatriation of tangible cultural heritage that meets the definitions within that statute. Nor does legislation exist that impairs tribal governance of intangible resources. Although US intellectual property laws typically do not protect traditional knowledge, there is no positive enactment of law that divests tribes of their rights to their traditional knowledge. Consequently, governance of Indigenous traditional knowledge should start within the Indigenous nations, and their laws should be protected by federal law, enabling application to nonmembers, including researchers, who often conduct the majority of their activities outside of the reservation.

Tribal cultural heritage, under this model, should be treated as a reserved right for purposes of tribal inherent sovereignty. Furthermore, the moral requirement of self-determination, as stated in the Declaration on the Rights of Indigenous Peoples, is that Indigenous peoples "freely determine their political status and freely pursue their economic, social, and cultural development." This means that tribal governments must decide, in the first instance, how to protect their cultural heritage. The United States must then protect tribal interests under federal law, and, finally, the interests of Indigenous peoples must be protected internationally under human rights principles.

In reality, however, the human rights directive of Indigenous self-determination, as it concerns Indigenous cultural heritage, is currently in grave tension with the forces of international trade law (Tsosie, 2012: 222). International trade law is best served by a robust public domain in which scientists and others freely innovate new technologies for commercial profit and gain, which is why the idea of a "genomic commons" is also appealing to researchers. In comparison, Indigenous cultural heritage, including traditional knowledge, is best protected under tribal cultural norms, which are often quite restrictive, based on the particular values that are at stake. Tribal governments are the ones that must decide whether commercialization of their knowledge or biological resources is appropriate, or whether selling or sharing this knowledge would impair the values that have enabled cultural survival for generations (Tsosie, 2012: 245).

There is not a great deal of international law or policy on the protection of intangible cultural heritage. The closest analogous case concerns governance of biodiversity.

Implementation Issues: The Case of Biodiversity

The Convention on Biological Diversity opened for signature on June 5, 1992 and entered into force on December 29, 1993. The United States signed the Convention on June 4, 1993, but the Senate never ratified it, an approach the United States takes toward many international conventions. It will sign on in principle, but will not effectuate the convention under US constitutional law, which requires ratification by the Senate and domestic legislation to implement the Treaty. Despite the internal challenges of full implementation, the United States, as a signatory, is entitled to participate as an observer in the international negotiations concerning the implementation of the Convention. For our discussion, it is interesting to see how the United States is responding to the challenge of implementing Article 8(j) of the Convention, which provides the following:

Each contracting Party shall, as far as possible and as appropriate: Subject to its national legislation, respect, preserve and maintain knowledge, innovations and practices of indigenous and local communities embodying traditional lifestyles

relevant for the conservation and sustainable use of biological diversity and promote their wider application with the approval and involvement of the holders of
such knowledge, innovations and practices and encourage the equitable sharing
of the benefits arising from the utilization of such knowledge, innovations and
practices. (Rio Convention, 1993)

After signing on in principle to this document, the United States assembled
an "interagency working group" to explore what the implementation of
this provision would entail. Specifically, the federal working group que-
ried "whether federal law imposes limits upon indigenous communities'
own efforts to protect indigenous knowledge through direct restrictions
on members' ability to reveal such knowledge to outside researchers"
(Indian Civil Rights Act, 1968).

The working group's initial assumption was that tribal restrictions on
members might violate the free speech norm of the First Amendment.
However, as they discovered, the First Amendment does not limit the
actions of tribal governments because those governments were not parties
to the Constitution. The free speech norm is applicable to tribal governments by statute, because it is embedded within the Indian Civil Rights Act
of 1968. However, according to the relevant case law, the constitutional
norms imposed by the ICRA are to be assessed under tribal law within
tribal court systems. Thus, it is not clear that the tribe would be unable to
regulate the conduct of its members seeking to breach confidentiality by
disclosing aspects of the group's traditional knowledge. In addition, the
working group noted that the answer to this question would obviously
depend upon whether the information could be viewed as tribal property,
rather than the property of an individual tribal member. The group also
considered whether the tribe had a strong interest in nondisclosure, similar to the interests of corporations under the trade-secret doctrine, which
protects the commercial investment of companies against actions by rogue
employees who would seek to alienate the information to competitors
for commercial gain. Again, the interests are not identical, suggesting that
there is a need for sui generis protection of Indigenous knowledge.

In an analogous case in Australia, for example, a court held that federal
copyright law should be extended in equity to protect the tribe's interests
in a traditional design representing its origin story. The court created the
"*Bulun Bulun* equity" doctrine *(Bulun Bulun v. R & T Textile Pty Ltd.,*
1998), which recognizes that the tribe is the traditional owner of the creation story and the design. The tribe had licensed a tribal member to paint
the picture for a public display of Indigenous art. However, that license
did not extend to permit a non-Indigenous corporation from reproducing
the design on T-shirts and other commercial products. Rather, the tribal

member was limited by his equitable license from the group to depict the creation story in a painting intended to educate the public about the tribe's traditional land claim.

In 2010, the US Interior Department convened a meeting of Indian law experts to discuss three related issues:

(1) Whether federal supremacy subordinates all aspects of enforcement related to intellectual property to US federal law, common law, and international treaties.
(2) Whether tribal governments have any authority to regulate intellectual property under tribal law.
(3) Whether an Indian treaty reservation of use-rights in off-reservation areas obligates the United States, as trustee, to protect the genetic integrity of the reserved resources.

I participated in that meeting, and my own response, as a scholar of federal Indian law and constitutional law, was that Indigenous nations retain full rights in their traditional knowledge and any associated resources, and they only give them up to the extent that they have expressly consented to do so, invoking the human rights norm of free, prior, and informed consent. In my view, the supremacy clause would only limit tribal governments to the extent that the expression or creation falls squarely within the parameters of US copyright, trademark, or patent law and the tribal action would violate the protections of federal law. Because traditional knowledge generally does not fall under the protection of federal laws, it ought to be fully protected under tribal law and under the federal trust responsibility.

I also believe that Indian treaties that secured tribal rights to hunt, fish, and gather in specific areas off the reservation obligate the United States, as trustee, to protect the genetic integrity of the reserved resources. Contamination of wild salmon runs by farmed salmon or bioengineered salmon, for example, can jeopardize the salmon resource as well as the cultural rights of the various Indigenous nations that have always had a relationship with salmon, often considering them to be "nonhuman persons." Thus, tribal rights to genetic resources may be embedded within the text of the treaties that the United States signed with particular Native nations.

The International Structure

The domestic laws of the United States, primarily those governing copyright, patent, and trademark, are of vital importance to determining what is protected as intellectual property. The theory is that the public domain is the repository for new inventions and creations, and the intellectual property system is carefully structured to avoid long-term monopolies on ideas and innovation. Protection is limited and intended to incentivize creation and innovation by allowing creators to gain some profit from their ideas before they go into the so-called knowledge commons known as the public domain.

International protections for artists and inventors are more difficult to secure because of jurisdictional constraints. So, the international trade structure is invoked to secure this protection voluntarily from member states. Intellectual property and trade are linked through the Agreement on Trade Related Aspects of Intellectual Property Rights (TRIPS, 1994), as well as related treaties between nation-states. TRIPS adopted minimum standards for intellectual property protection that are binding on all member states of the World Trade Organization (WTO). Prior to this, developing countries had little incentive to comply with the intellectual property protections that are so important to innovation in developed countries. However, after TRIPS, these countries are subject to sanctions and mandatory dispute resolution processes if they violate these protections. TRIPS has been criticized as an effort by the developed countries to impose Western intellectual property law on the entire world. This criticism inspired an inquiry into the potential human rights implications of the law, which, in some cases, aligned the issues of Indigenous peoples with those of developing countries in Asia and Africa. These nations also tend to possess ancient forms of knowledge, including medicinal knowledge, which is perceived to be of value to pharmaceutical companies and other commercial entities.

The World Intellectual Property Organization (WIPO) has played an important role in the dialogue about the need to protect aspects of folklore and traditional knowledge. In 2000, WIPO established the Intergovernmental Committee on Intellectual Property and Genetic Resources, Traditional Knowledge, and Folklore. This committee provides a structure for governments to discuss possible protections for TK and folklore. The Committee also undertook a study that proposed a hybrid system of TK protection, based on the intellectual property model. As demonstrated earlier, WIPO is currently convening meetings around a proposed treaty that would delineate protectable from nonprotectable aspects of TK.

It is unclear whether the current negotiations will result in a level of consensus that would allow a binding treaty to come into force. At this juncture, it is necessary to recognize that nation-states are negotiating according to their own respective concerns and interests, and Indigenous peoples' interests are largely subsumed within the position of the nation-state. In that respect, the United States may speak for all of the federally recognized tribal governments in the international negotiations because tribal governments lack the standing to appear on their own behalf. At a minimum, this arrangement should require the United States to engage in consultations with each federally recognized tribal government to ensure that they have the appropriate understanding of the position of the tribal governments on ownership of their TK.

In the consultation process, it will be necessary to observe the respective starting places of the United States and the Indigenous nations, because this will also inform the potential outcome. The United States will likely start from the perspective of free trade and intellectual property rights, according to the WIPO/WTO approach. The Indigenous nations may start from the perspective of their right to self-determination. The contours of the respective approaches are traced in the following section.

WIPO/WTO Approach

Currently, most discussions of TK are situated within the Western framework of international trade and intellectual property law. Under this structure, the predominant norm is free access to knowledge and ideas unless there is some reason to recognize a limited right to protection. The theory is that if we reward inventors with a limited-time economic advantage, they will have an incentive to invest in the development of useful products or processes. A robust public domain secures the benefits of innovation more broadly. Access is only limited to secure a legal right under intellectual property law or to secure an ethical norm, such as benefit-sharing with communities to avoid exploitation of their knowledge about medicinal plants.

This approach favors open access and benefit sharing in the form of economic benefits and limited rights. Although Indigenous peoples often seek to block outsiders in perpetuity from accessing their knowledge, there is a pervasive view that a perpetual right to exclude will disadvantage society (constructed at the global level). Under this utilitarian calculus, the costs and benefits are weighted in favor of the interests of society and the public.

Critics contend that if we prevent communities from claiming ownership at all, this may promote exploitation or create a unique disadvantage by excluding tribal groups from participating in the market, which is a human rights issue because it tracks the harms of colonialism. The solution is crafted on a property model, which allows government takings of Indigenous traditional knowledge if necessary to serve a broader good (sustainability, for example). Under this view, the interests of justice and fairness are served by compensating communities for takings of their knowledge. Proponents argue that if takings are allowed, Indigenous peoples will have an economic incentive to bargain for transfer of their technology and no incentive to try to exclude others from access. A collateral necessity is to assemble databases documenting Indigenous knowledge, on the theory that ownership and prior art must be proven factually and not merely asserted as a matter of right. Obviously, access to the database and breach of protocols regulating disclosure is a separate (but important) issue.

This model is problematic because it boxes Indigenous peoples into the Western structure, thus replicating the colonial model that allowed expropriation of land via the fiction of discovery. The injustices of the past should not be reproduced in the present, and therefore a better model can be constructed from the emerging norms about Indigenous self-determination.

The Self-Determination Model

Drawing inspiration from the United Nations Declaration on the Rights of Indigenous Peoples, and specifically the norm of self-determination, I suggest that the paramount duty of nation-states is to protect cultural integrity because it is the very nature of Indigenous peoples as distinctive cultural communities living on traditional lands that undergirds the notion of Indigenous rights.

Under this model, Indigenous knowledge is cultural property to be protected according to the norms of each Indigenous culture. If the group wants to participate in the market system, this option should be available. However, if they do not want to participate, they should not be forced to provide access. Without free, prior, and informed consent to a transfer, the harm to the community is likely to be extensive and the benefit to society might be negligible.

The Indigenous nation in the exercise of its right to self-determination should be recognized as having ownership of its traditional knowledge, along with the ability to exclude others from access and to gain damages for misuse of the traditional knowledge. This directive should, at a minimum, be the model for human genetic resources. Plant resources are more problematic to the extent that there has been widespread use of the technology by different groups in a region or country (as is the case with Basmati rice in India). In those cases, claims of national identity are likely to be appropriate, and, with respect to tribal groups, may necessitate inter-tribal cooperative efforts.

The Convention on Biological Diversity was an important first step because it specifically addressed the rights of Indigenous and local communities and called for nation-states to consult with those communities before entering into any scheme for benefit sharing. The process that is emerging within the United States is compatible because it is built on the notion embedded within federal Indian law that Indian nations are separate sovereigns with rights to lands and resources distinctive from those of the American public. In this capacity, the United States has a duty to consult with Indigenous peoples and develop just systems of governance for resources in which there are shared interests. The one-size-fits-all approach of US intellectual property law is insufficient to protect the rights and interests of Indigenous peoples, and a sui generis system of protection must be developed, in accordance with prevailing human rights norms.

Conclusion

I have argued for the development of a sui generis system of protection within the United States for traditional knowledge. This step is particularly important in the context of adaptation planning, given the predictions of experts on climate change. Sustainable development in an era of climate change involves land use, water conservation, energy resource development, and agriculture. Tribal governments have protectable interests in all of these resources, and they often possess associated traditional knowledge about the resource. This knowledge may be useful in an era of climate change to alert scientists to changes in the natural environment that jeopardize fish or wildlife resources, as demonstrated by the work of scientists in the Arctic – research that relies to a significant degree on knowledge possessed by Indigenous communities living within subsistence economies and reliant on hunting and fishing resources. In addition, scientists may use Indigenous botanical knowledge to innovate new pharmaceuticals or new strains of drought-resistant crops.

Currently, the regulation of traditional knowledge is considered an ethical issue, rather than a legal matter. Because Indigenous peoples do not have a property interest in the natural environment separate from their actual beneficial title to reservation lands and associated resources, they are not recognized as having a property interest in the knowledge about the environment. Therefore, scientists engaged in adaptation planning can freely innovate their discoveries based on information about the resource, and then they can gain the intellectual property right via the patent registration system, provided the discovery otherwise meets the statutory requirements for new and innovative products or processes.

The Convention on Biological Diversity injected an ethics of benefit sharing to guide the use of traditional knowledge. Each nation-state that signed this document pledged to recognize the value of traditional knowledge held by Indigenous peoples about biodiversity (the prime category of TEK), as well as local communities, and women, and to encourage the free sharing of such knowledge for research and development (broad access), conditioned upon the agreement of researchers to share any benefits that ensued. This ethical view has not been widely adopted in any enforceable way, with the limited exception of certain specific contractual agreements brokered by Latin American governments for particular Indigenous groups.

Thus, it is very likely that nation-states will have to come together at the international level and link the protections for Indigenous peoples to concrete goals within international trade policy. For the first time, there will be a synergy between the interests of Indigenous peoples and those of the developing countries. This development will pose a political challenge because the United States typically aligns its domestic policies with its international policies, which can work to the advantage of tribal governments in some cases. For example, the failure of the United States to sign onto any binding restriction on greenhouse gas emissions in the international climate accords allows for the expansion of coal, oil, and other forms of energy development on Indian reservations, as well as on public lands. This policy serves the interests of tribal governments engaged in fossil fuel production. However, with respect to traditional knowledge, the dynamic of exploitation and the history of colonialism have been a shared experience of Indigenous peoples and many developing countries. In comparison, the system of international trade has always served the interests of the industrialized nations. It will be quite instructive to see how the United States approaches the challenge of protecting the rights of Indigenous nations to their traditional knowledge.

WORKS CITED

"Agreement on Trade Related Aspects of Intellectual Property Rights," April 15, 1994.

Anaya, James. "Technical Review of Key Intellectual Property-Related Issues of the WIPO Draft Instruments on Genetic Resources, Traditional Knowledge and Traditional Cultural Expressions." *Intergovernmental Committee on Intellectual Property and Genetic Resources, Traditional Knowledge and Folklore*, Thirty-Third Session, Geneva, February 27 to March 3, 2017, WIPO/GRTKF/IC/33/INF/9 (December 6, 2016).

Bulun Bulun v. R & T Textiles Pty Ltd. (1998), 157 ALR 193.

"Indian Arts and Crafts Act," 25 U.S.C. 305 et seq.

"Indian Civil Rights Act of 1968," 25 U.S.C. 1301 et seq.

"Indian Commerce Clause," U.S. Constitution, Article I, sec. 8.

LaDuke, Winona. "Traditional Ecological Knowledge and Environmental Futures." *Colorado Journal of International Law and Policy*, 127, 1994, 127–48.

"Native American Graves Protection and Repatriation Act, 1990," 25 U.S.C. 3001 et seq.

Oliphant v. Suquamish Indian Tribe, 435 U.S. 191, 1978.

Riley, Angela K. "Indigenous Peoples and Intellectual Property Rights." *Intellectual Property Law and Information Wealth*, Vol. 4, edited by Peter K. Yu. Westport, CT: Praeger Publishers, 2007, 373–92.

"Rio Convention on Biological Diversity," Art. 8(j), 1760 UNTS 79; 31 ILM 818 (entered into force on December 29, 1993).

Tsosie, Rebecca. "International Trade in Indigenous Cultural Heritage: An Argument for Indigenous Governance of Cultural Property." *International Trade in Indigenous Cultural Heritage: Legal and Policy Issues*, edited by in Christoph B. Graber, Karolina Kruprecht, and Jessica C. Lai. Northampton, MA: Edward Elgar, 2012, 221–45.

  "Tribal Environmental Policy in an Era of Self-Determination: The Role of Ethics, Economics, and Traditional Ecological Knowledge." *Vermont Law Review*, 21, 1996, 225–333.

"United Nations Declaration on the Rights of Indigenous Peoples," G.A. Res. 61/295 (U.N. Doc. A/61/L67 and Add. 1) (adopted September, 13 2007).

14

Conclusion

Back in Our Tracks – Embodying Kinship as If the Future Mattered

Melissa K. Nelson

I recently returned from a tour of Tla-o-qui-aht Tribal Park in Nuu-Cha-Nulth territory in Tofino, Vancouver Island, British Columbia, Canada (Figure 2) where I felt fully immersed in the lived reality of Traditional Ecological Knowledge (TEK). It was a visceral sense of connection and belonging. I was inspired to be with so many elders who still retain the language and old ways of living in that lush, temperate rainforest and on those interconnected waters of river, bay, sound, and ocean. I was even more moved to meet with many young Native folks – children, teenagers (both high school and university students), graduate students, and young adults – eagerly interested in maintaining their beautiful languages, food-ways, canoe traditions, fishing practices, and governance systems. While feasting on traditionally prepared beach-fire-cooked first spring salmon, one twelve-year-old girl enthusiastically shared with me, "I am eating out of a shell with my hands instead of a plastic fork or paper plate because I'm keeping the Native ways going."

I was with a group of about thirty people as part of a Tribal Park Tour to remember the historic precedent set there over thirty years ago in 1984, when the Tla-o-qui-aht and Ahousaht First Nations (with great support from local environmental groups and others) asserted their aboriginal land rights, demanded an end to logging, and declared Meares Island Canada's first tribal park. We recognized that historic moment and enjoyed the beauty of that land, which is today three interlocking tribal parks committed to environmental stewardship, developing sustainable livelihoods, restorative justice, community healing, and traditional/ecological governance. We visited First Nations-owned restaurants, hotels, ecotour sites, carving sheds, and fishing areas. We canoed across the famous Clayoquot

FIGURE 2 Tla-o-qui-aht Tribal Park, Tofino, BC, Canada. (Photo by Melissa K. Nelson.)

Sound to Meares Island, learning from a young Nuu-Cha-Nulth woman, Tsimka Martin, about her people's rich experiences of living and working in their tribal homelands, some of it now a tribal park.

I was also fortunate to participate in a historic meeting of First Nations as several elders, chiefs, and community members joined the tour from the Tsilhqot'in Nation, an Athabaskan-speaking group of six communities in northern inland British Columbia. This small but mighty First Nation has recently received a lot of attention in local, national, and international media as they have experienced three major victories: the creation of Dasiqox Tribal Park, winning a game-changing Canadian supreme court case for aboriginal land title (*Tsilhqot'in Nation v. British Columbia*, 2014), and Marilyn Baptiste, a tribal member and former chief, receiving the prestigious Goldman Environmental Prize in 2015. Such legal and global recognition speaks to the shift in consciousness that is occurring in terms of recognizing the importance of Indigenous peoples and their TEK in helping to keep the planet healthy.

The Tla-o-qui-aht name of the Tribal Park is *hishuk ish ts'awalk*, "everything is one." The Tsilhqot'in name for their park is *nexwag-wez?an*, "there for us." Combining the meaning of these two tribal park names, we learn that "everything is one and it is there for us." Inherent in these concepts is the message that whatever we do to the land, which is our source of life, we do to ourselves. These tribal names communicate the critical importance of language in understanding and embodying an Indigenous environmental ethic.

Indigenous Ethics

Native languages, as the basis for Indigenous worldviews and lifeways, have their own words for the concept of "ethics." From the aforementioned examples, we see that these two First Nations have a holistic concept of oneness, and that land exists for us to take care of and provide for us. From my understanding of other Indigenous languages, words for ethics could be interpreted as responsibility, guardianship, mutual support, and spiritual obligation. Mark Paikuli-Stride, a Hawaiian farmer, interprets the Hawaiian word for land, *aina*, as "that which nourishes you" (Nelson, 2008: 305). Lenape scholar Jay T. Johnson investigates the Māori word, *kaitiakitanga*, meaning environmental guardianship: "The guardian invests his *mana* into the preservation of the resource and in turn derives from the resource *mana*, spiritual life and food to feed his or her community" (Johnson and Larsen, 2013: 130). Petuuche Gilbert, Acoma knowledge holder and relative of author Simon Ortiz shares, "[O]ur place is called Aakuu. It meant and still means 'prepared'" (Nelson, 2008: 36).

Given these Indigenous words and concepts, we see that environmental ethics are intrinsic within the terms and are deeply tied to perceptions of nourishment, investment of life-force, and a sense of preparedness. These ethics are tied to moral responsibility and justice, as in Western meanings, and they also carry a deeper, more fundamental requirement. That is, if we do not take care of "others," in a serious way, we will *not* take care of ourselves because from Indigenous languages and worldviews there is no artificial separation of self and other as there is under the Western notion of Cartesian dualism. To even utter the word *land* in Nuu-Cha-Nulth or Hawaiian or Acoma is to speak of our profound connection and obligation to place. Kinship and guardianship are necessary for our very survival because all life (if cared for) takes care of us, providing food, medicine, shelter, clothing, and so on. Accordingly, Indigenous words for self, identity, nation, land, and place are imbedded with ethical responsibility and point to humans' role as keepers of the green world.

This visceral, embodied, place-based ethic and concept of a relational and ecological self is diametrically opposed to the concept of the scientific self that is based on an abstract, objective, disembodied, and decontextualized knower (Dumont, 2008: 32–53). This distinction means that in any discussion about the importance of environmental ethics it is important to know what *type* of ethic we are talking about in terms of conceptions of self and place.

Thankfully, a growing awareness of the need for an environmental ethic has taken hold since the burgeoning environmental movement of the 1960s and 1970s, yet some environmental ethics still seem abstract, i.e., the value of clean air. After that value or ethic is expressed, the next question should be, "How do I help *create* clean air? Or *protect* clean air?" The Indigenous ethics of TEK are longstanding, intergenerational, and tied more to manners and behaviors than principles, in the sense that they are more about actions and hands-on activities than beliefs or ideals. All the chapters in this book explore the nuances and expressions of Indigenous and environmental ethics, especially the chapters by Jeannette Armstrong, Dennis Martinez, Robin Kimmerer, and Simon Ortiz.

Jeannette Armstrong concludes that her own tribally specific Syilx environmental ethic is inextricably tied to land-use practices and a social governance system. She illustrates how these three areas (ethics, land-use, and governance) must be integrated for an effectively applied and lived sustainability. She also boldly suggests that indigeneity, rather than being a property of cultural heritage and bloodline, is a lived philosophy sustaining the life-force of a specific place. She asserts that if humans were committed to fostering and embodying such an environmental ethics of place, this dedication would be a form of re-indigenization needed to shift from monocultures and dislocation to co-existence and environmental justice.

Dennis Martinez outlines how a truly sustainable environmental ethic, or what he calls a "conservation ethic," is not possible under individualistic, free-market capitalism committed to constant growth. Citing an in-depth case study of salmon and hatcheries, Martinez skillfully contrasts the philosophies and methods of both Western and Indigenous ethical-economic models. Using examples from both traditional agriculture and nonagricultural land-care practices, Martinez deconstructs the wilderness concept and illuminates the sophisticated science of "tending the wild" (Cronon, 1995; Anderson, 2013; Kimmerer, 2013). He concludes that an Indigenous redefinition of sustainability can be achieved through the eco-cultural restoration of traditional land-care practices that are based on a kincentric ecology, which is governed by five key principles: responsibility, restraint, biodiversity enhancement, adherence to natural law, and wealth distribution.

This same theme of kincentric ecology is echoed in the chapter by Robin Kimmerer and exemplified through Native peoples' relationships with plants. She describes how cultures of gratitude lead to cultures of reciprocity and demonstrates this with a story of sweetgrass, a revered native plant teacher with which she has conducted scientific studies to learn what helps it grow. Her research shows that sweetgrass populations that have been respectfully tended by human hands did much better than sweetgrass populations left alone, demonstrating that human tending and small-scale disturbances to plant communities can have beneficial impact. Kimmerer's example highlights the teachings of the Honorable Harvest, which makes clear the many benefits of TEK land management and eco-cultural restoration.

Award-winning poet Simon Ortiz provides an in-depth tribally specific example of the Acoma Pueblo people's complex and sophisticated relationship to land, providing a strong example of ethics in action, or what he calls Indigenous sustainability. Ortiz reminds us that for Pueblo people, language is the cultural foundation that secures a person's place upon the earth. The style of this chapter demonstrates the power of language through the use of Ortiz's native Keres language. For Ortiz and other Native people, land is the source of origin, and so one's connection to the land is literal and visceral, not symbolic or abstract. His chapter also provides a concrete example of TEK by outlining the science and technology behind the Hohokam-O'odham canal and irrigation system historically used in the Sonoran Desert. TEK matters, Ortiz concludes, because it is the foundation for Indigenous wholeness and it provides pragmatic tools for resiliently responding to environmental change.

The roots of Indigenous sustainability and ethics go back to cosmovisions – cosmology and cosmogony – the creation and origin stories that provide instructions for how and why we are here. As Gregory Cajete shares earlier: "Cosmology, the lived story of place, kinship, and environmental knowledge, forms the foundation for the expression of Native science in Native communities" (Chapter 2, p. 20). Within these diverse and complex cosmologies, epic narratives convey ethics and obligations, as well as specific directions or metaphoric "instructions" showing how to care for particular ecological features, such as rivers, medicine plants, and totem animals. Therefore, for Indigenous cultures rooted in their TEK, *not* having a moral relationship to the land is not an option if one wants to nurture life and help sustain it for future generations.

Tragically, these profound kinship ties and much of the sophisticated ecological knowledge and practices of Indigenous peoples were severely ruptured by multiple waves of destructive colonization. Today Native peoples are fiercely hanging on to their Indigenous knowledges and practices, and working to renew and restore them, despite ongoing threats to Native lands and livelihoods.

Cree scholar-activist Priscilla Settee clearly outlines the profound negative impacts that colonization has inflicted on the lands and lives of First Nations in Canada, specifically through changes in their food sovereignty. Through an in-depth review of agricultural economics and examples from resource extraction industries, Settee shows how once diverse, sustainable, and abundant native food sources and healthy First Nations/aboriginal communities were transformed into polluted landscapes and communities suffering from epidemic rates of diabetes, obesity, depression, and suicide. She states, "It is a simple equation that when land is taken, the local economy suffers along with the sense of native identity, and a people's physical and spiritual health deteriorates" (p. 177). Settee points out the major contributions Indigenous peoples' TEK has historically played in creating global food security with examples from Native agriculture. Additionally, she says that, despite her previously mentioned "simple equation," the Indigenous peoples of Canada are working hard today to create new community gardens and markets, organic agricultural policy, and innovative educational programs to restore Indigenous food sovereignty.

Whether working to restore Native foods, medicines, or languages, realizing an Indigenous sustainability, at root, has to do with understanding that humans are part of a kincentric world where we are all related and where the natural world has eyes and teeth – it is alive, can see us, and, if ignored, can harm us.[1] For Martinez, kincentricity is part of an "evolutionary cultural heritage" and "is about the reciprocal relationships contained in Indigenous stories of an 'Original Compact' made between the animals and humans" (p. 140). Through oral narratives and place-based stories, the elements of nature (mountains, trees, waterways, and so on) act as "text," providing cultural metaphors for

---

[1] The term *kincentrism* was coined by Dennis Martinez and Enrique Salmon in the 1990s and was first published in Enrique Salmon's germinal essay, "Kincentric Ecology: Indigenous Perceptions of the Human-Nature Relationship" (2000). "The Land Has Eyes, the land has teeth, and knows the truth" is a Rotuman proverb that was the basis for one of the first feature films ever made by a Native Rotuman filmmaker, *The Land Has Eyes* in 2004.

proper behavior. This practice is sometimes called a *moral landscape*, as Raramuri ecologist Enrique Salmon has stated: "... our morality is directed from the landscape" (Nelson, 2008: 100). Moral landscapes are part of a *native ecology* where each Indigenous nation has its own creation stories, original instructions, and TEK for taking care of its unique home ecosystems.

Before we learn how to harvest salmon, grow blue corn, or gather clay for medicine, we need to understand that these natural relatives (not resources) are gifts from the earth and ultimately gifts from a Creator or life-force beyond human control or comprehension, thus demanding great humility. Robin Kimmerer reminds us that "we inhabit a landscape of gifts" and these natural gifts of sun, water, air, soil, plants, and animals are ultimately not separate from us and certainly not inferior to us (Kimmerer, 2013, 2014). We need them to live and they were created by the same life-force that created us; therefore, we are equal parts of the web of life that sustains us.

Award-winning author Linda Hogan articulates the power of human-animal relationships in "The Radiant Life with Animals." In this chapter, Hogan poetically and powerfully communicates the emotional and spiritual bond humans can have with animals when we dare to be present and still, allowing animals to recognize the soul of the human. Through personal stories of encounters with animal beings (including whales, caribou, and eagles), Hogan shows us the potential depth of interspecies intimacy. "One of my grandmothers was an eagle ..." begins one story, demonstrating a profound kinship and love with the majestic bird too often feared for its fierceness. Through her stories, Hogan embodies the courage to love the more-than-human world. She concludes that, in order to address current environmental crises, humans must revive a more humanistic, compassionate, and respectful connection to other species with whom we share the planet.

Ingrained within Indigenous languages is the sense that an ethical relationship to place is not an intellectual concept; rather, it is a daily, embodied practice. Like all relationships, this one needs to be enacted, applied, responded to, cared for, and renewed as a way of being. It is best practiced in place over time, in local spaces where one has an opportunity to truly develop intimacy with particular mountains, valleys, forests, rivers, creeks, plants, and animals. This intimacy is the rich biocultural heritage of Indigenous place-based cultures that often have thousands of years of observations and experiences stored as oral narratives, native sciences, and place-based lifeways. This ethical relationship to ancestral places may be rooted in complex, philosophical cosmo-visions but is also manifested in practical, hands-on hard work on and with the land.

The Trouble of Terminology

These complex knowledge practices and ways of being have been called traditional knowledge, Indigenous knowledge systems, TEK, and Native Science, to name a few variations. They are also often referred to as "Indigenous ways of knowing," to imply a fluid diversity of ways and to make them more active and animate rather than static and rigid. Gregory Cajete's introductory chapter outlines the larger context of TEK as Native Science, and he articulates its many elements and processes that are resonant with the principles and practices outlined by the other authors.

In his chapter, "What Do Indigenous Knowledges Do for Indigenous Peoples?" Kyle Whyte refers "to all such English-language concepts as *Indigenous knowledges.*" For this book we focus on the term *Traditional Ecological Knowledge* (TEK), as it explicitly highlights a holistic *ecological* reality that allows the authors their own meanings and definitions, based on their tribal background and/or home ecosystem. Whyte is concerned about the ways TEK is often used and interpreted *by* non-Natives. For example, scientists looking for new evidence, sources of data, or ways to solve environmental problems often explore and appropriate the concept. He points out the lack of publications and discourse showing how Indigenous peoples are using TEK for their *own* planning and development, especially in regard to climate change, self-determination, and local resilience.

Whyte's chapter provides a solid examination of the terminology surrounding the concept of TEK and its various forms. He examines how and why the term came into being, as well as the beneficiaries and those who gain nothing or are even harmed by the misappropriation of traditional knowledge. Focusing mainly on the use of TEK by climate scientists, Whyte argues for a more careful and nuanced understanding and application of the term, especially in relation to governance, sovereignty, and larger political dimensions. Including contemporary Indigenous peoples in sustainability studies, not only their worldviews, is essential.

Just as the term *sustainability* has become almost meaningless because of its overuse and broad interpretations, TEK has also been problematized by numerous interpretations and uses, often by people outside Native cultures and skeptical of not only Indigenous knowledge but also Indigenous peoples themselves (Simpson, 2001; Agrawal, 2002). Additionally, TEK is being used in more superficial or even exploitive ways to satisfy diversity requirements or to hop on the academic bandwagon. This tokenism or "red-washing" is parallel to how *sustainability* has been exploited by corporations in the form of "green-washing." As I've written elsewhere, "As human beings deeply conditioned by technological modernity, we must be wary of the intellectual habit of objectification where 'tradition,' 'Indigenous science,' or 'TEK' may be reified, fragmented, and commodified for external exploitation" (Nelson, 2014: 190). Clearly, the concept of TEK is still problematic and contested both in academia and within Native communities. This book hasn't solved the debates but hopefully it illuminates and frames them for further discussion. Additionally, despite these tough issues, the authors all conclude that TEK is the seed of an important paradigm shift in science and the way humanity thinks of sustainability and the conservation of Earth.

TEK Influencing Mainstream Areas

We conclude that TEK is becoming a major conceptual force and area of study in academia, government, and conservation. Gregory Cajete refers to this time as the "Rise of the Indigenous Mind." It is clear that Indigenous peoples generally and TEK specifically are making new, significant contributions in the academy: from environmental ethics in philosophy to resource conservation, ecological services, and ethnobiology in the biological sciences and anthropology; from food security, agroforestry, and ethnoclimatology in the agricultural sciences to "green" planning in landscape design and architecture. TEK is now a recognizable academic acronym, conveying acceptance and legitimacy as an area of study and investigation across many disciplines. Some very innovative and exciting collaborations are occurring in this convergence of sciences, as authors Michael Paul Nelson and John Vucetich outline in Chapter 8, "Wolves and Ravens, Science and Ethics: Traditional Ecological Knowledge Meets Long-term Ecological Research."

Nelson and Vucetich begin their chapter by noting that different scholars emphasize different elements of TEK. Roughly, these elements map onto the subdisciplines of philosophy: epistemology (ways of knowing), metaphysics (conceptions of being), and ethics (notions of proper valuation and action). Much of the conversation surrounding TEK focuses on epistemology – asserting and demonstrating that Native peoples exhibit different ways of knowing about the world – and contrasting these ways with Western Scientific Ecological Knowledge (SEK). Nelson and Vucetich contend that most of the substantial differences between TEK and SEK actually have more to do with worldviews and ethics than with ideas in comparative epistemology. That is, an inclusive environmental metaphysic and corresponding ethic is what many find important and inspirational about TEK. What may be most distinctive about TEK – compared to SEK – is how knowledge is founded on a strong *sense of place*. Though a minority tradition within SEK, long-term ecological research (LTER) parallels the commitment to long-term place-based observations. However, while TEK embraces an inclusive ethical parallel, SEK has yet to develop a similar ethical correspondent. Focusing on specific case studies involving wolves and ravens, the essay suggests a possible environmental ethic consistent with long-term ecological research.

Some governmental agencies are also beginning to acknowledge and recognize TEK. On a 2014 MSNBC TV interview, former US Secretary of the Interior, Sally Jewell (2014), claimed, "In my role as Secretary of the Interior we will make sure that there's a platform for those tribal voices to be heard." In reference to Native Americans, she continued, "And I think they will make a very effective case because they know their lands better than we do."

"They know their lands better than we do." This is quite an admission coming from the US Secretary of the Interior, the official responsible for managing the National Park Service (NPS), Bureau of Land Management (BLM), and the Bureau of Indian Affairs (BIA), who also is authorized to help determine the legal status of US tribes. Although NPS, BLM, US Forest Service (USFS), and other federal agencies are beginning to acknowledge and incorporate TEK in local projects, there hasn't been a similar statement by a US Secretary of the Interior ever before. For an example of a USFS project incorporating TEK, one can find "Traditional Ecological Knowledge (TEK), Climate Change and Land Management," a tribal partnership between the Karuk Tribe and the USFS "to incorporate TEK in forestry, fire, fuels, and fisheries research and management" (USDA, nd).

"They know their lands better than we do" is a clear statement about the value of local Native knowledge systems, which recognize the profound ecological understanding, historic land tenure, and, ultimately, the sovereignty of tribal nations. Whether Secretary Jewell meant all of this with her comment is unclear, but the fact that she publicly acknowledged the superior ecological knowledge of countless generations of Native Americans was a major step forward in explicitly recognizing the TEK of First Peoples by a United States governmental agency.

TEK and Native ways of land management are also receiving substantial recognition in the area of conservation and protected areas
management at local, national, and international levels. New forms of
Native-based conservation are emerging in government, in the private
land trust movement, and globally through new models of Indigenous
conserved areas, biocultural territories, and among international groups
addressing land conservation, climate change, and biocultural research
(Middleton, 2011; Grossman and Parker, 2012 ; Maffi and Woodley,
2010). Additionally, considerable discussion and debate about "TEK
and sustainability" are taking place within international agencies such
as the United Nations Environmental Program (UNEP), the International
Union for the Conservation of Nature (IUCN), United Nations University,
and at global fora such as those addressing the UN Declaration on the
Rights of Indigenous Peoples (UN DRIP), the Convention on Biological
Diversity (CBD), and the Conference of the Parties (COP) meetings on
climate change (21st through 23rd sessions). Spaces for the definition,
application, and protection of Indigenous knowledge and the protection
of Indigenous peoples' rights are no longer always side events at these
meetings but, rather, are becoming significant themes and central topics
for debate, exploration, learning, and, hopefully, action.

In November 2014, I participated in the IUCN's World Parks Congress
(WPC) in Sydney, Australia, where 6,000 people met over a week to discuss the most pressing issues in parks and protected areas management.
According to the IUCN, protected areas cover about 15.4 percent of the
land's surface and 3.4 percent of the oceans', and most of these places are
ancestral homelands to Native peoples. Indigenous rights and issues were
more strongly represented at the WPC than ever before. Out of seven
thematic "streams," the seventh was dedicated to "Respecting Indigenous
and Traditional Knowledge and Culture" – a major recognition of the
importance of Indigenous peoples and parks. I served as a facilitator for
some of the lively dialogues associated with this stream.

Under the hot November sun of the Olympic Park at Sydney, I saw perhaps 500 or more dedicated Indigenous leaders and allies excited to share
their concerns, models, case studies, and questions regarding the future
of Indigenous rights and protected areas. The participants expressed a
profound interest in and commitment to a serious dialogue about how
we protect people and places together (biocultural diversity), highlighting
the rights of Indigenous peoples. For many of the traditional, land-based
tribal communities present, the issues of land rights and access to hunting

grounds, gathering sites, and sacred places are urgent matters of cultural survival.

Major changes are being made in some parks and protected areas – specifically co-management in Australia with traditional burning practices and other Indigenous techniques incorporated into land-care practices. TEK is being integrated into many other parks issues, including cultural heritage, sacred site protection, ethnobotany, and public education. In his chapter, Dennis Martinez writes about the changes that are occurring (and are still desperately needed) in protected areas management regarding Indigenous rights and TEK.

Despite this progress, the vast majority of the 6,000 participants at the WPC discussed parks management strategies as "conservation as usual," quite oblivious to Indigenous peoples' historic land tenure and contemporary issues and needs. It did seem that there was quite a bit of "redwashing" still going on with some parks that benefit and profit from evicting Indigenous peoples from their park homelands. Many parks are associated with Indigenous rights abuses and human rights violations, while the whole concept of parks and protected areas has colonial roots (Corry, 2015; Keller and Turik, 1999; Spence, 2000). Notwithstanding these ongoing disputes and the institutional resistance to eradicating the colonial legacy of protected areas, major strides *are* being made to increase respect for Indigenous rights in protected areas, which includes sharing decision-making power. Many Indigenous communities, and the TEK they hold, are finally earning respect as Earth scientists are being recognized for the valuable knowledge-practices they carry, which is necessary for the sustainable care of Earth's remaining intact ecosystems.

Native Women and Nature

For this book we gathered together some of the foremost experts on the topics of TEK and sustainability, with many participants coming to the topic through their own personal Native experiences and professional backgrounds in sustainability, land management, and traditional knowledge. Among the fifteen authors (excluding Dan Shilling and myself as co-editors and contributors) over half – eight – are Indigenous women, a total of nine women contributors. This gender ratio was deliberate. Not only has TEK been oppressed and marginalized as primitive knowledge but Native women's knowledge and practices *in particular* have been denigrated and made invisible.

A direct correlation exists between the exploitation of women and the earth, an area of study known as ecofeminism that is explored by philosopher Joan McGregor in her chapter, "Toward a Philosophical Understanding of TEK and Ecofeminism." McGregor presents a philosophical examination of TEK and its relationship to ecofeminism, focusing on the corresponding oppression of nature, women, and Indigenous peoples. In her survey she explores the conceptions of the self, power relations, spirituality and creativity, the underpinnings of Western science, and the role and responsibility of ethics in science and environmentalism.

Many of the authors note that Native women, historically and today, are often the holders and keepers of profound ecological knowledges about plants, agriculture, medicine and the healing arts, herbology, midwifery, water management, ethnomathematics, textile arts, and other areas that fit the TEK or Native Science model. Native women are the mothers of our nations, and as Mohawk midwife and environmental researcher Katsi Cook (2003) states, "women are the first environment." Being so connected to the environment through the water cycle, lunar cycle, and plant world, women's bodies are significantly impacted by environmental pollution; because of that many of them have become fierce warriors in the fields of environmental justice, health advocacy, and water protection (for example, see the Idle No More, Women Water Walker, and Standing Rock movements).

If Indigenous peoples are the "canaries in the mine," as Dennis Martinez asserts, then Indigenous women are truly at the frontlines of experiencing negative impacts in the environment. Women's bodies are the "first environment" that human's experience, and are also often targeted for exploitation just like "natural resources" (i.e., through sexual violence). As explicit caretakers for life, Native women are often the first to sound the alarm about subtle but significant changes in ancestral lands and waters. For these reasons, we felt it was critically important to recognize the knowledge and expertise of Indigenous women scholars and leaders working at the forefront of Native knowledge, environmental justice, and sustainability.

Global and Legal Considerations of TEK

To conclude the anthology, we addressed the global and legal implications of Indigenous sustainability with chapters focusing on larger economic and political processes affecting Indigenous peoples and their TEK. The one non-US-based chapter is by four Māori scholars from New Zealand.

Rachel Wolfgramm, Chellie Spiller, and Carla Houkamau are Māori women scholars, and Manuka Henare is a prominent Māori scholar and leader. They work to assert Indigenous models of sustainability in the business field.

In their chapter, "Home: Resistance, Resilience and Innovation from a Māori Economy Perspective," Wolfgramm et al. provide a Māori cosmovision and understanding of evolving realities of home and how those realities are tied to TEK and Māori economics. They place this topic within the larger context of New Zealand colonial history, Māori land dispossession, and present day tribunal agreements and settlements. Indigenous economic development and "Indigenous economics" are often considered contentious and loaded topics in many contemporary discussions, yet the Māori provide a refreshing example of an Indigenous group reclaiming their land rights, title, and resources in a successful process that has achieved a Māori asset base now estimated at NZ$50 billion (Maori Television, 2017). Wolfgramm et al. define *economy* in its true, etymological sense – the management of home as a physical space where home is defined as identity, community, a journey of social transformation, and a space for navigating futures. They argue that "the Māori economy is embedded in a holistic relational system where the natural, social, and spiritual worlds are interrelated and the well-being of the individual is central to the well-being of the collective" (p. 224).

They and other contributors do not shy away from the difficult and essential questions of economics, globalization, and sustainability. Instead, they delve deeply into the challenge of how to sustain and restore the biocultural diversity of Earth, including Indigenous peoples' sovereignty and rights, while also supporting the economic livelihoods of humans on a massively populated planet during the sixth greatest extinction event in history. In addition to Wolfgramm et al., authors Dennis Martinez, Priscilla Settee, and Robin Kimmerer examine the question of economic development with both heart-breaking and inspiring examples, ranging from the destructive impacts of capitalism to the promise of regenerative livelihoods, including examples from urban food cooperatives and salmon restoration.

Author Rebecca Tsosie, a globally recognized Indigenous law professor and attorney, delves into the complex legal definitions of "traditional knowledge" and "cultural sustainability" by exploring efforts to protect the intellectual sovereignty of Native Americans and other Indigenous peoples. Her chapter, "Indigenous Peoples and 'Cultural Sovereignty': The Role of Traditional Knowledge," explores if and how traditional knowledge should be protected under international law, US federal law, and tribal law. Her chapter clearly outlines the various legal definitions of "Indigenous," as well as the diverse categories of "traditional knowledge," both tangible and intangible. She shows that although "traditional knowledge is a valuable resource, as evidenced by international discussions on sustainability policy," it is currently "not recognized as a cultural resource that merits legal protection" (p. 229). Tsosie concludes that the ownership and regulation of traditional knowledge is currently considered an ethical issue rather than a legal matter, thus warranting and reinforcing the strong emphasis on ethics in this collection.

Personal Responsibility and Cultural Obligation

For scholars and activists working in their communities, this publication highlights the cultural responsibility and profound sacred obligations that guide their activities. We often see our work as preceding and beyond our careers. We see ourselves first as Acoma, Anishinaabe, Cree, Chickasaw, Māori, Okanagan, O'odham, Pueblo, Potawatomie, Tongan, Yaqui, which all means we are humans who belong to Earth and Sky and who have obligations to our ancestral lands and waters, to our places, to our homelands, to our communities, and to future generations. We are "plain members" of the land and are born into the responsibility of being keepers of the green world for all of our relations and for current and future generations.

This collective orientation became clear when we met in April 2013 to begin this book project (Figure 3). Thanks to support from the Amerind Museum in Dragoon, Arizona, and the School of Sustainability at Arizona State University, we were fortunate to hold a five-day seminar at the beautiful Amerind Museum on the edge of the Chiracahua Mountains in Southeast Arizona, to share our paper drafts, engage in dialogue and discussion, and provide feedback to one another's essays. We shared meals together, walks in the desert, informal late-night discussions, and generally grew to know each other and bond as a community of like-minded humans. It was during these days of dialogue and exploration that we learned about each other's histories and backgrounds, and although each story was unique, they all led to a place that embraces a life commitment to ecological sustainability and the TEK of Indigenous peoples.

This commitment is personal, professional, and, for many of us, cultural. It is a commitment to remembering and restoring diversity and the

FIGURE 3 Eleven of the eighteen book contributors met at the Amerind Museum for a seminar in 2013. (Photo by John Ware, former director of Amerind.)

health of the whole, not as an abstraction, but as a lived, participatory experience. Interestingly, the root of the word *abstract* means "out of our tracks" or "to drag away, detach" (etymology dictionary). What many of us in this book say is, if sustainability is to mean anything relevant for us, our more-than-human relatives, and future generations, then we must put our environmental ethics into action and get back in our tracks by re-rooting to specific landscapes. If we are able to embody kinship with our natural world and practice reciprocity as if the future mattered, then we may once again become keepers of the green world.

> A little too abstract,
> A little too wise,
> It is time for us to kiss the Earth again.
> —"Return," by Robinson Jeffers

WORKS CITED

Agrawal, Arun. "Indigenous Knowledge and the Politics of Classification." *International Social Science Journal*, 173, September 2002, 325–36. UNESCO.

Anderson, M. Kat. *Tending the Wild: Native American Knowledge and the Management of California's Natural Resources*. Berkeley: University of California Press, 2013.

Cook, Katsi. "Cook: Women are the first environment." *Indian Country Today Media Network*. December 23, 2003. [online] URL: http://indiancountrytoday-medianetwork.com/2003/12/23/cook-women-are-first-environment-89746

Corry, Stephen. "Op-Ed: The Colonial Origins of Conservation: The Disturbing History Behind US National Parks." *Truthout*, August 25, 2015.

Cronon, William. "The Trouble with Wilderness: Or Getting Back to the Wrong Nature." *Uncommon Ground: Rethinking the Human Place in Nature*, edited by William Cronon. New York: W. W. Norton, 1995, 69–90.

Dumont, Clayton. *The Promise of Poststructuralist Sociology: Marginalized Peoples and the Problem of Knowledge*. Syracuse: SUNY Press, 2008.

Grossman, Zoltan and Alan Parker. *Asserting Native Resilience: Pacific Rim Indigenous Nations Face the Climate Crisis*. Eugene: University of Oregon Press, 2012.

Jewell, Sally. Interview with Jose Diaz-Balart. *MSNBC Live*. December 3, 2014.

Johnson, Jay T. and Soren C. Larson. *A Deeper Sense of Place: Stories and Journeys of Collaboration in Indigenous Research*. Corvallis: Oregon State University Press, 2013.

Keller, Robert H. and Michael Turek. *American Indians and National Parks*. Tucson: University of Arizona Press, 1999.

Kimmerer, Robin Wall. *Braiding Sweetgrass: Indigenous Wisdom, Scientific Knowledge and the Teachings of Plants*. Minneapolis: Milkweed Editions, 2013.

"Returning the Gift." *Minding Nature Journal*, 7 (2), 2014. [online] URL: www.humansandnature.org/returning-the-gift

Maffi, Luisa and Ellen Woodley. *Biocultural Diversity Conservation: A Global Sourcebook*. New York: Routledge, 2010.

Maori Television." $50B Maori economy grows as Crown-Maori relationship evolves," June 28, 2017, https://www.maoritelevision.com/news/national/50b-maori-economy-grows-crown-maori-relationship-evolves

Middleton, Beth Rose. *Trust In the Land: New Directions in Tribal Conservation*. Tucson: University of Arizona Press, 2011.

Nelson, Melissa K., Ed. *Original Instructions: Indigenous Teachings for a Sustainable Future*. Rochester, VT: Bear & Company, 2008.

"Indigenous Science and Traditional Ecological Knowledge: Persistence in Place." *The World of Indigenous North America*, edited by Robert Warrior. New York: Routledge, 2014, 188–214.

Simpson, Leanne. "Traditional Ecological Knowledge: Marginalization, Appropriation, and Continued Disillusion." Indigenous Knowledge Conference, 2001.

Salmon, Enrique. "Kincentric Ecology: Indigenous Perceptions of the Human-Nature Relationship." *Ecological Applications*, 10 (5), 2000, 1327–32.

Spence, Mark David. *Dispossessing the Wilderness: Indian Removal and the Making of the National Parks*. Oxford, UK: Oxford University Press, 2000.

United States Department of Agriculture (USDA), US Forest Service. "Tribes and Climate Change Fact Research." [online] URL: www.fs.fed.us/research/docs/tribal-engagement/factsheets/pacific-southwest-california-tribal-factsheet.pdf

Index

Printed by Printforce, United Kingdom